www.wadsworth.com

wadsworth.com is the World Wide Web site for Wadsworth Publishing Company and is your direct source to dozens of online resources.

At *wadsworth.com* you can find out about supplements, demonstration software, and student resources. You can also send e-mail to many of our authors and preview new publications and exciting new technologies.

wadsworth.com
Changing the way the world learns®

Other titles by Louis P. Pojman:

Abortion Controversy: A Reader
Environmental Ethics, Second Edition
Ethics: Discovering Right and Wrong, Third Edition
Ethical Theory: Classical and Contemporary Readings, Third Edition
Introduction to Philosophy: Classical and Contemporary Readings, Second Edition
Life and Death: A Reader in Moral Problems, Second Edition
Philosophical Traditions: A Text with Readings
Philosophy of Religion: An Anthology, Third Edition
Philosophy: The Pursuit of Wisdom, Third Edition
Philosophy: The Quest for Truth, Fourth Edition
Theory of Knowledge: Classic and Contemporary Readings, Second Edition
What Can We Know? An Introduction to the Theory of Knowledge

LIFE AND DEATH

Grappling with the Moral Dilemmas of Our Time

Second Edition

Louis P. Pojman
United States Military Academy, West Point

Wadsworth Publishing Company
I(T)P® An International Thomson Publishing Company

Belmont, CA • Albany, NY • Boston • Cincinnati • Detroit • Johannesburg • London • Madrid • Melbourne
Mexico City • New York • Pacific Grove, CA • Scottsdale, AZ • Singapore • Tokyo • Toronto

Philosophy Editor: Peter Adams
Assistant Editor: Kerri Abdinour
Editorial Assistant: Mindy Newfarmer
Marketing Manager: Dave Garrison
Print Buyer: Stacey Weinberger
Permissions Editor: Bob Kauser
Production: Matrix Productions Inc.

Copyeditor: Jill Saxton
Cover Design: Cassandra Chu Design
Cover Image: *The Voyage of Life: Manhood,* Thomas
  Cole; National Gallery of Art, Washington;
  Ailsa Mellon Bruce Fund
Compositor: Linda Weidemann, Wolf Creek Press
Printer: Webcom

For permission to use material from this text, contact us:
web   www.thomsonrights.com
fax   1-800-730-2215
phone   1-800-730-2214

Printed in Canada
1 2 3 4 5 6 7 8 9 10

Wadsworth Publishing Company
10 Davis Drive
Belmont, CA 94002

International Thomson Editores
Seneca, 53
Colonia Polanco
11560 Mèxico D.F. Mèxico

International Thomson Publishing Europe
Berkshire House
168-173 High Holborn
London, WC1V 7AA, United Kingdom

International Thomson Publishing Asia
60 Albert Street #15-01
Albert Complex
Singapore 189969

Nelson ITP, Australia
102 Dodds Street
South Melbourne
Victoria 3205 Australia

International Thomson Publishing Japan
Hirakawa-cho Kyowa Building, 3F
2-2-1 Hirakawa-cho, Chiyoda-ku
Tokyo 102, Japan

Nelson Canada
1120 Birchmount Road
Scarborough, Ontario
Canada M1K 5G4

International Thomson Publishing Southern Africa
Building 18, Constantia Square
138 Sixteenth Road, P.O. Box 2459
Halfway House, 1685 South Africa

Library of Congress Cataloging-in-Publication Data
Pojman, Louis P.
    Life and death : grappling with the moral dilemmas of our time / Louis Pojman. — 2nd ed.
        p.   cm.
    Includes bibliographical reference and index.
    ISBN 0-534-50824-3 (alk. paper)
    1. Death—Moral and ethical aspects.   I. Title.
BJ1409.5.P64   1999
179.7—dc21   99-10720

Dedicated to
my brother Kenneth

Contents

Preface

This book about contemporary moral dilemmas seeks to throw light on the subject from a philosophical point of view. Sophisticated technology creates new possibilities that our ordinary moral beliefs were not made to handle. On the one hand, although once thought possible only in science fiction, medical technology can extend physical life and health for long periods, using an array of expensive treatments. We have cloned animals and seem on the verge of cloning human beings—something thought inconceivable a generation ago. On the other hand, military expertise can destroy life at a magnitude never before imagined except in science fiction. In our day science fiction is fast becoming fact.

With the weakening of religious authority and the emergence of cultural pluralism, a multitude of possibilities present themselves on issues that go to the very heart of our personal and social existence. Society is deeply divided on the matters of life and death discussed in this book: the sanctity of life versus the quality, the meaning of death and dying, suicide, euthanasia, abortion, artificial procreation such as in vitro fertilization and cloning, the death penalty, animal rights, world hunger, and war. This book subjects these vital issues to philosophical analysis, attempting to replace heat with light.

Nothing is more important for our age, nothing is more inspiring for the thoughtful person, nothing is more challenging for our society than to think clearly, comprehensively, and imaginatively about the moral life. Little guidance is given ordinary people to enable them to evaluate and construct good moral reasoning. It is with the hope of shedding light on the moral life and equipping ordinary men and women to reflect critically on the moral dilemmas of our time that I have written this book.

Some seven years have passed since I wrote the first edition of this work. I'm delighted to have the opportunity to bring out this enlarged, new edition. Some teachers have asked for more ethical theory, especially on relativism, egoism, and the major theories, so that this book can be used in comprehensive ethics courses. I have added three more chapters to the theoretical area of the work as well as a chapter on human cloning and genetic engineering, the latest challenge to moral thinking. I have revised and updated every chapter.

An anthology, *Life and Death: A Reader,* with selections on each topic discussed herein, accompanies this book and could well be used as a companion volume. However, this book provides sufficient material for an entire course.

Joseph Betz, Forrester Church, Joseph DeMarco, John Jagger, Stephen Kaufman, Jim Landesman, Len Mitchell, Laura Purdy, Henry Sackin, Mary Anne Warren, and especially Bob Ginsberg were very helpful in reading the manuscript that lead to the first edition. Dan Crawford of the University of Nebraska; Tim Moses of Lake City College, Florida; Robert Mellert of Brookdale Community College, Maryland; Mark Schersten of Siena Heights College; Tim Moses of Lake City Community College; and Tziporah Kasachkoff of City University of New York Graduate Center made helpful suggestions that greatly improved this second edition of the book. Peter Adams and Jake Warde were very supportive in organizing the material for this edition. Most of all, I am grateful to my wife, Trudy, a hospice nurse, who helped me with the material concerning issues in death and dying and who has given me an example of how to live. The work is dedicated to my brother and friend, Kenneth.

Louis P. Pojman
United States Military Academy
West Point, NY 10928
June 22, 1998

Welcome to Moral Philosophy:

A Word to the Student

We are discussing no small matter,
but how we ought to live.

SOCRATES

Philosophy is the passionate pursuit of truth—literally, the love of wisdom. It begins with wonder at the mysteries and paradoxes of existence and seeks to arrive at informed judgments that enhance our understanding and lend meaning to life. It is revolutionary in that it often disrupts the received opinion of an age, calling on us to think new thoughts, critically, comprehensively, honestly, even when they disturb deeply held biases. Its weapons are the swords of reason and imagination. Like science and mathematics it is a highly rational activity, centered in argument and analysis and disciplined thinking, but like art and drama, it appeals to imagination and life experience in creating probing thought experiments, counter-examples to conclusions, and interdisciplinary applications of principles.

This book is a philosophical exploration into the moral status of crucial issues connected with our being alive and having to face the reality of death (either our own or that of others). Its topics include the idea of the sanctity of life versus the quality of life, the meaning of death, abortion, suicide, euthanasia, the death penalty, animal rights (do animals have a right to life?), and war. The last chapter deals with the very definition of "death." The issues are interrelated, all having as an underlying theme the question of what makes life valuable in the first place. To set the stage for our discussion I begin this work with an introductory chapter on the nature of ethics. I have introduced the amount of ethical theory necessary for your work on the specific issues that make up the bulk of this work.

Philosophy is an ongoing process of seeking deeper understanding of issues that are difficult but vital to the human condition. As such it seldom arrives at a final word on any subject. This is sometimes frustrating to students who desire exact and reliable answers to problems, but wisdom consists not in final dogmatic solutions but in a growing understanding of the issues and considered judgments in favor of one side or the other. As such, I have set forth my best thinking on these life-and-death issues, but I make no pretense to have said anything approaching finality. Although I try to present opposing sides of the issue as fairly as possible, I have sometimes made clear where I think the best arguments lead. In the conclusion of the work I have completed this process so that you will know where I come down on the issues. No doubt you will disagree with some of my reasoning. Fine! My reasoning is offered as a stimulant to get you to think these matters out for yourself and arrive at your own *considered judgments*. But I emphasize that it is a *considered* judgment that must be aimed at, not simply an emotional bias or unexamined intuition. I encourage you to take issue with me, even where you suspect my arguments are sound, to attack these arguments, to improve upon them, and to develop better arguments of your own. For these problems of life and death are your problems. Let the arguments set forth in this work be rungs on a ladder that helps you ascend to a higher understanding of the issues, which when reached can be replaced with your own better formulations.

Indeed, I invite you to write me with your responses to my thoughts. I will endeavor to reply.

The intellectual life, that which makes us more than mere animals, is noble and exhilarating. It provides a quality of understanding that is intrinsically good yet can also aid in making life more enjoyable. My wish for you is that applying the intellect to these moral dilemmas will be a worthwhile experience that will excite you to a life of philosophical reflection.

Introduction

"Doctor Death's" Suicide Machine

Two thousand miles away from her home in Oregon on the afternoon of June 4, 1990, in a 1968 Volkswagen van, Janet Adkins, a vibrant fifty-four-year-old schoolteacher who had been diagnosed as having Alzheimer's disease, pressed the button of a suicide machine and died. A retired sixty-two-year-old pathologist from Royal Oak, Michigan, Dr. Jack Kevorkian, having been turned away from motels, funeral homes, vacant office space, and even the local Unitarian church, equipped his rusty 1968 Volkswagen van with a cot, clean sheets, and his newly invented suicide machine. The contraption consisted of an intravenous tube and three bottles. One contained a saline solution, another held thiopental sodium to induce sleep, and the third contained potassium chloride, which stops the heart.

Mrs. Adkins had first noticed memory slips and a waning of ability to play her beloved piano and flute some three years previously. A year before her death she had been diagnosed as having Alzheimer's disease, an irreversible degeneration of the brain cells that can lead to severe memory loss, dementia, and death. "That just hit her like a bombshell," said her husband, Norman. "Her mind was her life." She had believed for a long time that people had a right to die when life offered greatly diminished quality, and she had joined the Hemlock Society, an organization dedicated to assisting terminally ill people commit suicide.

After experimental treatment failed, she decided to seek a way to end her life. Having consulted with her family and minister, and having received the strong support of her husband, she made inquiries about assisted suicide. Eventually she heard about Dr. Kevorkian's suicide machine. Flying to Michigan, one of the few states where it is not illegal to assist in a suicide, she met Dr. Kevorkian. He spent a few days with Mr. and Mrs. Adkins, monitored the machine inside the van, and notified the police when the ordeal was completed. He had only one regret—that Mrs. Adkins's organs could not be donated because her body remained in the van for several hours before it was removed. "The medical examiner wouldn't let us touch the body," he said.

> They were there for four hours walking around and scratching their heads. You could have sliced her liver in half and saved two babies and her bone marrow could have been taken, her heart, two kidneys, two lungs, a pancreas. Think of the people that could have been saved. If you were waiting for a new heart, you'd be all for what I'm doing. She had a good strong heart. I know. I watched it on the screen.

The news of Mrs. Adkins's suicide sent earthquake tremors through the nation. *The New York Times* condemned the act and, unsuccessfully, called for Dr. Kevorkian's arrest. Others dubbed him "Dr. Death." Medical ethicists generally were appalled. Susan M. Wolf of the Hastings Center of Medical Ethics said, "Even the staunchest proponent of physician-assisted suicide should be horrified at this case because there were no procedural protections." Dr. Joanne Lynn of George Washington University said that the claim that Mrs. Adkins's "decision to take her life was made with a clear mind was incompatible with her having Alzheimer's disease." A spokesperson for the American Medical Association announced that this act violated the mutual trust of the doctor-patient relationship.

"Our patients should not be concerned that we are going to make a value judgment that their lives are no longer worth living."

Even a representative for the Hemlock Society, the organization dedicated to the cause of voluntary euthanasia, gave only qualified endorsement of Janet Adkins's suicide. "It was unfortunate that Janet Adkins died before she had to die," *The New York Times* reported Cheryl K. Smith, lawyer for the National Hemlock Society, as saying. "She should have been able to wait until it was time to die." If society would only accept voluntary euthanasia for those who have lost all quality of life, Mrs. Adkins could have trusted to others to help her die when she had become incompetent.

Less sympathetically, Dr. John Kiley claimed in the *National Review* that Mrs. Adkins really suffered from a philosophical disorder worse than Alzheimer's disease—a fear of facing the truth. "She was in fatal flight from her terrifying *thought* about Alzheimer's disease. [Dr. Kevorkian] suffers from his own philosophical disease: playing God." The editor went on to say that Mrs. Adkins died "tackily." "The advance promotion for abortion and infanticide imagines them impelled by necessity and performed under ideal conditions. But in time the routine reality becomes sleazier. If life has no intrinsic value, why should the end of life have any grace?"

Twenty-three years after the epoch-making Karen Ann Quinlan case, America is still wrestling with the question of whether terminally ill patients and others facing greatly diminished quality of life have the right to die. Ironically, it was a machine that assisted Janet Adkins in her death—if Dr. Kevorkian had slipped her the poison directly, he would have been arrested and accused of murder—for it is the very burgeoning of medical technology with its ventilators, artificial hearts, and other machines that can keep people "alive" almost indefinitely. A person may be permanently comatose, persistently vegetative, or without a live cerebral cortex (the brain organ in

which resides consciousness and the ability to reason and remember), but legally he or she is still alive—and the mounting doctor and hospital bills prove it.

Is the editor of the *National Review* correct in claiming that people like Mrs. Adkins are moral cowards who cannot face God-given reality? Or that physicians like Dr. Kevorkian are guilty of assuming the authority of God in assisting in suicide? Would such lethal cooperation between physician and patient lead to a confusion of the doctor's role, traditionally one of "promoting life"? Assuming that we grant terminally ill people a right to die, should a new profession be created, "the thanatologist" or "euthanist," whose function is to assist in suicides? He or she would probably have to be salaried rather than provide "service for fee," lest there be a temptation to solicit patients.

What is the moral difference, if any, between unplugging a respirator and plugging in a suicide machine? Is there a moral difference between purposefully allowing someone to die (when you can easily make a difference) and actively causing that person to die—given the same attitude towards the patient in both instances?

And just what is this idea of sanctity of life that the editorials of both *The New York Times* and the *National Review* cite as the grounds for opposing the suicide machine? Is the *National Review* correct that tacky suicides are related to our views on abortion and represent a loss of faith in the sanctity of life? Is the Roman Catholic Church correct when it says, "A right to death does not exist. Love for life, even a life reduced to a ruin, drives one to protect life with every possible care"?[1] Is life sacred? What does that concept mean in the light of today's technological labyrinth? Janet Adkins's suicide raises all of these questions.

In this book we will be looking at some concrete moral problems, matters of life and death: the idea of sanctity of life, the criteria for death, suicide, euthanasia, abortion, cloning, the death penalty, animal rights, and war. The solutions, if there are such, to these problems must be wrested with great effort in the light of the best moral thinking available. All of our rational and imaginative powers must be brought to bear on these issues, but the reward in terms of understanding and guidance is worth the toil.

I have tried to present opposite sides of each issue as fairly as possible. Regarding the specific moral problems, I have largely let the flow of the arguments follow their own courses and have not set forth my own views on the matters. For those who are interested in how I come down on these questions, I have written a conclusion, where I spell out some of my views.

I do, however, defend two major theses in this book. The first is that morality is made for humanity, not humanity for morality. That is, moral principles serve for our (and other ani-

mals') well-being. Hence, I reject moral relativism and espouse a broadly based moral objectivism. I set forth an overview of the purposes of morality in the first chapter. My second thesis is that the quality-of-life principle should override the sanctity-of-life principle, which, in its absolutist form, (as I will argue in the fourth chapter), is an invalid principle. The quantity of life does not count as much as the quality.

Before we turn to specific moral problems we need to take a look at the nature of morality itself.

Endnote

1. Vatican theologian Gino Concetti, quoted in Joseph and Julia Quinlan's *Karen Ann: The Quinlans Tell Their Story,* with Phyllis Battelle (New York: Doubleday, 1977), p. 211.

Chapter 1

What Is Ethics?

We are discussing no small matter, but how we ought to live.

SOCRATES, in Plato's *Republic*

What is it to be a moral person? What is the nature of morality, and why do we need it? What is the good, and how shall I know it? Are moral principles absolute or simply relative to social groups or individual decisions? Is it in my interest to be moral? Is it sometimes in my best interest to act immorally? What is the relationship between morality and religion? What is the relationship between morality and law? What is the relationship between morality and etiquette?

These are some of the questions that we shall be examining in this chapter. We want to understand the foundation and structure of morality. We want to know how we should live.

The terms *moral* and *ethics* come from Latin and Greek, respectively (*mores* and *ethos*), deriving their meaning from the idea of custom. Although philosophers sometimes distinguish these terms, *morality* referring to the customs, principles and practices of a people or culture, and *ethics* referring to the whole domain of morality and moral philosophy, I shall use them interchangeably in this book, using the context to make any differences clear.

Moral philosophy refers to the systematic endeavor to understand moral concepts and justify moral principles and theories. It undertakes to analyze such concepts as 'right', 'wrong', 'permissible', 'ought', 'good', and 'evil' in their moral contexts. Moral philosophy seeks to establish principles of right behavior that may serve as action guides for individuals and groups. It investigates which values and virtues are paramount to the worthwhile life or society. It builds and scrutinizes arguments in ethical theories, and it seeks to discover valid principles (e.g., 'Never kill innocent human beings') and the relationship between those principles (e.g., does saving a life in some situations constitute a valid reason for breaking a promise?).

Morality As Compared with Other Normative Subjects

Moral precepts are concerned with norms—not what is, but what *ought* to be. How should I live my life? What is the right thing to do in this situation? Should I always tell the truth? Do I have a duty to report a student whom I have seen cheating in class or a coworker whom I have seen stealing office supplies? Should I tell my friend that his spouse is having an affair? Is premarital sex morally permissible? Ought a woman ever to have an abortion? Should we permit the cloning of human beings? Morality has a distinct action-guiding or *normative* aspect[1], which it shares with other practical institutions, such as religion, law, and etiquette.

Moral behavior, as defined by a given religion, is often held to be essential to the practice of that religion. But neither the practices nor the precepts of morality should be identified with religion. The practice of morality need not be motivated by religious considerations, and moral precepts need not be grounded in revelation or divine authority, as religious teachings invariably are. The most salient characteristic of ethics—by which I mean both philosophical morality (or morality, as I will simply refer to it) and moral philosophy—is that it is grounded in reason and human experience.

To use a spatial metaphor, secular ethics is horizontal, omitting a vertical or transcendental dimension. Religious ethics has a vertical dimension, being grounded in revelation or divine authority, though generally using reason to supplement or complement revelation. These two differing orientations often generate different moral principles and standards of evaluation, but they need not. Some versions of religious ethics, which posit God's revelation of the moral law in nature or conscience, hold that reason can discover what is right or wrong even apart from divine revelation.

Morality is also closely related to law, and some people equate the two practices. Many laws are instituted to promote well-being, resolve conflicts of interest, and enhance social harmony, just as morality does, but ethics may judge that some laws are immoral without denying that they are valid laws. For example, laws may permit slavery or irrelevant discrimination against people on the basis of race or sex. A Catholic or antiabortion advocate may believe that the laws permitting abortion are immoral.

In a recent television series, *Ethics in America* (PBS, 1989), James Neal, a trial lawyer, was asked what he would do if he discovered that his client had committed a murder some years back, for which another man had been convicted and would soon be executed. Mr. Neal said that he had a legal obligation to keep this information confidential and that if he divulged it, he would be disbarred. Does he have a moral obligation that overrides his legal obligation and demands that he take action to protect the innocent man from being executed?

Furthermore, some aspects of morality are not covered by law. For example, although it is generally agreed that lying is usually immoral, there is no law against it (except under special conditions, such as in cases of perjury or falsifying income tax returns). Sometimes college newspapers publish advertisements for "research assistance," and know in advance that the companies will aid and abet plagiarism. The publishing of such research paper ads is legal, but it is doubtful whether it is morally correct. In 1964, thirty-eight people in Queens, New York, watched from their apartments for some 45 minutes as a man beat up a woman, Kitty Genovese. They did nothing to intervene, not even call the police. These people broke no law, but surely they were morally culpable for not calling the police or shouting at the assailant.

There is one other major difference between law and morality. In 1351 King Edward of England promulgated a law against treason that made it a crime merely to think homicidal thoughts about the king. But, alas, the law could not be enforced, for no tribunal can search the heart and fathom the intentions of the mind. It is true that *intention,* such as malice aforethought, plays a role in the legal process in determining the legal character of the act once the act has been committed, but preemptive punishment for people presumed to have bad intentions is illegal. If malicious intentions

(called in law *mens rea*) were criminally illegal, would we not all deserve imprisonment? Even if it were possible to detect intentions, when should the punishment be administered? As soon as the subject has the intention? But how do we know that he will not change his mind? Furthermore, is there not a continuum between imagining some harm to X, wishing harm to X, desiring harm to X, and intending harm to X?

Although it is impractical to have laws against bad intentions, such intentions are still bad, still morally wrong. Suppose I plan to push Uncle Charlie off a 1,000-foot cliff when we next hike together so that I can inherit his wealth, but I never have a chance to do it (Uncle Charlie breaks his leg and forswears hiking). I have not committed a crime, but I have committed a moral wrong. Law generally aims at setting an important but minimal framework in a society of plural values.

Finally, law differs from morality in that physical and financial sanctions[2] (e.g., imprisonment and fines) enforce the law but only the sanctions of conscience and reputation enforce morality.

Morality also differs from etiquette, which is concerned with form and style rather than the essence of social existence. Etiquette determines what is polite behavior rather than what is right behavior in a deeper sense. It represents society's decisions as to how we are to dress, greet one another, eat, celebrate festivals, dispose of the dead, express gratitude and appreciation, and, in general, carry out social transactions. Whether we greet each other with a handshake, a bow, a hug, or a kiss on the cheek varies in different social systems. Whether we uncover our heads in holy places (as males do in Christian churches) or cover them (as females do in Catholic churches and males do in synagogues), none of these rituals has any moral superiority.

People in Russia wear their wedding rings on the third finger of the right hand, whereas we wear them on our left hands. People in England hold their fork in their left hand when they eat, whereas people in other countries hold it in their right hand or in whichever hand they feel like holding it, while people in India typically eat without a fork at all, using the forefingers of their right hand to convey food from their plate to their mouth.

Polite manners grace our social existence, but they are not what social existence is about. They help social transactions to flow smoothly, but they are not the substance of those transactions.

At the same time, it can be immoral to disregard etiquette. Whether to shake hands when greeting a person for the first time or put one's hands together and forward as one bows, as people in India do, is a matter of cultural decision, but once the custom is adopted, the practice takes on the importance of a moral rule, subsumed under the wider principle of showing respect to people. Similarly, there is no moral necessity to wear clothes, but we have adopted the custom partly to keep us warm in colder climates and partly out of modesty. However, there is nothing wrong with nudists who decide to live together naked in nudist colonies, although it may well be the case that running nude in classrooms, stores, and along the road, would constitute such offensive behavior as to count as morally insensitive. There was a scandal on the beaches of South India, where American tourists swam in bikinis, shocking the more modest Indians. There was nothing immoral in itself about wearing bikinis, but given the cultural context, the Americans, in willfully violating etiquette, were guilty of moral impropriety.[3]

Law, etiquette and religion are all important institutions, but each has limitations. The limitation of the law is that you can't have a law against every social malady nor can you enforce every desirable rule. The limitation of etiquette is that is doesn't get to the heart of what is of vital importance for personal and social existence. Whether or not one eats with one's fingers pales in significance compared with the importance of being honest, trustworthy, or just. Etiquette is a cultural invention, but morality claims to be a discovery.

The limitation of the religious injunction is that it rests on authority, and we are not always sure of or in agreement about the credentials of the authority, nor about how the authority would rule in ambiguous or new cases. Since most religions are not founded on reason but on revelation, you cannot use reason to convince someone who does not share your religious views that your view is the right one. I hasten to add that when moral differences are caused by fundamental moral principles, it is unlikely that philosophical reasoning will settle the matter. Often, however, our moral differences turn out to be rooted in world views, not moral principles. For example, the antiabortionist and pro-choice advocate often agree that it is wrong to kill innocent persons, but they differ on the facts. The antiabortionist may hold a religious view that states that the fetus has an eternal soul and thus possess a right to life, while the pro-choice advocate may deny that anyone has a soul and hold that only self-conscious, rational beings have a right to life.

The following chart characterizes the relationships among ethics, religion, law, and etiquette.

Subject	Normative Disjuncts	Sanctions
Ethics	Right—Wrong—Permissible as defined by conscience or reason	Conscience—Praise and Blame Reputation
Religion	Right—Wrong (Sin)—Permissible as defined by religious authority	Conscience—Eternal Reward and Punishment caused by a supernatural agent or force
Law	Legal and Illegal as defined by a judicial body	Punishments determined by the legislative body
Etiquette	Proper and Improper as defined by culture	Social Disapprobation and Approbation

In summary, morality distinguishes itself from law and etiquette by going deeper into the essence of rational existence. It distinguishes itself from religion by seeking reasons, rather than authority, to justify its principles. The central purpose of moral philosophy is to secure valid principles of conduct and values that can be instrumental in guiding human actions and producing good character. As such, it is the most important activity known to humans, for it has to do with how we are to live.

Domains of Ethical Assessment

It might seem at this point that ethics concerns itself entirely with rules of conduct based solely on an evaluation of acts. However, the situation is more complicated than this. Following are the four domains of ethical assessment:

Domain	Evaluative Terms
1. Action, the act	Right, wrong, obligatory, permissible
2. Consequences	Good, bad, indifferent
3. Character	Virtuous, vicious, neutral
4. Motive	Good will, evil will, neutral

Let us examine each of these domains.

(1) TYPES OF ACTION

The most common distinction may be the classification of actions as right and wrong, but the term *right* is ambiguous. Sometimes it means "obligatory" (as in "*the right* act"); sometimes it means "permissible" (as in "a right act"). Usually philosophers define *right* as permissible, including under that category what is obligatory.

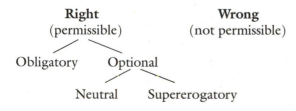

Right   **Wrong**
(permissible)   (not permissible)

Obligatory   Optional

Neutral   Supererogatory

(I) A 'right act' is an act that is permissible. It may be either (a) optional or (b) obligatory.

   a. An *optional* act is neither obligatory nor wrong. It is not your duty to do it, nor is it your duty not to do it. Neither doing it nor not doing it would be wrong.

   b. An *obligatory* act is one that morality requires; it is not permissible to refrain from doing it. It would be wrong not to do it.

(II) A 'wrong act' is one that carries an obligation, or a duty, to refrain from doing. It is an act you ought not to do. It is not permissible to do it.

Let us briefly illustrate these concepts. The act of lying is generally seen as wrong (prohibited), whereas telling the truth is generally seen as obligatory. But some acts do not seem to be either obligatory or wrong. Whether you decide to take a course in art history or English literature, or whether you write your friend a letter with a pencil or a pen seem morally neutral. Either is permissible. Whether you listen to pop music or classical music is not usually considered morally significant. Listening to both is allowed, and neither is obligatory. A decision to marry or remain single is of great moral significance (It is, after all, an important decision about how to live one's life). The decision reached, however, is usually considered to be morally neutral or optional. Under most circumstances, to marry (or not to marry) is thought to be neither obligatory nor wrong, but permissible.

Within the range of permissible acts is the notion of 'supererogatory' or highly altruistic acts. These acts are not required or obligatory, but they exceed what morality requires, going "beyond the call of duty." You may have an obligation to give a donation to help people in dire need, but you are probably not obliged to sell your car, let alone become destitute, in order to help them.

Theories that place the emphasis on the nature of the act are called *deontological* (from the Greek word for duty). These theories hold that there is something inherently right or good about such acts as truth telling and promise keeping and something inherently wrong or bad about such acts as lying and promise breaking. Illustrations of deontological ethics include the Ten Commandments found in the Bible (Exodus 20), natural law ethics such as those found in the Roman Catholic church, and Immanuel Kant's theory of the Categorical Imperative, which we discuss below.

(2) CONSEQUENCES

We said above that lying is generally seen as wrong and telling the truth is generally seen as right. But consider this situation: In your home you are hiding an innocent Jewish woman named Sarah, who is fleeing Nazi officers. When the Nazis knock on your door and you open it, they ask if Sarah is in your house. What should you do? Should you tell the truth or lie? Those who say that morality has something to do with consequences of actions would prescribe lying as the morally right thing to do. Those who deny that we should look at the consequences when there is a clear and absolute rule of action would say that we should either keep silent or tell the truth. When no other rule is at stake, of course, the rule-oriented ethicist will allow the foreseeable consequences to determine a course of action. Theories that focus primarily on consequences in determining moral rightness and wrongness are called *teleological* ethical theories (from the Greek *telos*, meaning "goal directed"). The most famous of these theories is Utilitarianism, set forth by Jeremy Bentham (1748–1832) and John Stuart Mill (1806–1873), which enjoins us to do the act that is most likely to have the best consequences: do the act that will produce the greatest happiness for the greatest number. We will discuss Utilitarianism in Chapter 4.

(3) CHARACTER

While some ethical theories emphasize principles of action in themselves and some emphasize principles involving consequences of action, other theories, such as Aristotle's ethics, emphasize character or virtue. According to Aristotle, it is most important to develop virtuous character, for if and only if we have good people can we ensure habitual right action. Although it may be helpful to have action-guiding rules, what is vital is the empowerment of character to do good. Many people know that cheating or gossiping or overindulging in food or alcohol is wrong, but they are incapable of doing what is right. A virtuous person may not be consciously following moral law when he or she does what is right and good. Although virtues are not central to other types of moral theories, most moral theories include virtues as important. Most reasonable people, whatever their notions about ethics, would judge that the people who watched Kitty Genovese being assaulted lacked good character. Different moral systems emphasize different virtues and emphasize them to different degrees.

(4) MOTIVE

Finally, virtually all ethical systems, but especially Kant's system, accept the relevance of *motive*. It is important to the full assessment of any action that the intention of the agent be taken into account. Two acts may be identical, but one may be judged morally culpable and the other excusable. Consider John's pushing Joan off a ledge, causing her to break her leg. In situation A he is angry and intends to harm her; in situation B he sees a knife flying in her direction and intends to save her life. In A what he did was clearly wrong, whereas in B he did the right thing. On the other hand, two acts may have opposite results but the action may be equally good judged on the basis of intention. For example, two soldiers may try to cross enemy lines to communicate with an allied force. One is captured through no fault of his own, and the other succeeds. In a full moral description of any act, motive will be taken into consideration as a relevant factor.

The Purposes of Morality

What is the role of morality in human existence? I believe that morality is necessary to stave off social chaos, what Thomas Hobbes called a "state of nature," wherein life becomes "solitary, poor, nasty, brutish and short," a "war of all against all," a lose-lose situation. It is a set of rules that, if followed by nearly everyone, will promote the flourishing of nearly everyone. These rules restrict our freedom but only in order to promote greater freedom and well-being. More specifically, morality seems to have these five purposes:

1. To keep society from falling apart
2. To ameliorate human suffering
3. To promote human flourishing
4. To resolve conflicts of interest in just and orderly ways
5. To assign praise and blame, reward and punishment and guilt

None of these is the sole purpose of morality, but each is part of a comprehensive purpose that enables us to live a good life in a just society. The first purpose, keeping society from falling apart, is a necessary but not sufficient condition for a good society, for a tyrant could keep the society together through oppression. Likewise, the second purpose, ameliorating suffering, is a vital component. One of the reasons we cooperate with each other is to come to each other's aid in time of need, but this is not the sole aim of society or morality. The third goal, promoting human flourishing, signifies enabling people to reach their potential, to live happily. It may be as central to morality as any of the five purposes, but even here, we would not want happiness at any price. Suppose the price we had to pay for our happiness was treat-

ing other people unjustly. One thinks of Ursula LeGuin's short story "The Ones Who Walk Away from Omelas," which describes the town Omelas in which the flourishing of the community is dependent on the torturing of a child. People with a sensitive conscience walk away from such "happiness." We would reject such a social arrangement as morally incomplete. Hence, the fourth goal, justice. But justice isn't the *whole* of morality, either. We could imagine two different social arrangements, equally fair, but in which one went beyond mere justice and promoted high altruism, thereby making people more fulfilled. Finally, morality has the function of holding people responsible for their actions, of assigning praise and blame in accordance with the springs of our actions.

Imagine what society would be if everyone or nearly everyone did whatever he or she pleased without obeying moral rules. For example, I make a promise to you to help you with your philosophy homework tomorrow if you fix my car today. You believe me, so you fix my car. Then you are deeply angry when I laugh at you on the morrow as I drive away to the beach instead of helping you with your homework. Or you lend me money, but I run off with it. Or I lie to you or harm you when it is in my interest, or even kill you when I feel the urge.

Parents would abandon children and spouses betray each other whenever it was convenient. Under such circumstances, society would break down. No one would have an incentive to help anyone else because reciprocity (a moral principle) was not recognized. Great suffering would go largely unameliorated, and people would not be happy. We would not flourish or reach our highest potential.

Once while visiting a city in the former Soviet Union, I rented a fifth-floor apartment in which the stairwell lacked lighting. It was difficult navigating stairs at night in complete darkness. I inquired as to why there were no lightbulbs in the stairwells, only to be told that the residents stole them, believing that if they did not take them, their neighbors would. Absent a dominant authority, the social contract had been eroded and everyone struggled alone in the darkness.

We need moral rules to guide our actions in ways that light our paths and prevent and reduce suffering, that enhance human (and animal?) well-being, that allow us to resolve our conflicts of interests according to recognizably fair rules and to assign responsibility for actions so that we can praise, blame, reward, and punish people according to the way their actions reflect moral principles.

Even though these five purposes are related, they are not identical, and different moral theories emphasize different purposes in different ways. Utilitarianism fastens on human flourishing and the amelioration of suffering, whereas contractual systems rooted in rational self-interest accent the role of resolving conflicts of interest. Contractualism, such as set forth by Thomas

Hobbes, emphasizes the first and fourth purposes: survival and the resolution of conflicts of interest in just and orderly ways. A complete moral theory would include a place for each of these purposes. Its goal would be to internalize the rules that promote these principles in each person's life, producing a virtuous person, someone who is "a jewel that shines in [morality's] own light," to paraphrase Kant. The goal of morality is to create happy and virtuous people, the kind that create flourishing communities. That's why it is the most important subject on earth.

Which of these views of classical ethics is correct? This will be a major question throughout this work. But there is one basic question to which we must attend before we can have any intelligent discussion of ethics at all—the question of ethical relativism. Are moral principles objectively and universally valid, or are they simply valid relative to culture or individual choice?

Study Questions

1. Illustrate the differences among ethics, law, religion, and etiquette. How are these concepts related? Do you think either law, religion or etiquette are more important than morality in guiding human action? Explain your answer.
2. Discuss the four domains of morality. Which domains do you consider are more crucial than others, or do you think they are all equally important? Explain your answer.
3. What are the purposes of morality? Which ones seems more important than others? Do you agree that these are the central purposes? Are there others?

For Further Reading

Frankena, William, *Ethics* (Englewood Cliffs, NJ: Prentice-Hall, 1973).

Kagan, Shelly, *Normative Ethics* (Boulder, CO: Westview Press, 1997).

Mackie, J.L., *Ethics: Inventing Right and Wrong* (New York: Penguin, 1976).

Pojman, Louis, ed., *Ethical Theory* (Belmont, CA: Wadsworth Publishing Co., 1998).

Pojman, Louis, *Ethics: Discovering Right and Wrong* (Belmont, CA: Wadsworth Publishing Co., 1998).

Rachels, James, *Elements of Moral Philosophy* (New York: McGraw-Hill, 1993).

Singer, Peter, *The Expanding Circle: Ethics and Sociobiology* (Oxford University Press, 1983).

Taylor, Richard, *Good and Evil* (Buffalo, NY: Prometheus, 1970).

Williams, Bernard, *Morality* (New York: Harper, 1972).

Wilson, James Q., *The Moral Sense* (New York: Free Press, 1993).

Endnotes

1. The term *normative* means seeking to make certain types of behavior a norm or standard in a society. *MerriamWebster's Collegiate Dictionary* defines it as "of, or relating or conforming to or prescribing norms or standards."

2. A *sanction* is a mechanism for social control, used to enforce society's standards. It may consist of rewards or punishment, praise or blame, approbation or disapprobation.

3. Although Americans pride themselves on tolerance, pluralism, and awareness of other cultures, custom and etiquette can be—even among people from similar backgrounds—a bone of contention. A friend of mine, John, tells of an experience early in his marriage. He and his wife, Gwen, were hosting their first Thanksgiving meal. He had been used to small celebrations with his immediate family, whereas his wife had been used to grand celebrations. He writes, "I had been asked to carve, something I had never done before, but I was willing. I put on an apron, entered the kitchen, and attacked the bird with as much artistry as I could muster. And what reward did I get? [My wife] burst into tears. In her family the turkey is brought to the *table,* laid before the [father], grace is said, and *then* he carves! 'So I fail patriarchy,' I hollered later. 'What do you expect?'"

Chapter 2

Ethical Relativism

Who's to Judge What's Right and Wrong?

In the nineteenth century Christian missionaries sometimes used coercion to change the customs of pagan tribal people in parts of Africa and the Pacific Islands. Appalled by the customs of public nakedness, polygamy, working on the Sabbath, and infanticide, they paternalistically went about reforming the pagans. They clothed them, separated wives from their husbands in order to create monogamous households, made the Sabbath a day of rest, and ended infanticide. In the process they sometimes created social malaise, causing the estranged women to despair and their children to be orphaned. The natives often did not understand the new religion, but they accepted it in deference to the white man's power. The white people had guns and medicine.

Since the nineteenth century we've made progress in understanding cultural diversity and realize that the social dissonance caused by do-gooders was a bad thing. In the last century or so, anthropology has exposed our penchant for *ethnocentrism,* the prejudicial view that interprets all of reality through the eyes of our cultural beliefs and values. We have come to see enormous variety in social practices throughout the world.

Eskimos allow their elderly to die by starvation; we believe that this is morally wrong. The Spartans of ancient Greece and Dobu of New Guinea believe that stealing is morally right; we believe it is wrong. Many cultures, past and present, have practiced or still practice infanticide. A tribe in East Africa once threw deformed infants to hippopotamuses; our society condemns infanticide. Ruth Benedict describes a tribe in Melanesia that views cooperation and kindness as vices, and Colin Turnbull has documented that the Ik in Northern Uganda have no sense of duty toward their children or parents. There are societies that consider it a duty for children to kill (sometimes strangle) their aging parents. Eskimos sometimes abandon their elderly as they move on to new locations. Sexual practices vary over time and clime. Some cultures permit, while others condemn, homosexual behavior. Some cultures, including Moslem societies, practice polygamy;

Christian cultures view it as immoral. Some cultures accept cannibalism; we detest it. While our culture has generally encouraged meat eating, not to mention the killing of animals for sport, Hindus and Jains (a religion in India) look upon the killing of animals as immoral, and the eating of meat as wrong. *Cultural Relativism* is well documented, and custom seems king o'er all.

Today we condemn ethnocentrism, the uncritical belief in the inherent superiority of one's own culture, as a variety of prejudice tantamount to racism and sexism. What is right in one culture may be wrong in another; what is good east of the river may be bad west of the same river; and what is a virtue in one nation may be seen as a vice in another. Thus it behooves us not to judge others but to be tolerant of diversity.

This rejection of ethnocentrism in the West has contributed to a general shift in public opinion about morality. For a growing number of Westerners, consciousness-raising about the validity of other ways of life has led to a gradual erosion of belief in moral *objectivism,* the view that universal moral principles are valid for all people at all times and in all climes. For example, in polls taken in my ethics and introduction to philosophy classes over the years (in three different universities in three areas of the country), students affirmed a version of Ethical Relativism over moral absolutism by a two-to-one ratio, with hardly 3 percent seeing anything between these two polar opposites. Of course, I'm not suggesting that all of these students have a clear understanding of what relativism entails, for many of those who say that they are ethical relativists also state on the same questionnaire that "abortion except to save the mother's life is always wrong," that "capital punishment is always morally wrong," or that "suicide is never morally permissible." The apparent contradictions signal confusion on the matter.

In this section I examine the central notions of ethical relativism and look at the implications that seem to follow from it. Then I set forth the outlines of a very modest objectivism, which holds to the objective validity of moral principles but takes into account many of the insights of relativism.

1. *An Analysis of Relativism*

Ethical Relativism is the theory that there are no universally valid moral principles, but that all moral principles are valid relative to culture or individual choice. It is to be distinguished from moral skepticism, the view that there are no valid moral principles at all (or at least that we cannot know whether there are any), and from all forms of moral objectivism or absolutism. The following statement by John Ladd is a typical characterization of the theory.

> Ethical relativism is the doctrine that the moral rightness and wrongness of actions varies from society to society and that there are no absolute universal moral standards binding on all men at all times. Accordingly, it holds that whether or not it is right for an individual to act in a certain way depends on or is relative to the society to which he belongs.[1]

If we analyze this passage, we derive the following argument:

1. What is considered morally right and wrong varies from society to society, so that there are no moral principles accepted by all societies.
2. All moral principles derive their validity from cultural acceptance.
3. Therefore, there are no universally valid moral principles—objective standards that apply to all people everywhere and at all times.

1. The first thesis, which may be called the *Diversity thesis* and identified with *Cultural Relativism,* is simply an anthropological thesis, which registers the fact that moral rules differ from society to society. As noted in the introduction of this essay, there is enormous variety in what may count as a moral principle in a given society. The human condition is malleable in the extreme, allowing any number of folkways or moral codes. As Ruth Benedict has written:

> The cultural pattern of any civilization makes use of a certain segment of the great arc of potential human purposes and motivations, just as we have seen . . . that any culture makes use of certain selected material techniques or cultural traits. The great arc along which all the possible human behaviors are distributed is far too immense and too full of contradictions for any one culture to utilize even any considerable portion of it. Selection is the first requirement.[2]

It may or may not be the case that no single moral principle is held in common by every society, but if there are any, they seem to be few, at best. Certainly it would be very hard to derive one single "true" morality on the basis of observation of various societies' moral standards.

2. The second thesis, the *Dependency thesis,* asserts that individual acts are right or wrong depending on the nature of the society from which they emanate. Morality does not occur in a vacuum, but what is considered morally right or wrong must be seen in a context, depending on the goals, wants, beliefs, history, and environment of the society in question. As William Graham Sumner says, "We learn the [morals] as unconsciously as we learn to walk and hear and breathe, and they never know any reason why the [morals] are what they are. The justification of them is that when we wake to consciousness of life we find the facts which already hold us in the bonds of tradition, custom, and habit."[3] Trying to see things from an independent, noncultural point of view would be like taking out our eyes in order to examine their contours and qualities. We are simply culturally determined beings.

We could, of course, distinguish a weak and a strong thesis of dependency. The nonrelativist can accept a certain relativity in the way moral principles are *applied* in various cultures, depending on beliefs, history, and environment. For example, Orientals show respect by covering the head and uncovering the feet, whereas Occidentals do the opposite, but both adhere to a principle of respect for deserving people. They just apply the principle of respect differently. Drivers in Great Britain drive on the left side of the road, while those in the rest of Europe and the United States drive on the right side, but both adhere to a principle of orderly progression of traffic. The application of the rule is different, but the principle in question is the same principle in both cases. However, the ethical relativist must maintain a stronger thesis, one that insists that the very validity of the principles is a product of the culture and that different cultures invent different valid principles. The ethical relativist maintains that even beyond the environmental factors and differences in beliefs, there is a fundamental disagreement among societies.

In a sense, we all live in radically different worlds. Each person has a different set of beliefs and experiences, a particular perspective that colors all of his or her perceptions. Do the farmer, the real estate dealer, and the artist, looking at the same spatiotemporal field, see the *same* field? Not likely. Their different orientations, values, and expectations govern their perceptions, so different aspects of the field are highlighted for each and some features are missed. Even as our individual values arise from personal experience, so social values are grounded in the peculiar history of the community. Morality, then, is just the set of common rules, habits, and customs that have won social approval over time; they seem part of the nature of things—facts. There is nothing mysterious or transcendent about these codes of behavior. They are the outcomes of our social history.

There is something conventional about *any* morality, so every morality really depends on a level of social acceptance. Not only do various societies adhere to different moral systems, but the very same society can (and often does) change its moral views over time and place. For example, the southern United States now views slavery as immoral, whereas just over 100 years

ago, it did not. We have greatly altered our views on abortion, divorce, and sexuality as well.

3. The conclusion that there are no absolute or objective moral standards binding on all people follows from the first two propositions. Cultural Relativism (the Diversity thesis) plus the Dependency thesis yields ethical relativism in its classic form. If there are different moral principles from culture to culture, and if all morality is rooted in culture, it follows that there are no universal moral principles valid for all cultures and all people at all times.

2. Subjective Ethical Relativism (Subjectivism)

Some people think that even this conclusion is too tame and maintain that morality is not dependent on the society but on the individual him- or herself. As students sometimes maintain, "Morality is in the eye of the beholder." Ernest Hemingway wrote, "So far, about morals, I know only that what is moral is what you feel good after and what is immoral is what you feel bad after and judged by these moral standards, which I do not defend, the bullfight is very moral to me because I feel very fine while it is going on and have a feeling of life and death and mortality and immortality, and after it is over I feel very sad but very fine."[4]

This form of moral subjectivism has the sorry consequence that it makes morality a useless concept for, on its premises, little or no interpersonal criticism or judgment is logically possible. Hemingway may feel good about killing bulls in a bullfight, while Albert Schweitzer or Mother Teresa may feel the opposite. No argument about the matter is possible. The only basis for judging Hemingway or anyone else wrong would be if he failed to live up to his own principles, but of course, one of Hemingway's principles could be that hypocrisy is morally permissible (he feels good about it), so it would be impossible for him to do wrong. For Hemingway hypocrisy and nonhypocrisy are both morally permissible. On the basis of Subjectivism it could very easily turn out that Adolf Hitler is as moral as Gandhi, so long as each believes he is living by his chosen principles. Notions of moral good and bad or right and wrong cease to have interpersonal evaluative meaning. You may not like it when your teacher gives you an F on your test paper while she gives your neighbor an A for one exactly similar, but there is no way to criticize her for injustice. Justice is not one of her elected principles.

Absurd consequences follow from Subjective Ethical Relativism. If it is correct, morality reduces to aesthetic tastes over which there can be neither argument nor interpersonal judgment. Although many students say that they hold this position, there seems to be a conflict between it and some of their other moral views (e.g., that Hitler is really morally bad or that capital punishment is always wrong). There seems to be a contradiction between Subjectivism and the very concept of morality, which it is supposed to characterize, for morality has to do with 'proper' resolution of interpersonal conflict and the amelioration of the human predicament. Whatever else it does, it has a minimal aim of preventing a state of chaos in which life is "solitary, poor, nasty, brutish, and short" (Thomas Hobbes). But if so, Subjectivism is no help at all in doing this, for it doesn't rest on social *agreement* of principle (as the conventionalist maintains) or on an objectively independent set of norms that bind all people for the common good.

Subjectivism treats individuals as billiard balls on a societal pool table where they meet only in radical collisions, each aiming for its own goal and striving to do the other one in. This atomistic view of personality is belied by the fact that we develop in families and mutually dependent communities in which we share a language, institutions, and habits, and that we often feel each other's joys and sorrows. As John Donne said, "No man is an island, entire of itself; every man is a piece of the continent."

Radical individualistic relativism seems incoherent. If so, it follows that the only plausible view of ethical relativism must be one that grounds morality in the group or culture. This form of relativism is called *conventionalism,* and to it we now turn.

3. *Conventional Ethical Relativism (Conventionalism)*

Conventional Ethical Relativism, the view that there are no objective moral principles but that all valid moral principles are justified by virtue of their cultural acceptance, recognizes the social nature of morality. That is precisely its power and virtue. It does not seem subject to the same absurd consequences that plague Subjectivism. Recognizing the importance of our social environment in generating customs and beliefs, many people suppose that ethical relativism is the correct ethical theory. Furthermore, they are drawn to it for its liberal philosophical stance. It seems to be an enlightened response to the sin of ethnocentricity, and it seems to entail or strongly imply an attitude of tolerance toward other cultures. As Benedict says, in recognizing ethical relativity "we shall arrive at a more realistic social faith, accepting as grounds of hope and as new bases for tolerance the coexisting and equally valid patterns of life which mankind has created for itself from the raw materials of existence."[5] The most famous of those holding this position is anthropologist Melville Herskovits, who argues even more explicitly than Benedict that ethical relativism entails intercultural tolerance.

(1) If morality is relative to its culture, then there is no independent basis for criticizing the morality of any other culture but one's own.

(2) If there is no independent way of criticizing any other culture, we ought to be *tolerant* of the moralities of other cultures.

(3) Morality is relative to its culture.

Therefore (4) we ought to be tolerant of the moralities of other cultures.[6]

Tolerance is certainly a virtue, but is this a good argument for it? I think not. If morality simply is relative to each culture, then if the culture does not have a principle of tolerance, its members have no obligation to be tolerant. Herskovits seems to be treating the *principle of tolerance* as the one exception to his relativism, as an absolute moral principle. However, from a relativistic point of view, there is no more reason to be tolerant than to be intolerant, and neither stance is objectively morally better than the other.

Not only do relativists fail to offer a basis for criticizing those who are intolerant, but they also cannot rationally criticize anyone who espouses what they might regard as a heinous principle. If, as seems to be the case, valid criticism supposes an objective or impartial standard, relativists cannot morally criticize anyone outside their own culture. Adolf Hitler's genocidal actions, so long as they are culturally accepted, are as morally legitimate as Mother Teresa's works of mercy. If Conventional Relativism is accepted, racism, genocide of unpopular minorities, oppression of the poor, slavery, and even the advocacy of war for its own sake are as equally moral as their opposites. If a subculture decided that starting a nuclear war was somehow morally acceptable, we could not morally criticize these people.

Any actual morality, whatever its content, is as valid as every other, and more valid than ideal moralities since the latter aren't adhered to by any culture.

Ethical relativism has other disturbing consequences. It seems to entail that reformers are always (morally) wrong since they go against the tide of cultural standards. William Wilberforce was wrong in the eighteenth century to oppose slavery, the British were immoral in opposing *suttee* in India (the burning of widows, which is now illegal). The Early Christians were wrong in refusing to serve in the Roman army or bow down to Caesar, since the majority in the Roman Empire believed that these two acts were moral duties. In fact, Jesus himself was immoral in breaking the law of his day by healing on the Sabbath and by advocating the principles

of the Sermon on the Mount, since it is clear that few in his time (or in ours) accepted them.

Yet we normally feel just the opposite, that a reformer is a courageous innovator who is right, who has the truth, in contrast to the mindless majority. Sometimes an individual must stand alone with the truth, risking social censure and persecution. As Dr. Stockman says in Ibsen's *Enemy of the People,* after he loses the battle to declare his town's profitable polluted tourist spa unsanitary, "The most dangerous enemy of the truth and freedom among us—is the compact majority. Yes, the damned, compact and liberal majority. The majority has *might*—unfortunately—but *right* it is not. Right—are I and a few others." Yet if relativism is correct, the opposite is necessarily the case. Truth is with the crowd and error with the individual.

Similarly, Conventional Ethical Relativism entails disturbing judgments about the law. Our normal view is that we have a *prima facie* duty to obey the law because law, in general, promotes the human good. According to most objective systems, this obligation is not absolute, but relative to the particular law's relation to a wider moral order. Civil disobedience is warranted in some cases where the law seems to be in serious conflict with morality. However, if Ethical Relativism is true, neither law nor civil disobedience has a firm foundation. On the one hand, from the side of the society at large, civil disobedience will be morally wrong so long as the culture agrees with the law in question. On the other hand, if you belong to the relevant subculture that doesn't recognize the particular law in question, disobedience will be morally mandated. The Ku Klux Klan, which believes that Jews, Catholics, and Blacks are evil or undeserving of high regard, are, given conventionalism, morally permitted or required to break the laws that protect these endangered groups. Why should I obey a law that my group doesn't recognize as valid?

To sum up, unless we have an independent moral basis for law, it is hard to see why we have any general duty to obey it; and unless we recognize the priority of a universal moral law, we have no firm basis to justify our acts of civil disobedience against "unjust laws." Both the validity of law and morally motivated disobedience of unjust laws are annulled in favor of a power struggle.

An even more basic problem with the notion that morality depends on cultural acceptance for its validity is that the notion of a culture or society is notoriously difficult to define. This is especially so in a pluralistic society like our own, in which the notion seems to be vague, with unclear boundary lines. One person may belong to several societies (subcultures) with different value emphases and arrangements of principles. A person may belong to the nation as a single society with certain values of patriotism, honor, courage, and law (including some which are controversial but have majority acceptance, such as the law on abortion). He or she may also belong to a church that opposes some of the laws of the state. He may also be an integral member of a socially mixed community in which different principles hold sway, and he may belong to clubs and a family in which still other rules are followed. Relativism seems to tell us that where he is a member of societies with conflicting moralities, he must be judged both wrong and not-wrong, whatever he does. For example, if Mary is a U.S. citizen and a member of the Roman Catholic Church, she is wrong (qua Catholic) if she chooses to have an abortion and not-wrong (qua citizen of the United States) if she acts against the teaching of the church on abortion. As a member of a racist university fraternity, KKK, John has no obligation to treat his fellow Black student as an equal, but as a member of the University community itself (where the principle of equal rights is accepted) he does have the obligation. As a member of the surrounding community (which may reject the principle of equal rights) he again has no such obligation, but as a member of the nation at large (which accepts the

principle) he is obligated to treat his fellow with respect. What is the morally right thing for John to do? The question no longer makes much sense in this moral Babel. It has lost its action-guiding function.

Perhaps the relativist would adhere to a principle which states that in such cases the individual may choose one group as primary. If Mary chooses to have an abortion, she is choosing to belong to the general society relative to that principle. And John must likewise choose between groups. The trouble with this option is that it seems to lead back to counterintuitive results. If Gangland Gus of Murder, Incorporated feels like killing Bank President Ortcutt and wants to feel good about it, he identifies with the Murder, Incorporated society rather than with the general public morality. Does this justify the killing? In fact, couldn't one justify anything simply by forming a small subculture that approved of it? Charles Manson would be morally pure in killing innocents simply by virtue of forming a little coterie. How large must the group be in order to be a legitimate subculture or society? Does it need ten or fifteen people? How about just three? Come to think about it, why can't my burglary partner and I found our own society with a morality of its own. Of course, if my partner dies, I can still claim that I was acting from an originally social set of norms. But why can't I dispense with the interpersonal agreements altogether and invent my own morality, since morality, on this view, is only an invention anyway? Conventionalist Relativism seems to reduce to Subjectivism, and Subjectivism leads, as we have seen, to the demise of morality altogether.

However, while we may fear the demise of morality, as we have known it, this in itself may not be a good reason for rejecting relativism, that is, for judging it false. Alas, truth is not always edifying. But the consequences of this position are sufficiently alarming to prompt us to look carefully for some weakness in the relativist's argument. So let us examine the premises and conclusions listed at the beginning of this chapter as the three theses of relativism.

1. *The Diversity Thesis*

   What is considered morally right and wrong varies from society to society, so there are no moral principles accepted by all societies.

2. *The Dependency Thesis*

   All moral principles derive their validity from cultural acceptance.

3. *Ethical Relativism*

   Therefore, there are no universally valid moral principles—objective standards that apply to all people everywhere and at all times.

Does any one of these seem problematic? Let us consider the first thesis, the Diversity Thesis, which we have also called Cultural Relativism. Perhaps there is not as much diversity as anthropologists such as Sumner and Benedict suppose. One can also see great similarities between the moral codes of various cultures. E. O. Wilson has identified over a score of common features, and before him Clyde Kluckhohn has noted some significant common ground.

> Every culture has a concept of murder, distinguishing this from execution, killing in war, and other "justifiable homicides." The notions of incest and other regulations upon sexual behavior, the prohibitions upon untruth under defined circumstances, of restitution and reciprocity, of mutual obligations between parents and children—these and many other moral concepts are altogether universal.[7]

Colin Turnbull, whose description of the sadistic, semidisplaced Ik in Northern Uganda was seen as evidence of a people without principles of kindness and cooperation, has produced evidence that underneath the surface of this dying society, there is a deeper moral code from a time when the tribe flourished, a code that occasionally surfaces and shows its nobler face.

On the other hand, enormous cultural diversity exists, and many societies have radically different moral codes. Cultural Relativism seems to be a fact, but even so, it does not by itself establish the truth of Ethical Relativism. Cultural diversity in itself is neutral between theories. The objectivist could concede complete cultural relativism but still defend a form of universalism; he or she could argue that some cultures simply lack correct moral principles.

A denial of complete Cultural Relativism (i.e., an admission of some universal principles) does not disprove Ethical Relativism. Even if we did find one or more universal principles, this would not prove that they had any objective status. We could still *imagine* a culture that was an exception to the rule and be unable to criticize it. The first premise doesn't by itself imply Ethical Relativism, and its denial doesn't disprove Ethical Relativism.

We turn to the crucial second thesis, the Dependency Thesis. Morality does not occur in a vacuum, but what is considered morally right or wrong must be seen in a context, depending on the goals, wants, beliefs, history, and environment of the society in question. We distinguished a weak from a strong thesis of dependency. The weak thesis says that the application of principles depends on the particular cultural predicament, whereas the strong thesis affirms that the principles themselves depend on that predicament. The nonrelativist can accept a certain relativity in the way moral principles are applied in various cultures, depending on beliefs, history, and environment. For example, a raw environment with scarce natural resources may justify the Eskimos' brand of euthanasia to the objectivist, who in another environment would consistently reject that practice. The members of a tribe in the Sudan throw their deformed children into the river because of their belief that such infants *belong* to the hippopotamus, god of the river. We believe that they have a false belief about this, but the point is that the same principles of respect for property and respect for human life are operative in these contrary practices. These people differ with us only in belief, not in substantive moral principle. This is an illustration of how nonmoral beliefs (e.g., deformed children belong to the hippopotamus) when applied to common moral principles (e.g., give to each his due) generate different actions in different cultures. In our own culture, differences in the nonmoral beliefs about the status of a fetus generate opposite moral prescriptions. The fact that moral principles are weakly dependent doesn't show that Ethical Relativism is valid. In spite of this weak dependency on nonmoral factors, there could still be a set of general moral norms applicable to all cultures and even recognized in most, but disregarded at a culture's own expense.

What the relativist needs is a strong thesis of dependency, that somehow all principles are essentially cultural inventions. But why should we choose to view morality this way? Is there anything to recommend the strong thesis over the weak thesis of dependency? The relativist may argue that in fact we don't have an obvious impartial standard from which to judge. "Who's to say which culture is right and which is wrong?" But this seems dubious. We can reason and perform thought experiments to make a case for one system over another. We may not be able to *know* with certainty that our moral beliefs are closer to the truth than those of another culture or those of others within our own culture, but we may be *justified* in believing that they are. If we can be closer to the truth regarding factual or scientific matters, why can't we be closer to the truth on moral matters? Why can't a culture simply be confused or wrong about its moral perceptions? Why can't we say that a society like the Ik, which sees nothing wrong with watching its own children fall into fires, is less moral in that regard than a culture that cher-

ishes children and grants them protection and equal rights? To take such a stand is not to commit the fallacy of ethnocentrism, for we are seeking to derive principles through critical reasoning, not simply uncritical acceptance of one's own mores.

4. The Case for Moral Objectivism

If nonrelativists are to make their case, they will have to offer a better explanation of cultural diversity and why we should nevertheless adhere to moral objectivism. One way of doing this is to appeal to a divine law and to human sin, which causes deviation from that law. Although I think that human greed, selfishness, pride, self-deception and other maladies have a great deal to do with moral differences and that religion may lend great support to morality, I don't think that a religious justification is necessary for the validity of moral principles. In any case, in this section I shall outline a modest nonreligious objectivism, first by appealing to our intuitions and second by giving a naturalist account of morality that transcends individual cultures.

First, I must make it clear that I am distinguishing Moral *Absolutism* from Moral *Objectivism*. The absolutist believes there are non-overridable moral principles that ought never to be violated. Kant's system is a good example of this. One should never break a promise, no matter what. Act utilitarianism also seems absolutist, for the principle of doing that act that has the most promise of yielding the most utility, is non-overridable. An objectivist need not posit any non-overridable principles, at least not in unqualified general form, and so need not be an absolutist. As Renford Bambrough put it,

> To suggest that there is a *right* answer to a
> moral problem is at once to be accused of or
> credited with a belief in moral absolutes. But
> it is no more necessary to believe in moral

absolutes in order to believe in moral objectivity than it is to believe in the existence of absolute space or absolute time in order to believe in the objectivity of temporal and spatial relations and of judgements about them.[8]

In the Objectivist's account, moral principles are what William Ross refers to as *prima facie* principles, valid rules of action that should generally be adhered to, but which may be overridden by another moral principle in cases of moral conflict. For example, although a principle of justice may generally outweigh a principle of benevolence, there are times when enormous good can be done by sacrificing a small amount of justice, so an objectivist would be inclined to act according to the principle of benevolence. There may be some absolute or non-overridable principles, but there need not be any (or many) for objectivism to be true.[9]

If we can establish or show that it is reasonable to believe in the existence of at least one objective moral principle that is binding on all people everywhere in some ideal sense, we shall have shown that relativism is probably false and that a limited objectivism is true. Actually, I believe that there are many qualified general ethical principles that are binding on all rational beings, but one will suffice to refute relativism. The principle I've chosen is the following:

A. It is morally wrong to torture people for the fun of it.

I claim that this principle is binding on all rational agents, so if an agent, S, rejects A, we should not let that affect our intuition that A is a true principle but rather try to explain S's behavior as perverse, ignorant, or irrational. For example, suppose Adolf Hitler doesn't accept A. Should that affect our confidence in the truth of A? Is it not more reasonable to infer that Adolf is morally deficient, morally blind, ignorant, or irrational than to suppose that his noncompliance is evidence against the truth of A?

Suppose further that there is a tribe of Hitlerites somewhere who enjoy torturing people. The whole culture accepts torturing others for the fun of it. Suppose that Mother Teresa or Gandhi tries unsuccessfully to convince them that they should stop torturing people altogether, and they respond by torturing them. Should this affect our confidence in A? Would it not be more reasonable to look for some explanation of Hitlerite behavior? For example, we might hypothesize that this tribe lacks a developed sense of sympathetic imagination, which is necessary for the moral life. Or we might theorize that this tribe is on a lower evolutionary level than most *Homo sapiens*. Or we might simply conclude that the tribe is closer to a Hobbesian state of nature than are most societies, and as such probably would not survive. We need not know the correct answer as to why the tribe was in such bad shape in order to maintain our confidence in A as a moral principle. If A is a basic or core belief for us, we will be more likely to doubt the Hitlerites' sanity or ability to think morally than to doubt the validity of A.

We can perhaps produce other candidates for membership in our minimally basic objective moral set. For example:

1. Do not kill innocent people.

2. Do not cause unnecessary pain or suffering.

3. Do not cheat or steal.

4. Keep your promises and contracts.

5. Do not deprive another person of his or her freedom.

6. Do justice, treating equals equally and unequals unequally.

7. Tell the truth.

8. Help other people, at least when the cost to oneself is minimal.

9. Show gratitude for services rendered; that is, reciprocate.

10. Obey just law.

These ten principles are examples of the *Core Morality,* principles necessary for the good life. They are not arbitrary, for we can provide reasons that they are necessary for social cohesion and human flourishing. Principles such as the Golden Rule, not killing innocent people, treating equals equally, truth telling, promise keeping, and the like are central to the fluid progression of social interaction and the resolution of conflicts that ethics determines (at least minimal morality is central, even though there may be more to morality than simply these kinds of concerns). For example, language itself depends on a general and implicit commitment to the principle of truth telling. Accuracy of expression is a primitive form of truthfulness; hence, every time we use words correctly, we are telling the truth. Without this behavior, language wouldn't be possible. Likewise, without the recognition of a rule of promise keeping, contracts are of no avail and cooperation is less likely to occur. Without the protection of life and liberty, we could not secure our other goals.

A morality would be adequate if it contained a requisite set of these objective principles or the core morality, but there might be more than one adequate morality that contained different rankings of these principles and other principles consistent with Core Morality. That is, there may be a certain relativity to secondary principles (whether to opt for monogamy rather than polygamy, whether to include a principle of high altruism in the set of moral duties, whether to allocate more resources to medical care than to environmental concerns, whether to institute a law to drive on the left or the right side of the road, and so forth), but in every morality a certain core will remain. It may be applied somewhat differently because of differences in environment, belief, tradition, and the like.

The core moral rules are analogous to the set of vitamins necessary for a healthy diet. We need an adequate amount of each vitamin—some humans more of one than another—but

in prescribing a nutritional diet, we don't have to set forth recipes, specific foods, place settings, or culinary habits. Gourmets will meet the requirements differently than will ascetics and vegetarians, but the basic nutrients may be had by all without rigid regimentation or an absolute set of recipes.

Stated more positively, an objectivist who bases his or her moral system on a common human nature with common needs and desires might argue for objectivism somewhat in this manner:

1. Human nature is relatively similar in essential respects, having a common set of needs and interests.

2. Moral principles are functions of human needs and interests, instituted by reason to promote the most significant interests and needs of rational beings (and perhaps others).

3. Some moral principles promote human interests and meet human needs better than others.

4. The principles that meet essential needs and promote the most significant interests of humans in optimal ways can be said to be objectively valid moral principles.

5. Therefore, since there is a common human nature, there is an objectively valid set of moral principles, applicable to all humanity.

If we leave out any reference to a common human nature, the argument is even simpler:

1. Objectively valid moral principles are those that meet the needs and promote the most significant interests of their adherents.

2. Some principles are such that adherence to them meets the needs and promotes the most significant interests of persons.

3. Therefore, there are some objectively valid moral principles.

Either argument satisfies objectivism, but the former makes it clearer that it is our common human nature that generates the common principles. However, some philosophers might not like to be tied down to the concept of a common human nature, in which case the second version of the argument may be used. It has the advantage that, even if it turns out that we do have somewhat different natures or that other creatures in the universe have somewhat different natures, some of the basic moral principles will still survive.

If this argument succeeds, there must be ideal moralities (not simply adequate ones). Of course, there might still be more than one ideal morality, which presumably an ideal observer would choose under optimal conditions. This observer may conclude that out of an infinite set of moralities, two, three, or more combinations would tie for first place. One expects that these would be similar, but there is every reason to believe that all of them would contain the set of core principles.

Of course, we don't know what an ideal observer would choose, but we can imagine that the conditions under which such an observer would choose would be conditions of maximal knowledge about the consequences of action types and impartiality, second-order qualities that ensure that agents have the best chance of making the best decisions. If this is so, the more we learn to judge impartially and the more we know about possible forms of life, the better chance we have to approximate an ideal moral system. If there is a possibility of approximating ideal moral systems with an objective core and other objective components, then ethical relativism is certainly false. We can confidently dismiss it as an aberration and get on with the job of working out better moral systems.

Let me make my appeal to your intuitions in another way to make the same point. Imagine that you have been miraculously transported to the dark kingdom of hell, and there you get a glimpse of the sufferings of the damned. What is their punishment? Well, they have eternal back itches that ebb and flow, but they cannot scratch their backs, for their arms are paralyzed in a frontal position. Therefore they writhe with itchiness through eternity. Just as you are beginning to feel the itch in your own back, you are suddenly transported to heaven. What do you see in the kingdom of the blessed? Well, you see people who have eternal back itches and cannot scratch their own backs, but they are all smiling instead of writhing. Why? Because everyone has his or her arms stretched out to scratch someone else's back. Arranged in one big circle, they have turned hell into a heaven of ecstasy.

If Ethical Relativism is false and moral objectivism true, why is Ethical Relativism so popular?

One of the main reasons for the appeal of Ethical Relativism is that we have become aware of the evils of ethnocentrism, which has plagued the relations of Europeans and Americans with people of other cultures. We are now more conscious of the frailty of many aspects of our moral repertoire, so now there is a tendency to wonder, "Who's to judge what's really right or wrong?" However, the move from a reasonable cultural relativism, which rightly causes us to rethink our moral systems, to an ethical relativism, which causes us to give up the heart of morality altogether, is an instance of the fallacy of confusing factual or descriptive statements with normative ones. Cultural relativism doesn't entail ethical relativism. The very reason that we are against ethnocentrism constitutes the same basis for our being for an objective moral system: impartial reason draws us to it.

We may well agree that cultures differ and that we ought to be cautious in condemning what we don't understand, but this in no way implies that there are not better and worse ways of living. We can understand and excuse, to some degree at least, those who differ from our best notions of morality without abdicating the notion that cultures without principles of justice or promise keeping or protection of the innocent are morally poorer for these omissions.

In sum, I have argued (1) that Cultural Relativism (the fact that there are cultural differences regarding moral principles) does not entail Ethical Relativism (the thesis that there are no objectively valid universal moral principles); (2) that the Dependency thesis (that morality derives its legitimacy from individual cultural acceptance) is mistaken; and (3) that there are universal moral principles based on a common human nature and a need to solve conflicts of interest and flourish.

Note that if either form of ethical relativism is correct, we will have no basis for arguing against anyone else's view of how he or she should act with regard to the environment. If subjective ethical relativism is correct, each individual may choose his or her own moral perspective. If conventional ethical relativism is correct, all we have to do is identify with a specific culture to justify our treatment of the environment—no matter how degrading, no matter how much suffering it causes, no matter how selfish. If the arguments in the last two chapters are correct, morality has a set of purposes that generate a set of principles to reach those purposes.

So "Who's to judge what's really right or wrong?" *We are.* We are to do so on the basis of the best reasoning we can bring forth and with sympathy and understanding.

Study Questions

1. Explain the difference between cultural and ethical relativism. Are there criteria by which we can say some cultures are morally better than others?
2. Explain the difference between subjectivism and conventionalism. Discuss their strengths and weaknesses. Why is relativism so appealing to many people?
3. Discuss the difference between absolutism and objectivism. What is the meaning of *prima facie* duty?
4. What are the implications of the debate over ethical relativism and objectivism for our treatment of the environment? Can one be a relativist and still promote global environmental ethics? Explain your answer.

For Further Reading

Bambrough, Renford, *Moral Skepticism and Moral Knowledge* (London: Routledge & Kegan Paul, 1979).

Benedict, Ruth, *Patterns of Culture* (New York: New American Library, 1934).

Brink, David, *Moral Realism and the Foundation of Ethics* (Cambridge: Cambridge University Press, 1989).

Gert, Bernard, *Morality: A New Justification of the Moral Rules* (Oxford: Oxford University Press, 1988).

Harman, Gilbert and Judith Jarvis Thomson, *Moral Relativism and Moral Objectivity* (London: Blackwell, 1996).

Mackie, J. L., *Ethics: Inventing Right and Wrong* (New York: Penguin, 1977).

Pojman, Louis, ed., *Ethical Theory* (Belmont, CA: Wadsworth Publishing Co., 1998).

Quinton, Anthony, *Utilitarianism Ethics* (London: MacMillan, 1973).

Sumner, William Graham, *Folkways* (Boston: Ginn and Company, 1906).

Endnotes

1. John Ladd, *Ethical Relativism* (Wadsworth, 1973).

2. Ruth Benedict, *Patterns of Culture* (New York: New American Library, 1934), 219.

3. *Folkways,* New York, 1906, section 80. Ruth Benedict indicates the depth of our cultural conditioning this way. "The very eyes with which we see the problem are conditioned by the long traditional habits of our own society." "Anthropology and the Abnormal," *The Journal of General Psychology* (1934): 59-82.

4. Ernest Hemingway, *Death in the Afternoon* (New York: Scribner's, 1932), 4.

5. Benedict, *Patterns of Culture,* 257.

6. Melville Herskovits, *Cultural Relativism* (Random House, 1972).

7. Clyde Kluckhohn, "Ethical Relativity: Sic et Non," *Journal of Philosophy,* LII (1955).

8. Renford Bambrough, *Moral Skepticism and Moral Knowledge* (London: Routledge & Kegan Paul, 1979), 33.

9. W.D. Ross, *The Right and the Good* (Oxford: Oxford University Press, 1931).

Chapter 3

Egoism, Self-Love, and Altruism

Nice guys finish last.

LEO DUROCHER

The achievement of his own happiness is man's highest moral purpose.

AYN RAND

Children are sometimes brought up feeling guilty if they are concerned about their own good. They are taught that self-love is selfishness, a sinful attitude. To do things for oneself is evil. Indeed, I was brought up in a strict religious community in which children were made to feel they were sinful. The proper attitude toward oneself was one of humility ("Blessed are the poor in spirit, for theirs is the kingdom of heaven") and self-effacement ("Unless a person hates his own life, he cannot enter the kingdom of God").[1]

Sometimes such an upbringing results in self-hatred, low self-esteem, a lack of self-confidence, masochism, and pervasive, irrational guilt. Let's call this attitude the morality of self-effacement.

Lise, in Fyodor Dostoevsky's *Brothers Karamazov,* breaks her engagement with the saintly Alyosha, explaining to him that he is too gentle for her needs:

> I was just thinking for the thirtieth time what a good thing it is that I broke off our engagement and decided not to become your wife. You wouldn't be much of a husband, you know. . . . I want someone to marry me, tear me to pieces, betray me, and then desert me. I don't want to be happy.[2]

Shortly afterward we read,

> Lise unlocked the door, opened it a little, put her finger in the crack, and slammed the door as hard as she could. Ten seconds later she released her hand, went slowly to her chair, sat down, and looked intently at her blackened, swollen finger and the blood that was oozing out from under the nail. Her lips quivered. "I'm vile, vile, vile, a despicable creature."[3]

At the exact opposite extreme is the morality of self-exaltation, or the morality of meism. One is to love oneself first. Ayn Rand's *The Virtue of Selfishness,* Robert Ringer's *Looking Out for Number One,* and David Seabury's *The Art of Selfishness* advise us to love ourselves first, even if it means hurting others. Perhaps no one

was more candid about the legitimacy of *egoism* than Friedrich Nietzsche (1844–1900), who taught that you should strive to satisfy your own will to power even to the extent of exploiting and dominating others before they dominated you: "What is strong wins. That is the universal law. To speak of right and wrong per se makes no sense at all. No act of violence, rape, exploitation, destruction, is intrinsically 'unjust,' since life itself is violent, rapacious, exploitative, and destructive and cannot be conceived otherwise."[4]

But Nietzsche's version of egoism is an extreme one. A less virulent version is found in Thomas Hobbes's (1588–1679) classic *Leviathan* (1651). Hobbes believes egoism is the proper foundation for the moral and political life. Human nature is basically self-interested, so that it makes no sense to ask people to be altruistic. All apparent altruistic acts are, if you look deeply into the heart of people, merely disguised acts of selfishness. Nevertheless, out of enlightened egoism arises objective moral norms and a legitimate political system, the Leviathan.

Hobbes's argument goes like this. Suppose we existed outside of any society without laws or agreed-on morality in a "state of nature." There are no common ways of life, no means of settling conflicts of interest except violence, no reliable expectations of how other people will behave—except that, as psychological egoists, they will follow their own inclinations and perceived interests, tending to act and react and overreact in fearful, capricious, and violent ways.

The result of life in the state of nature is chaotic anarchy. Reason advises us not to depend on anyone except ourselves, for others will let us down if it is in their interests to do so. I must always be on my guard, protecting my vital interests. But I see that others are thinking the same thing—perhaps they are ganging up on me. This increases my fear of others and leads, in turn, to preventive or preemptive aggression, which leads to "a war of all against all."

During the time men live without a common Power to keep them all in awe they are in that condition called War; and such a war, as is of every man against every other man. . . . To this war every man against every man, this is consequent; that nothing can be Unjust. The notions of Right and Wrong, Justice and Injustice have no place.

In such a state, life is "solitary, poor, nasty, brutish, and short."⁵

But reason tells us that a war of all against all is really in no one's interest. It would be better for all of us, individually and collectively, if we adopted certain minimal rules that would override immediate self-interests whenever self-interests were a threat to others. So the notion of a mutually agreed-on moral code arises from a situation of rational self-interest.

Of course, the moral code will not work if only some obey it, because those who do will be slaughtered like sheep before waiting wolves. Reason can support morality only when the presumption about other people's behavior is reversed. Hobbes thought that this could be achieved only by the creation of a *Leviathan*, an absolute ruler with absolute power to enforce his laws. But this is incorrect. The minimal moral society may be achieved by a people democratically if common rules or ways of life are taught to all members of the society, inculcated in them early in life, and enforced by the group.

The members must be able to count on one another to obey these rules even when it is not in their immediate self-interest. Nonetheless, it is still rational to violate the rules whenever two conditions obtain: You calculate that you can get away with it, and your infraction will not seriously threaten the stability of the social system as a whole, sending you back toward the state of nature.

To prevent such violations, Hobbes proposed a strong central government with a powerful police force and a sure and effective system of punishment. The threat of being caught and punished should function as a deterrent to

crime. People must believe that offenses against the law are not in their overall interest. Is Hobbes correct in his account of human nature? Is he correct in his view that ethical egoism is the correct moral theory?

What is the place of self-regard, self-interest, or self-love in the moral life? Is everything we do really done out of self-interest, meaning that morality is necessarily egoistic? Is some form of egoism the best moral theory? Or is egoism really diametrically opposed to true morality? What is the relationship of egoism to morality?

There are two versions of egoism: individual egoism and universal ethical egoism, both of which claim to tell how to live the moral life.

Individual ethical egoism is the view that everyone ought always to serve my self-interest. That is, moral rightness is defined solely in terms of what is good for me, whether or not it is good for anyone else. Of course, every one of us may put his own name in the place of "me." Say, for example, that Aunt Ruth is an individual ethical egoist; thus, all moral rightness consists entirely in what is good for Aunt Ruth. It would follow that whether or not a mother in India loves her child is morally irrelevant, for it has no effect on Aunt Ruth. Now that Aunt Ruth is dead, morality is dead, for it has no object.

Interestingly enough, while individual ethical egoism seems implausible, it may be the central position of many religious people who define ethics as that which serves God's interests and pleases him. For mere mortals, individual ethical egoism seems a partial and absurd theory. What makes you so special that all of us have an obligation to grant your interests as our primary concern?

Universal ethical egoism is the theory that everyone ought always to serve his or her own self-interest. That is, everyone ought to do what will maximize one's own expected utility or bring about one's own happiness, even when it means harming others. Brian Medlin defines ethical egoism this way: "Everyone (including the speaker) ought to look after his own interest and to disregard those of other people except insofar as their interests contribute towards his own."[6] Jesse Kalin defines it thus: For everyone (x) and for every act (y), "x ought to do y if and only if y is in x's overall self-interest."[7] This has all the earmarks of a legitimate ethical theory. It is a universal theory, applying to everyone equally and without bias, which is not the case with individual egoism. It is not egotistical but prudential, and it favors long-term interests over short-term interests. In its most sophisticated form, it urges everyone to *try* to win in the game of life and recognizes that to do this, some compromises are necessary. Indeed, the universal egoist will admit that to some extent we must all give up a certain freedom and cooperate with others to achieve our ends.

We will consider three arguments for universal ethical egoism: the economist argument, the Ayn Rand argument, and the Hobbesian argument. We want to know whether any of them give us an argument for an adequate moral theory based on egoism.

The Economist Argument

Economists, following Adam Smith (1723–1790), often argue that individual self-interest in a state of competition in the marketplace produces a state of optimal goodness for society at large because the peculiar nature of self-interested competition causes each competitor to produce a better product and sell it at a lower price than his or her competitors. Enlightened self-interest leads, as though by an invisible hand, to the best overall situation.

The *economist argument*, essentially not an argument for ethical egoism, is really an argument for utilitarianism (see chapter 4), which makes use of self-interest to attain, paradoxically, the good of all. Its goal is social utility, but it places its faith in an invisible hand, inherent in the free-enterprise system, to use enlightened self-interest to reach that goal. We might say that it is a two-tier system. On the highest level,

it is utilitarian; on a lower level of day-to-day action, it is practical egoism. It tells us not to worry about the social good but only our own good; in that way, we will attain the highest social good possible.

There may be some truth in such a two-tier system, but two objections arise. First, it is at best unclear whether you can transpose the methods of economics (which are debatable) into the realm of personal relations. Personal relations may have a different logic than economic relations. The best way to maximize utility in an ethical sense may be to give one's life for others rather than kill another person, as an egoist may enjoin. Second, it is not clear that classical laissez-faire capitalism works. Since the 1929 depression, most economists have altered their faith in classical capitalism, and most Western nations have supplemented capitalism with some government intervention. Similarly, although self-interest may often lead to greater social utility, it may get out of hand and need to be supplemented by a concern for others. Just as classical capitalism has been altered to allow government intervention—resulting in a welfare system for the worst-off people, public education, Social Security, and Medicare—an adequate moral system may need to draw attention to the needs of others and direct us to meeting those needs even where we do not see it to be in our immediate self-interest.

The Ayn Rand Argument

In her book *The Virtue of Selfishness*, Ayn Rand (1905–1982), describing her "objectivist ethics" as egoistic, argues that selfishness is a virtue and altruism is a vice, a totally destructive idea that leads to the undermining of individual worth:

> Man's proper values and interests, that *concern with his own interests* is the essence of a moral existence, and that *man must be the beneficiary of his own moral actions*. . . . If a man accepts the ethics of altruism, his first concern is not how to live his life, but how to sacrifice it. . . .

Altruism erodes men's capacity to grasp the value of an individual life; it reveals a mind from which the reality of a human being has been wiped out. . . . Altruism holds *death* as its ultimate goal and standard of value—and it is logical that renunciation, resignation, self-denial, and every other form of suffering, including self-destruction, are the virtues it advocates.[8]

In her novel *The Fountainhead,* Rand paints Howard Rourk, her hero, as an egoist who is dedicated to his own happiness and Ellsworth Toohey, the altruistic philanthropist, as a scoundrel. Altruism, in the hands of the likes of Toohey, Rand avers, calls on one to sacrifice his or her life, not to find happiness, which is the highest goal of life.

According to Rand, the perfection of one's abilities in a state of happiness is the highest goal for humans. We have a moral duty to attempt to reach this goal. Because the ethics of altruism prescribes that we sacrifice our interests and lives for the good of others, it is incompatible with the goal of happiness. Ethical egoism prescribes that we seek our own happiness exclusively, and as such it is consistent with the happiness goal. Therefore, ethical egoism is the correct moral theory.

The *Ayn Rand argument* for the virtues of selfishness is flawed by the fallacy of a false dilemma. It simplistically assumes that absolute altruism or absolute egoism are the only alternatives, but this is an extreme view of the matter. There are plenty of options between these two positions. Even a predominant egoist would admit that, analogous to the *hedonistic paradox,* sometimes the best way to reach self-fulfillment is for us to forget about ourselves and strive to live for goals, causes, or other persons. Even if altruism is not required as a duty, it may be permissible in many cases. Furthermore, self-interest may be compatible with concern for others. Even the Second Commandment, "Love your neighbor as yourself," set forth by Moses and Jesus, states not that you must always sacri-

fice yourself for the other person but that you ought to love your neighbor *as* yourself (Leviticus 19:18; Matthew 22:39). Self-interest and self-love are morally good things, but not at the expense of other people's legitimate interests. When there is moral conflict of interests, a fair process of adjudication must take place.

Actually, Rand slides back and forth between advocating selfishness and self-interest. Most of the time, if I understand her, she is really advocating self-interest, in which case nonegoists can agree with her. Her villain, her paradigmatic altruist Ellsworth Toohey, is not an altruist at all, but an insecure, envious ideologue who manipulates others for his causes.

The Hobbesian Argument

As we noted earlier, Hobbes thought that we were fundamentally egoistical. We might as well recognize this fact and work it into our moral theory. It is permissible to live self-interested lives since we cannot do otherwise without unreasonable effort. However, enlightened common sense tells us that we should aim at fulfilling our long-term versus our short-term interests, so we need to refrain from immediate gratification of our senses, from doing things that would break down the social conditions that enable us to reach our goals. We should even, perhaps, generally obey the Golden Rule, "Do unto others as you would have them do unto you," for doing good unto others helps ensure that they do good unto us. However, sometimes we should cheat when our doing so will maximize agent utility, and sometimes we should harm others when it is in our overall self-interest to do so.

Sometimes this version of egoism is based on the notion that all values are essentially owned by an agent and that each of us has our own hierarchy and specific set of values, so each of us has different reasons for acting. There are no agent-neutral values, identical in all persons. Naturally, we have to cooperate with others in the pursuit of our projects, but ultimately we are alone in the world, the only persons who know exactly what the values are. Sometimes we may have to harm others in order to realize our projects.

Hobbes's argument is flawed by ideological pessimism. It assumes that we cannot do any better than be egoists, so we should be as enlightened about our egoism as possible. But this cynicism about human nature seems extreme. Although there is a tendency toward self-interest, humans are capable of disinterested action, benevolence, and even high altruism. As David Hume (1711–1776) said, "There is some benevolence, however small, infused into our bosom; some spark of friendship for humankind; some particle of the dove kneaded into our frame, along with the elements of the wolf and serpent."⁹ There is a great variation in people regarding their ability to act disinterestedly, kindly, and altruistically. Some seem innocently other-regarding, whereas others seem pugnacious Scrooges from birth on.

Arguments Against Ethical Egoism

Not only do the arguments for ethical egoism have drawbacks, but there are also four arguments against this doctrine.

THE PUBLICITY ARGUMENT

On the one hand, it seems necessary that something be a moral theory to publicize one's moral principles. Unless principles are put forth as universal prescriptions that are accessible to the public, they cannot serve as guides to action or as helps in resolving conflicts of interest. On the other hand, it is not in the egoist's self-interest to publicize them. Egoists would rather that the rest of us be altruists. (Why did Nietzsche and Rand write books, announcing their positions—were the royalties taken in by announcing ethical egoism worth the price of letting the "cat out of the bag"?)

It would be a bad thing for an egoist to argue for his position, and even worse that he

or she should convince others of it! However, it is perfectly possible to have a private morality that does not resolve conflicts of interest (for that, the egoist publicizes standard principles of traditional morality). So, if you're willing to pay the price, you can accept the solipsistic-directed norms of egoism.

If the egoist is prepared to pay the price, egoism could be a consistent system but have some limitations. Although the egoist can cooperate with others in limited ways and perhaps even have friends—as long as their interests don't conflict with his—he has to be very careful about preserving his isolation. The egoist can't give advice or argue about his position, not sincerely at least. He must act alone, atomistically or solipsistically, in moral isolation, for to announce one's adherence to the principle of egoism would be dangerous to his project. He can't teach his children or justify himself to others or forgive others.

THE PARADOX OF EGOISM

The situation, however, may be even worse than the sophisticated, self-conscious egoist supposes. Can the egoist have friends? And if limited friendship is possible, can she ever be in love or experience deep friendship? Suppose the egoist discovers that in the pursuit of the happiness goal, deep friendship is in her best interest. Can she become a friend? What is necessary to deep friendship? A true friend is one who is not always preoccupied about her own interest in the relationship but who forgets about herself altogether, at least sometimes, in order to serve or enhance the other person's interest. "Love seeketh not its own" is an altruistic disposition, the very opposite of egoism. One can go on to argue that friendship is a necessary ingredient for psychological health. Since egoists cannot have true friends, they cannot attain psychological health. Since any theory that undermines psychological health is an inadequate moral theory, ethical egoism must be rejected. So the paradox of egoism is that to reach the goal of egoism, one must give up egoism and become to some extent an altruist, the very antithesis of egoism.

Does the egoist have a reply to this criticism? Perhaps she can construct a split-level egoism. On the *higher* level, I am committed to advancing my own good above all else, whatever the effect on others. But I may conclude that to maximize personal utility, I must have friends. Because having friends requires having altruistic dispositions, I must on a *lower* or *practical* level be selectively *altruistic,* rather than egoistic.

I leave it to you to decide whether such split-level egoism is really egoism and whether one can even maintain it.

RELEVANT DIFFERENCE ARGUMENT

This argument, based on a concept of universalizability and developed by James Rachels, goes like this: All difference of treatment between people must be justified by some relevant difference in description of the people or their acts. For example, I am justified in paying Mary twice as much as John because she is working twice as long and producing twice as many widgets, but I am not justified in paying Mary twice as much as Sam simply because Mary is an African American and Sam is an Asian American. Race is an irrelevant difference. Racism, sexism, and fanatical nationalism are all prejudices that violate the relevant difference principle. This principle applies to egoism as well: What makes you so different from everyone else that you will allow your preferences to count for more than other rational beings? It seems unjust.[10]

Of course, the egoist will reject the relevant difference principle in his or her behavior and so allow racism, sexism, and other forms of discrimination. I've heard egoists deny that they are racists, but the truth is, there is no reason to prohibit them from being called racists. If it's in my interest to be a racist, I *ought* to be one, and if it's not, then I *ought* not to be one. It all depends on whether being thus serves my interest.

If it does, the version of egoism set forth above requires that we be racists.

THE COUNTERINTUITIVE CONSEQUENCES ARGUMENT

The final argument against ethical egoism is that it leads to consequences that seem abhorrent. If we followed its dictates, we would be prohibited from doing acts that seem obviously good. It is an absolute ethics that not only permits egoistic behavior but also demands it. Helping others at one's own expense is not only not required but also morally wrong. Whenever I do not have good evidence that my helping you will end up to my advantage, I must refrain from helping you. In New York City (Queens) in March 1964, not only did the thirty-eight people who watched Kitty Genovese being beaten and repeatedly stabbed to death have *no* obligation to call for help, but they also would have been wrong to do so. If I can save the whole of Europe and Africa from destruction by pressing a little button, as long as there is nothing for me to gain by it, it is wrong for me to press that button. The Good Samaritan was, by this logic, a vicious man in helping the injured victim and not collecting on it. It is certainly hard to see why the egoist should be concerned about environmental matters if he or she is profiting from polluting the environment (e.g., if the egoist gains 40 hedons in production *P*, which produces pollution that, in turn, causes others 1000 dolors—units of suffering—but he only suffers 10 of those dolors himself, by an agent-maximizing calculus, he is morally obligated to produce *P*). There is certainly no obligation to preserve scarce natural resources for future generations. "Why should I do anything for posterity?" the egoist asks. "What has posterity ever done for me?"

In the text above, I have described a strong version of ethical egoism. One could accuse me of attacking a straw man if it weren't for the fact that people like Rand, Kalin, and others defend this strong position, making serving one's self-interest a necessary and sufficient condition for moral obligation. But perhaps there is a weaker form of ethical egoism that states that it is always *permissible* to do whatever is in your (the agent's) self-interest. The problem with this is that it seems either to reduce morality to subjectivism (discussed in the last chapter) or to eliminate any normativity from ethics altogether. If it's always permissible to do what is in my self-interest, it is also permissible to do what is not in my self-interest. Unless we are given supplementary guidance, this seems to leave *every* act as permissible!

Evolution and Altruism

If sheer, unadulterated egoism is an inadequate moral theory, does that mean that we ought to aim at complete altruism, total self-effacement for the sake of others? What is the role of self-love in morality? An interesting place to start is with the new field of sociobiology, which posits the theory that social structures and behavioral patterns, including morality, have a biological base, explained by evolutionary theory.

In the past, linking ethics to evolution meant justifying exploitation. Social Darwinism justified imperialism and the principle that "might makes right" by saying that the law of nature is the survival of the fittest. This philosophy lent itself to a promotion of ruthless egoism. This is nature's law, "nature red in tooth and claw." Against this view, ethologists such as Robert Ardrey and Konrad Lorenz argue for a more benign view of the animal kingdom—reminiscent of Rudyard Kipling—where the animal kingdom survives by cooperation, which is at least as important as competition. In Ardrey and Lorenz's view, it is the group or species, not the individual, that is of primary importance.

With the onset of sociobiology in the work of E. O. Wilson, but particularly with the work of Robert Trivers, J. Maynard Smith, and Richard Dawkins, a theory has come to the fore that combines radical individualism with limited altruism. It is not the group or species that is of evolutionary importance, but the gene or, more precisely, the gene type. Genes, the parts of the chromosomes that carry the blueprints for all our natural traits (e.g., height, hair color, skin color, and intelligence), copy themselves as they divide and multiply. In conception they combine with the genes of the member of the opposite sex to form a new individual.

In his fascinating sociobiological study, Richard Dawkins describes human behavior as determined evolutionarily by stable strategies set to replicate the gene.[11] This is not done consciously, of course, but it's the invisible hand that drives the consciousness. We're essentially gene machines.

Successful morality can be seen as an evolutionary strategy for gene replication. Here's an example. Birds are afflicted with life-endangering parasites. Because they cannot use limbs to pick them off their heads, they—like much of the animal world—depend on the ritual of mutual grooming. Nature has evolved two different types of birds in this regard: those who are disposed to groom anyone (the nonprejudiced type?) and those who refuse to groom anyone but who present themselves for grooming. The former type of bird Dawkins calls "Suckers" and the latter "Cheaters."

In a geographic area with harmful parasites where there are only Suckers or Cheaters, Suckers will do fairly well, but Cheaters will not survive for want of cooperation. However, in a Sucker population in which a mutant Cheater arises, the Cheater will prosper and his gene type will multiply. As the Suckers are exploited, they will gradually die out, but if they become too few to groom the Cheaters, the Cheaters will start to die off, too, and eventually they will become extinct.

Why don't birds all die off, then? Well, somehow nature has come up with a third type, call them "Reciprocators." Reciprocators groom only those who reciprocate in grooming them. They groom one another and Suckers, but not

Cheaters. In fact, once a Cheater is caught, he is marked forever. There is no forgiveness. It turns out then that unless there are a lot of Suckers around, Cheaters have a hard time of it—harder even than Suckers! But it is the Reciprocators that prosper. Unlike Suckers, they don't waste their time messing with unappreciative Cheaters, so they are not exploited, and they have ample energy to gather food and build better nests for their loved ones.

J. L. Mackie argues that the real name for a Sucker is "Christian," one who believes in complete altruism, even turning the other cheek to one's assailant and loving one's enemy. Cheaters are ruthless egoists who can survive only if there are enough naïve altruists around. Whereas Reciprocators are *reciprocal* altruists who have a rational morality based on cooperative self-interest, Suckers like Socrates and Jesus advocate "turning the other cheek and repaying evil with good."[12] Instead of a rule of reciprocity: "I'll scratch your back if you'll scratch mine," the extreme altruist substitutes the Golden Rule: "If you'd like the other fellow to scratch your back, you scratch his—even if he won't reciprocate."

The moral of the story is this: the Altruist's morality (so interpreted) is rational only given the payoff of eternal life (with a scorekeeper, as Woody Allen says). Take that away, and it looks like a Sucker system. What replaces the "Christian" vision of submission and saintliness is the reciprocal altruist's tit-for-tat morality, the willingness to share with those willing to cooperate.

Mackie may caricature the position of the religious altruist, but he misses the subtleties of wisdom involved (Jesus said, "Be as wise as serpents but as harmless as doves"). Nevertheless, Mackie does remind us that there is a difference between core morality and complete altruism. We have duties to cooperate and reciprocate, but no duty to serve those who manipulate us and no obvious duty to sacrifice ourselves for people outside our domain of special responsibility. We have a special duty of high altruism toward those in the close circle of our concern, namely, our family and friends.

Conclusion

Martin Luther once said that humanity is like a man who is mounting a horse and always falls off on the opposite side, especially when he tries to overcompensate for his previous exaggerations. So it is with ethical egoism. Trying to compensate for an irrational, guilt-ridden, complete Sucker altruism of the morality of self-effacement, it falls off the horse on the other side, embracing a Cheater's preoccupation with self-exaltation that robs the self of the deepest joys in life. Only a person who mounts properly, avoiding both extremes, is likely to ride the horse of happiness to its goal.

Study Questions

1. Distinguish between individual and universal ethical egoism. Which theory appeals to you more? Does either constitute an adequate ethical theory? Explain your answer.
2. Discuss the three arguments in favor of ethical egoism and the four against it. Which side has the best arguments? Why?
3. What is the relationship between ethics and evolution? How does this relationship throw light on egoism? What is the significance of reciprocity for ethics?
4. Can an ethical egoist have friends? Some philosophers, beginning with Plato, have argued that ethical egoism is irrational, since it precludes psychological health. In an article entitled "Ethical Egoism and Psychological Dispositions" (*American Philosophical Quarterly* 17, 1980), Laurence Thomas sets forth the following argument.

1. A true friend could never, as a matter of course, be disposed to harm or to exploit a friend [definition of a friend].

2. An egoist could never be a true friend to anyone [for the egoist must be ready to exploit others whenever it is in his or her interest].

3. Only someone with an unhealthy personality could never be a true friend to anyone [definition of a healthy personality; that is, friendship is a necessary condition for a healthy personality].

4. Ethical egoism requires that we have a kind of disposition which is incompatible with our having a healthy personality [from 1–3].
   Conclusion: Therefore, from the standpoint of our psychological makeup, ethical egoism is unacceptable as a moral theory.
   Do you agree with Thomas? Explain your answer.

5. In this chapter, we have argued against various forms of egoism. Can you think of a version of ethical egoism that can meet the objections presented?

For Further Reading

Baier, Kurt, *The Moral Point of View* (Ithaca, NY: Cornell University Press, 1958). A good discussion of egoism and related issues.

Gauthier, David, *Morality by Agreement* (Oxford: Clarendon Press, 1986). The best defense of a contractualist position based on enlightened self-interest in the literature.

Pojman, Louis, ed., *Ethical Theory: Classical and Contemporary Readings*, 3rd ed., (Belmont, CA: Wadsworth, 1998). Contains several important readings in this area.

Rachels, James, *The Elements of Moral Philosophy*, (New York: Random House, 1986). Chapters 5 and 6 are two of the best discussions of egoism in the literature.

Rand, Ayn, *The Virtues of Selfishness*, (New York: Signet Books, 1964). An example of ethical egoism, wherein altruism is considered a virtue.

Singer, Peter, *The Expanding Circle: Ethics and Sociobiology*, (Oxford: Oxford University Press, 1983). A good discussion of egoism in the light of sociobiology.

Endnotes

1. Luke 14:26. "If any man come to me and hate not his father and his mother and his wife and children and brethren and sisters, yea and his own life also, he cannot be my disciple." Some interpretations of this difficult passage argue that Jesus is saying that in *comparison* to one's devotion to God, which should be absolute, other relationships should be secondary or nonabsolute.

2. Fyodor Dostoevsky, *The Brothers Karamazov*, trans. Andrew MacAndrews (New York: Bantam Books, 1970), 697.

3. Ibid., 703.

4. Friedrich Nietzsche, *Genealogy of Morals*, trans. Walter Kaufmann (New York: Random House, 1966), 208. Some may accuse Nietzsche of "nihilism," of undermining ethics altogether, but I think that Nietzsche believed in an elitist morality in which the "superior" egoists cooperate with one another in their struggle against the herd, the mediocre masses of humanity.

5. Thomas Hobbes, *Leviathan*, ch. 13.

6. Brian Medlin, "Ultimate Principles and Ethical Egoism," in *Australasian Journal of Philosophy* (1957).

7. Jesse Kalin, "In Defense of Ethical Egoism," *Philosophical Review* (1968).

8. Ayn Rand, *The Virtues of Selfishness* (New York: Signet Books, 1964), ix, 27–34, 80ff.

9. David Hume, *An Enquiry Concerning the Principles of Morals* (1751), conclusion.

10. James Rachels, *The Elements of Moral Philosophy* (New York: Random House, 1986), ch. 6.

11. Richard Dawkins, *The Selfish Gene* (Oxford: Oxford University Press, 1976), ch. 10.

12. J. L. Mackie, "The Law of the Jungle: Moral Alternatives and Principles of Evolution," *Philosophy* 53 (1978).

Chapter 4

Classical Ethical Theories

Suppose you are on an island with a dying millionaire. As he lies dying, he entreats you for one final favor: "I've dedicated my whole life to football and have gotten endless pleasure, and some pain, rooting for the Dallas Cowboys for 50 years. Now that I am dying, I want to give all my assets, $2 million, to the Dallas Cowboys. Would you take this money [he indicates a box containing the money in large bills] back to Dallas and give it to the Dallas Cowboys' owner, so that he can buy better players?" You agree to carry out his wish, at which point a huge smile of relief and gratitude breaks out on his face as he expires in your arms. After returning to Dallas, you see a newspaper advertisement placed by the World Hunger Relief Organization (whose integrity you do not doubt) pleading for $2 million to be used to save 100,000 people dying of starvation in East Africa. Not only will the $2 million save their lives, but it will also be used to purchase small technology and the kinds of fertilizers necessary to build a sustainable economy. You reconsider your promise to the dying Cowboys fan in the light of this consideration. What should you do with the money?

Suppose there are two men who are starving to death on a raft floating in the Pacific Ocean. One day they discover some food in an inner compartment of a box on the raft. They have reason to believe that the food will be sufficient to keep one of them alive until the raft reaches a certain island where help is available, but that if they share the food both of them will most likely die. One man is a brilliant scientist who has in his mind the cure for cancer. The other man is undistinguished. Otherwise, there is no relevant difference between the two men. What is the morally right thing to do? Share the food and hope against the odds for a miracle? Flip a coin to see which man gets the food? Give the food to the scientist?

What is the right thing to do in these kinds of situations?

If you decide to act on the principle of promise keeping or not stealing in the case of

the millionaire's money, or if you decide to share the food in the case of the two men on the raft on the basis of the principle of fairness or equal justice, then you adhere to a type of moral theory called *deontology*.

If, on the other hand, you decide to give the money to the World Hunger Relief Organization in order to save an enormous number of lives and restore economic solvency to the region, you side with a type of theory called *teleology* or *consequentialist ethics*. Similarly, if you decide to give the food to the scientist because he would probably do more good with his life, you side with the teleologist.

Traditionally, two major types of ethical systems have dominated the field, one in which the locus of value is the act or kind of act and the other in which the locus of value is the outcome or consequences of the act. The former type of theory is called *deontological* (from the Greek *deon*, meaning "duty," and *logos*, meaning "logic"), and the latter is called *teleological* (from the Greek *teleos*, meaning "having reached one's end" or "finished"). Whereas teleological systems see the ultimate criterion of morality in some nonmoral value that results from acts, deontological systems see certain features in the act itself as having intrinsic value. For example, a teleologist would judge whether lying was morally right or wrong by the consequences it produced, but a deontologist would see something intrinsically wrong in the very act of lying.

As we mentioned earlier, a teleologist is a person whose ethical decision-making aims solely at maximizing nonmoral goods such as pleasure, happiness, welfare, and the amelioration of suffering. That is, the standard of right or wrong action for the teleologist is the comparative consequences of the available actions. The act that produces the best consequences is right. Whereas the deontologist is concerned only with the rightness of the act itself, the teleologist asserts that there is no such thing as an act that has intrinsic worth. Whereas for the deontologist there is something intrinsically bad about lying, for the teleologist the only thing wrong with lying is the bad consequences it produces. If you can reasonably calculate that a lie will do even slightly more good than telling the truth, you have an obligation to lie. In the next section, we will consider the dominant version of teleological ethics, utilitarianism. In the following section, we'll examine deontological ethics, especially Immanuel Kant's ethics as the major form of deontological ethics.

Utilitarianism

The Greatest Happiness for the Greatest Number.

FRANCIS HUTCHESON

One of the earliest examples of utilitarian reasoning is recorded in the New Testament, where Caiaphas, the High Priest, advised the Council to deliver Jesus to the Romans for execution: "You know nothing at all; you do not understand that it is expedient that one man should die for the people, and that the whole nation should not perish" (John 11:50). Sometimes Jesus himself is interpreted as adhering to utilitarianism, such as when he breaks the Sabbath laws in order to do good, saying that "the Sabbath was made for man, not man for the Sabbath" (Mark 2:27).

However, as a moral philosophy, *utilitarianism* begins with the work of Scottish philosopher Francis Hutcheson (1694–1746) and comes into its classical stage in the persons of English social reformers Jeremy Bentham (1748–1832) and John Stuart Mill (1806–1873). They were the nonreligious ancestors of the twentieth-century secular humanists, optimistic about human nature and our ability to solve our problems without recourse to providential grace. Engaged in a struggle for legal as well as moral reform, they were impatient with the rule-bound character of law and morality in eighteenth- and nineteenth-century Great Britain and tried to make the law serve human needs and interests.

Bentham's concerns were mostly practical rather than theoretical. He worked for a thorough reform of what he regarded as an irrational and outmoded legal system. He might well have paraphrased Jesus, making his motto "Morality and Law were made for man, not man for Morality and Law." What good was adherence to outworn deontological rules that served no useful purpose and kept the poor from enjoying a better life? What good were punitive codes that served only to satisfy sadistic lust for vengeance?

The changes the utilitarians proposed were not done in the name of justice; rather, even justice must serve the human good. The poor were to be helped, women were to be liberated, and criminals rehabilitated if possible, not in the name of justice but because doing so would bring about more utility: ameliorate suffering and promote more pleasure or happiness.

Their view of punishment is a case in point. Whereas deontologists believe in retribution—that all the guilty should be punished in proportion to the gravity of their crimes—the utilitarians' motto is "Don't cry over spilt milk!" They believe that the guilty should be punished only if the punishment would serve some deterrent (or preventive) purpose. Rather than punish John in exact proportion to the heinousness of his deed, we ought to find the right punishment that will serve as the optimum deterrent.

The proper amount of punishment to be inflicted upon the offender is the amount that will do the most good (or least harm) to all those who will be affected by it. The measure of harm inflicted on John should be preferable to the harm avoided by fixing that penalty rather than one slightly lower. If punishing John will do no good (because John is not likely to commit the crime again and no one will be deterred by the punishment), John should go free.

It is the *threat* of punishment that is the important thing! Every act of punishment is to that extent an admission of the failure of the threat. If the threat were successful, there would be no punishment to justify. Of course, utilitarians believe that, given human failing, punishment is vitally necessary as a deterrent, so the guilty will seldom if ever be allowed to go free.

Utilitarianism has two main features: the consequentialist principle (or its teleological aspect) and the utility principle (or its hedonic aspect). The *consequentialist principle* states that the rightness or wrongness of an act is determined by the goodness or badness of the results that flow from it. It is the end, not the means, that counts. The end justifies the means. The *utility principle* states that the only thing that is good in itself is some specific type of state (e.g., pleasure, happiness, or welfare). Hedonistic utilitarianism views pleasure as the sole good and pain as the only evil. To quote Bentham, the first one to systematize classical utilitarianism, "Nature has placed mankind under the governance of two sovereign masters, pain and pleasure. It is for them alone to point out what we ought to do, as well as what we shall do."[1] An act is right if it promotes a balance of pleasure over pain or prevents pain, and an act is wrong if it brings about more pain than pleasure or prevents pleasure from occurring.

Although applying his theory mainly to humanity, Bentham included animals within the scope of moral considerability.

> The day may come when the rest of the animal creation may acquire those rights which never could have been witholden from them but by the hand of tyranny. The French have already discovered that the blackness of the skin is no reason why a human being should be abandoned without redress to the caprice of a tormentor. It may one day come to be recognized that the number of legs, the [type] of the skin . . . are insufficient for abandoning a sensitive being to the same fate. What else is it that should trace the insuperable line? Is it the faculty of reason, or perhaps the faculty of discourse? But a full grown horse or dog is beyond comparison a more rational, as well as a more conversable animal, than an infant of a

day, or a week, or even a month, old. But suppose they were otherwise, what would it avail? The question is not, Can they reason? Nor Can they *talk*, but, *Can they suffer?*[2]

Sentience is the sole criterion for moral considerability. If an animal can suffer, can experience pleasure and pain, it is worthy of our concern. At the least, we may not do it harm without cause. Bentham's utilitarianism is not really an anthropocentric but a *sentience-centric* system. This will be an important consideration when we come to Chapter 13 on animal rights.

Bentham invented a scheme for measuring pleasure and pain, which he called the *hedonic* calculus. The quantitative score for any pleasure or pain experience comes about by giving sums to seven aspects of an experience in terms of pleasure and pain. The seven aspects of a pleasurable or painful experience are its intensity, duration, certainty, nearness, fruitfulness, purity, and extent. By adding up the sums of each possible act in terms of pleasure and pain and comparing them, we can decide on which act to perform. With regard to our example of deciding between giving the dying man's money to the Cowboys or the starvation victims, we should add up the likely pleasures to all involved in terms of these seven qualities. Suppose that we find that by giving the money to the East African famine victims we will cause at least 3 million *hedons* (units of happiness), but by giving the money to the Cowboys, we will probably cause fewer than 1,000 hedons. So we would have an obligation to give the money to the famine victims.

There is something appealing about Bentham's utilitarianism. It is simple in that there is only one principle to apply: Maximize pleasure and minimize suffering. It is commonsensical in that we think that morality really is about ameliorating suffering and promoting benevolence. It is scientific: Simply make quantitative measurements and apply the principle impartially, giving no special treatment to yourself or to anyone else because of race, gender, or religion.

However, Bentham's philosophy may be too simplistic in one way and too complicated in another. It may be too simplistic in that there are values other than pleasure, such as freedom and wisdom, and it seems too complicated in that its hedonic calculus is encumbered with too many variables and problems in attempting to give scores to the variables. What score does one give cool drink on a hot day or a warm shower on a cool day? How do you compare a five-year-old's delight over a new toy with a fifty-year-old's delight with a new lover? Can I take your second car from you and give it to Beggar Bob, who does not own a car and would enjoy it more than you? And if it's simply the overall benefits of pleasure that we are measuring, might it not turn out that if Jack or Jill would be "happier" in the Pleasure or Happiness machine or on drugs than in the real world, we have an obligation to see to it that these conditions obtain? Because of these considerations, Bentham's version of utilitarianism was even in his own day referred to as the "pig philosophy": a pig enjoying his life would constitute a higher moral state than a slightly dissatisfied Socrates.

It was to meet these sorts of objections and save utilitarianism from the charge of being a pig philosophy that Bentham's brilliant successor John Stuart Mill sought to distinguish happiness from mere sensual pleasure. His version of utilitarianism, *eudaimonistic* (from the Greek *eudaimona,* meaning "happiness") utilitarianism, defines happiness in terms of certain types of higher-order pleasures or satisfactions such as intellectual, aesthetic, and social enjoyments, as well as of minimal suffering. That is, there are two types of pleasures: the lower or elementary (e.g., eating, drinking, sexual activity, resting, and sensuous titillation) and the higher (e.g., the intellectual, creative, and spiritual). Although the lower pleasures are perhaps more intensely gratifying, they also lead to pain when overindulged in. The spiritual or achieved pleasures tend to be more protracted, continuous, and gradual.

Mill argues that the higher or more refined pleasures are superior to the lower ones. "A being of higher faculties requires more to make him happy, is capable probably of more acute suffering, and certainly accessible to it at more points, than one of an inferior type," but still he is qualitatively better off than the person without these higher faculties. "It is better to be a human being dissatisfied than a pig satisfied; better to be Socrates dissatisfied than a fool satisfied."[3]

Humans are the kind of creatures who require more to be truly happy. We want the lower pleasures but also deep friendship, intellectual ability, culture, ability to create and appreciate art, knowledge, and wisdom. But, one may object, how do we know that it really is better to have these higher pleasures? Here Mill imagines a panel of experts and says that of those who have had wide experience of pleasures of both kinds, almost all give a decided preference to the higher type. Since Mill was an empiricist, one who believed all knowledge and justified belief was abased in our experience, he had no recourse but to rely on the composite consensus of human history. People who experience both rock music and classical music will, if they appreciate both, prefer Bach and Beethoven to the Rolling Stones or Dancing Demons. We generally move up from appreciating simple things (e.g., nursery rhymes to more complex poetry rather than the other way around).

Mill has been criticized for not giving a better reply, for being an elitist and unduly favoring the intellectual over the sensual, but he has a point. Don't we generally agree, if we have experienced both the lower and the higher types of pleasure, that although a full life would include both, a life with only the former is inadequate for human beings? Isn't it better to be Socrates dissatisfied than the pig satisfied? And better still to be Socrates satisfied?

The point is not merely that humans would not be satisfied with what satisfies a pig but also that somehow the quality of these pleasures is *better.* What does it mean to speak of better pleasure? Is Mill unwittingly assuming some nonhedonic notion of intrinsic value to make this distinction? That is, knowledge, intelligence, freedom, friendship, love, health, and so forth are good things in their own right. Or is Mill simply saying that the lives of humans are generally such that we can predict that they will be happier with the more developed, refined, spiritual values? Which thesis would you be inclined to defend?

THE STRENGTHS AND WEAKNESSES OF UTILITARIANISM

Utilitarianism does have two very positive features. The first attraction or strength is that it is a system with a single absolute principle, with a potential answer for every situation. Do what will promote the most utility! It's good to have a simple action-guiding principle, applicable for every occasion—even if it may be difficult to apply (life is not simple). The second strength is that utilitarianism seems to get at the substance of morality. It is not merely a *formal system,* offering only formal principles (broad guidelines for choosing substantive principles, such as the Golden Rule, the rule to "Let your conscience be your guide," or "Never do what you cannot will to make a universal law"), but has a *material* core: promoting human and animal happiness and ameliorating suffering. The first virtue gives one a clear decision procedure for arriving at our answer about what to do. The second virtue appeals to our sense that morality is made for humans (and other animals) and that it is not so much about rules as about helping people and alleviating the suffering in the world.

This seems to be common sense. Utilitarianism gives us clear and reasonable guidance in everyday matters. We should try to make our colleges, our towns, our families, as well as our nation and world, better places than they are. We should help people and ameliorate their suffering whenever it does not cost us unduly. In the case of deciding what to do with the $2 million of the dead millionaire, something in us

says that it is absurd to keep a promise to a dead man when it means allowing hundreds of thousands of famine victims to die (how would we like it if we were in their shoes?). Far more good can be accomplished by helping the needy than by giving the money to the Cowboys!

However, utilitarianism has problems that must be addressed before one can give it a clean bill of health.

Problem 1: How Can We Know the Consequences of Actions? Sometimes utilitarians are accused of playing God. They seem to hold to an ethical theory that demands godlike powers, that is, knowledge of the future. Of course, we normally do not know the long-term consequences of our actions, for life is too complex and the consequences go on into the indefinite future. One action causes one state of affairs that, in turn, causes another state of affairs indefinitely, so that calculation becomes impossible. Recall the nursery rhyme:

> For want of a nail
> The shoe was lost;
> For want of a shoe
> The horse was lost;
> For want of a horse
> The rider was lost;
> For want of a rider
> The battle was lost;
> For want of a battle
> The kingdom was lost;
> And all for the want
> Of a horseshoe nail.

Poor, unfortunate blacksmith! What utilitarian guilt he must bear all the rest of his days.

Of course it is ridiculous to blame the loss of one's kingdom on the poor unsuccessful blacksmith, and utilitarians are not so foolish as to hold him responsible for the bad situation. Instead, following C. I. Lewis, they distinguish three different kinds of consequences: actual consequences of an act, consequences that could reasonably have been expected to occur, and intended consequences.[+] An act is *ab-*

solutely right if it has the best actual consequences. An act is *objectively* right if it is reasonable to expect that it will have the best consequences. An act is *subjectively* right if its agent intends or actually expects it to have the best consequences. It is the second kind of rightness (*objective rightness*), based on reasonable expectations, that is central here, for only the subsequent observer of the consequences is in a position to determine the actual results. The most that the agent can do is use the best information available and do what a reasonable person would expect to have the best overall results. Suppose, for example, that while Stalin's aunt was carrying little baby Josef up the stairs to her home, she slipped and had to choose between dropping infant Josef, allowing him to be fatally injured, or breaking her arm. According to the formula just given, it would have been absolutely right for her to let him be killed, but it would not have been within her power to know that. She did what any reasonable person would do—save the baby's life at the risk of some injury to herself. She did what was objectively right. The utilitarian theory is that by doing what reason judges to be the best act based on likely consequences, we will, in general, actually promote the best consequences.

Problem 2: The No-Rest Objection According to utilitarianism, one should always do the act that promises to promote the most utility. But there are usually an indefinite set of possible acts from which to choose, and even if I can be excused from considering all of them, I can be fairly sure that there is often a preferable act that I could be doing. For example, when I am about to go to the movies with a friend, I should ask myself if helping the homeless in my community wouldn't promote more utility. When I am about to go to sleep, I should ask myself whether I could at this moment be doing something to help save the ozone layer. And why not simply give all of my assets (beyond what is absolutely necessary to keep me

alive) to the poor to promote utility? How would a sophisticated utilitarian respond to this criticism?

Problem 3: The Absurd Implications Objection W. D. Ross argued that utilitarianism is to be rejected because it is counterintuitive. If we accepted it, we would have to accept an absurd implication. Consider two acts, *A* and *B,* that will both result in 100 hedons (units of pleasure of utility). The only difference is that *A* involves telling a lie and *B* involves telling the truth. The utilitarian must maintain that the two acts are of equal value, but this seems counterintuitive, at least at first glance. Most of us think that telling the truth is an intrinsically good thing. Who is right here?

Similarly, in Arthur Koestler's *Darkness at Noon,* Rubashov writes of the Communist philosophy in the Soviet Republic:

> History has taught us that often lies serve her better than the truth; for man is sluggish and has to be led through the desert for forty years before each step in his development. And he has to be driven through the desert with threats and promises, by imaginary terrors and imaginary consolations, so that he should not sit down prematurely to rest and divert himself by worshipping golden calves.[5]

According to this interpretation, orthodox Soviet communism justifies its lies and atrocities by utilitarian ideas. Something in us revolts at this kind of value system. Truth is sacred and must not be sacrificed on the altar of expediency.

Problem 4: The Justice Objection Suppose that in a racially volatile community a rape and murder is committed. You are the sheriff who has spent a lifetime working for racial harmony. Now, just when your goal is about to be realized, this incident occurs. The crime is thought to be racially motivated, and a riot is about to break out, which will very likely result in the death of several people and create long-lasting racial antagonism. You are able to frame a tramp for the crime so that a trial will show that he is guilty. He will then be executed. There is every reason to believe that a speedy trial and execution will head off the riot and save the community. Only you (and the real criminal, who will keep quiet about it) will know that an innocent man has been tried and executed. What is the morally right thing to do? The utilitarian seems committed to framing the tramp, but many would find this appalling.

Consider this hypothetical situation. You are a utilitarian physician who has five patients under your care. One needs to have a heart transplant, one needs two lungs, one needs a liver, and the last two need kidneys. Now into your office comes a healthy bachelor needing a flu shot. You judge him to be a perfect sacrifice for your five patients. Doing a utility calculus, there is no doubt in your mind that you could do more good by injecting the healthy man with a sleep-inducing drug and using his organs to save your five patients.[6]

This cavalier view of justice offends us. The very fact that utilitarians even countenance such actions, that they would misuse the legal system or the medical system to carry out their schemes seems frightening. It reminds us of the medieval Roman Catholic bishop's justification for heresy hunts, inquisitions, and religious wars:

> When the existence of the Church is threatened, she is released from the commandments of morality. With unity as the end, the use of every means is sanctified, even cunning, treachery, violence, simony, prison, death. For all order is for the sake of the community, and the individual must be sacrificed to the common good.[7]

UTILITARIAN RESPONSES TO STANDARD OBJECTIONS

The preceding objections are weighty and too complicated to attempt to refute here, but we can allow the utilitarian to make an initial defense. What sorts of responses are open to utilitarians? Well, it seems that a sophisticated version of utilitarianism can offset at least some of the force of these criticisms. Utilitarians can use the *multilevel strategy,* which goes like this: we must split considerations of utility into two levels, the lower level dealing with a set of rules that we judge to be most likely to bring about the best consequences most of the time. We'll call this the *rule-utility* feature of utilitarianism. Normally, we have to live by the best rules our system can devise, and rules of honesty, promise keeping, and justice will be among them.

But sometimes the rules conflict or clearly will not yield the best consequences. In these infrequent cases, we will need to suspend or override the rule in favor of the better consequences. We call this the *act-utility* feature of utilitarianism. It constitutes the second level of consideration and is referred to only when there is dissatisfaction with the rule-utility feature. An example of this might be the rule against breaking a promise. Normally, the most utility will occur through keeping one's promises, but consider this situation: I have promised to meet you at the movies tonight at 7 o'clock. Unbeknown to you, on the way to our rendezvous I come across an accident and am able to render great service to the injured parties. Unfortunately, I cannot contact you, and you are inconvenienced as you wait patiently in front of the theater for an hour. I have broken a utility rule in order to maximize utility and am justified in so doing.

Here is another example, set forth by Judith Jarvis Thomson. You are a trolley car driver who sees five workers on the track before you. You suddenly realize that the brakes have failed. Fortunately, the track has a spur leading off to the right, and you can turn the trolley onto it. Unfortunately, there is one person on the right-hand track. You can turn the trolley to the right, killing one person, or you can refrain from turning the trolley, in which case five people will die.[8] Under traditional views, a distinction exists between killing and letting die, between actively killing and passively allowing death, but the utilitarian rejects this distinction. You should turn the trolley, causing the lesser evil, for the only relevant issue is expected utility. So the normal rule against actively causing an innocent to die is suspended in favor of the utility principle.

This is the kind of defense the sophisticated utilitarian is likely to lodge against all of the preceding criticisms. The utilitarian responds to Problem 2, the no-rest objection, by insisting that a rule prescribing rest and entertainment is actually the kind of rule that would have a place in a utility-maximizing set of rules. The agent should aim at maximizing his or her own happiness as well as other people's happiness. For the same reasons, it is best not to worry too much about the needs of those not in one's primary circle. Although one should be concerned about the needs of future and distant people, it actually would promote disutility for the average person to become preoccupied with these concerns. But, the utilitarian would remind us, we can surely do a lot more for suffering humanity than we now are doing.

With regard to Problem 3, Ross's absurd implications objection, the utilitarian can agree that there is something counterintuitive in the calculus of equating an act involving a lie with one involving honesty; but, he argues, we must be ready to change our culture-induced moral biases. What is so important about truth telling or so bad about lying? If it turned out that lying really promoted human welfare, we'd have to accept it. But that's not likely. Our happiness is tied up with a need for reliable information (truth) on how to achieve our ends. So truthfulness will be a member of the rule-utility set. But where lying clearly promotes utility without undermining the general adherence to the rule, we simply ought to lie. Don't we already accept lying to a gangster or telling "white" lies to spare people's feelings?

With regard to Rubashov's utilitarian defense of communism and its inhumanity or the medieval defense of the Inquisition, the utilitarian replies that this abuse of utilitarianism only illustrates how dangerous the doctrine can be in the hands of self-serving bureaucrats. Any theory can be misused in this way.

We turn to the most difficult objection, the claim that utilitarianism permits injustice, as seen in the example of the sheriff framing the innocent derelict. The utilitarian counters that justice is not an absolute—mercy, benevolence, and the good of the whole society sometimes should override it. However, the sophisticated utilitarian insists that it makes good utilitarian sense to have a principle of justice that is generally obeyed. It is not clear what the sheriff should do in the racially torn community. More needs to be said, but if we could be certain that it would not start a precedent of sacrificing innocent people, it may be right to sacrifice one person for the good of the whole. Wouldn't we all agree, the utilitarian continues, it is sometimes best to harm an innocent person in order to prevent great evil? The trolley car case is one example. Here is another.

Virtually all standard moral systems have a rule against torturing innocent people. But suppose a maniac is about to set off a nuclear bomb that will destroy New York City. He is scheduled to detonate the bomb in one hour. His psychiatrist knows the lunatic well and assures us that there is one way to stop him: torture his ten-year-old daughter and show it on television. Suppose, for the sake of the argument, there is no way to simulate the torture. Would you not consider torturing the child in this situation? (Just in case you don't think New York City is worth saving, imagine that the lunatic has a lethal gas that will spread throughout the globe and wipe out *all* life within a few weeks.)

Is it not right to sacrifice one innocent person to stop a war or save the human race from destruction? We seem to proceed on this assumption in wartime, in every bombing raid, especially in the dropping of the atomic bomb on Hiroshima and Nagasaki. We seem to be following this rule in our decision to drive automobiles and trucks even though we are fairly certain that the practice will result in the death of thousands of innocent people each year.

On the other hand, the sophisticated utilitarian may argue that in the case of the sheriff's framing of the innocent derelict, justice should not be overridden by current utility concerns, for human rights themselves are outcomes of utility consideration and should not lightly be violated. That is, because we tend to subconsciously favor our own interests and biases, we institute the principle of rights to protect ourselves and others from capricious and biased acts that would in the long run have great disutility. So we must not undermine institutional rights too easily—we should not kill the bachelor in order to provide a heart, two lungs, a liver, and two kidneys to the five patients—at least not at the present time, given people's expectations of what will happen to them when they enter hospitals. But neither should we worship rights! They are to be taken seriously but not given ultimate authority. The utilitarian cannot foreclose the possibility of sacrificing innocent people for the greater good of humanity. If slavery could be humane and resulted in great overall utility, utilitarians would accept it.

We see, then, that sophisticated, multileveled utilitarianism has responses to all criticisms leveled on it. For most people most of the time, ordinary moral principles should be followed, for they actually maximize utility in the long run. But we should not be tied down to this rule: "Morality was made for man, not man for morality." The purpose of morality is to promote flourishing and ameliorate suffering, and where these can be done by sacrificing a rule, we should do them. Whether this is an adequate defense, I must leave you to decide.

Deontological Ethics

Act only on that maxim whereby thou canst at the same time will that it would become a universal law.

IMMANUEL KANT

What makes a right act right? The teleological answer to this question is that good conse-

quences make it right. Moral rightness and wrongness are determined by nonmoral values (e.g., happiness or utility). To this extent, the end justifies the means. The deontological answer to this question is quite the opposite. The end *never* justifies the means. Indeed, you must do your duty whatever the consequences, simply because it is your duty. You must do your duty disinterestedly, as though it were the last act of your life, simply because it is your duty. Danish philosopher Soren Kierkegaard (1813–1855) described his childhood experience of sensing his duty to learn his first-grade grammar lesson: "It was as if heaven and earth might collapse if I did not learn my lesson, and on the other hand as if, even if heaven and earth were to collapse, this would not exempt me from doing what was assigned to me."[9]

It is not the consequences that determine the rightness or wrongness of an act but certain features in the act itself. For example, there is something right about truth telling and promise keeping even when acting thusly may bring about some harm, and there is something wrong about lying and promise breaking even when acting thusly may bring about good consequences. Acting unjustly is wrong even if it maximizes expected utility. Referring to our examples in the introduction of this chapter, as a deontologist you would very likely keep your promise and give the $2 million to the Cowboys and share or flip a coin for the food on the raft.

There are several different deontological ethical systems. Religious ethics based on God's commands are deontological systems. The Ten Commandments in the Hebrew Bible (Old Testament) are an example. Ethical Intuitionism is another example. The intuitionist claims we can consult our hearts and consciences in order to discern correct moral rules. Oxford University philosopher W. D. Ross (1877–1971) held that moral principles are self-evident upon reflection to any normal person, but they may not be absolute. He called them *prima facie* (Latin for "at first glance") or conditional duties. Ross contrasted *prima facie* duties with *actual* duties. He listed seven *prima facie* moral principles: (1) promise-keeping; (2) fidelity (3) gratitude for favors; (4) beneficence; (5) justice; (6) self-improvement; and (7) nonmaleficence. If we make a promise, for example, we put ourselves into a situation in which a duty to keep promises is a moral consideration. It has presumptive force, and if there is no conflicting *prima facie* duty that is relevant, the promise becomes an actual duty.

What about situations of conflict? For an absolutist, an adequate moral system can never produce moral conflict, nor can a basic moral principle be overridden by another moral principle. But Ross is no absolutist. He allows for the overriding of principles. For example, suppose you have promised your friend that you will help her with her ethics homework at 3 P.M. As you are going to meet her, you encounter a lost, crying child. There is no one else around to help the little boy, so you help him find his way home. But in doing so, you miss your appointment. Have you done the morally right thing? Yes. You have broken your promise, but with good cause. You had an overriding duty to help the lost child. Whether intuitionism is a satisfactory system is a difficult question. One problem with it is that people with different upbringings and cultures have different intuitions, so it may not be as reliable a guide as one would like. But intuitionism is important for environmental ethics. Systems such as Albert Schweitzer's *Reverence for Life* and Holmes Rolston's *Intrinsic Value in Nature* seem to be intuitionist.

IMMANUEL KANT'S RATIONALIST DEONTOLOGICAL SYSTEM

The most famous deontological ethical system is Immanuel Kant's *Categorical Imperative*. Immanuel Kant (1724–1804), the greatest philosopher of the German Enlightenment and one of the most important philosophers of all time, was both an *absolutist* and a *deontological rationalist*. He believed that we could use reason to work out an absolute (non-overridable) consistent set of moral principles.

Kant was born in Konigsberg, Germany in 1724 and died there in 1804, never having left the surroundings of the city. His father was a saddlemaker. His parents were Pietists in the Lutheran church. The Pietists were a sect in the church, much like present-day Quakers, who emphasized sincerity, deep feeling, and the moral life rather than theological doctrine or orthodox belief. Pietism is a religion of the heart, not the head, of the spirit rather than ritual. However, Kant, as an intellectual, emphasized the head as much as the heart, but it was a head that was concerned about the moral life, especially good will.

THE GOOD WILL

The only thing that is intrinsically good, good in itself and without qualification, is the good will. All other virtues, both intellectual and moral, can serve the vicious will and thus contribute to evil. None of these are good in themselves, but good only for a further purpose. They can be united in themselves, but only for further purposes. They are valuable only if accompanied by good will. Even success and happiness are not good in themselves. Honor can lead to pride. Happiness without good will is not worthwhile. Is honor with deceit worth attaining? No. Nor is utilitarianism plausible, for if we have a quantity of happiness to distribute, is it just to distribute it equally, regardless of virtue? Should we not distribute it discriminately, according to moral goodness? Happiness should be distributed in proportion to one's moral worth, and happiness without moral worth is not inherently valuable.

How good is Kant's argument for the good will? Could we imagine a world where non-moral virtues were always and necessarily put to good use, where it was simply impossible to use a virtue such as intelligence for evil? Is happiness any less good simply because it can be distributed incorrectly? Can't the good will itself be put to bad use, as with the misguided do-gooder? As the aphorism goes, "The road to hell is paved with good intentions." Could

Adolf Hitler have had good intentions in carrying out his dastardly programs? Can't the good will have bad effects?

We may agree that the good will is a great good, but it is not obvious on Kant's account that it is the *only* inherently good thing, for even as intelligence, courage, and happiness can be put to bad uses, so can the good will. Even as it seems not to count against the good will that it can be put to a bad use, neither should it count against the other virtues that they can be put to bad uses. The good will may be a necessary element to any morally good action, but is it also a *sufficient* condition to moral goodness?

Perhaps we can reinterpret Kant in such a way as to preserve his central insight. There does seem to be something morally valuable about the good will, apart from any consequences. Consider this illustration: Two soldiers volunteer to cross enemy lines to make contact with their allies on the other side. They both start off and do their best to make their way through the enemy's area. One succeeds, but the other doesn't and is captured. Aren't they both morally praiseworthy? The success of one in no way detracts from the goodness of the other. Judged from a commonsense moral point of view, their actions are equally good; judged from a utilitarian or consequentialist view, the successful act is far more valuable than the unsuccessful one. Here one can distinguish the agent's worth from the value of the consequences and make two separate, nonconflicting judgments.

Duty and Moral Law

Kant wants to remove moral truth from the zone of contingency and empirical observation and place it securely in the area of *necessary truth,* that is, truth that is absolute and universal. Morality's value is not based on the fact that it has instrumental value, that it often secures nonmoral goods such as happiness, but it is valuable in its own right.

Even if it should happen that, owing to special disfavor of fortune, or the niggardly provision of a step-motherly nature, this [Good] will should wholly lack power to accomplish its purpose, if with its greatest efforts it should yet achieve nothing, and there should remain only the good will . . .; then, like a jewel, it would still shine by its own light, as a thing which has its whole value in itself. Its usefulness or fruitfulness can neither add to nor take away anything from this value.[10]

All mention of duties (or obligations) can be translated into the language of imperatives or commands. As such, moral duties can be said to have imperative force. Kant distinguishes two kinds of imperatives: hypothetical and categorical. The formula for a hypothetical injunction is

If you want to *A,* then do *B.*

Two examples are "If you want to get a good job, get a good education" and "If you want to be happy, stay sober and live a balanced life."

The formula for a categorical injunction is simply Do *B!*

That is, do what reason discloses to be the intrinsically right thing to do, for example, "Tell the truth!" *Hypothetical,* (means–ends) *imperatives* are not the kind of imperatives that characterize moral actions. Categorical or unqualified imperatives are the right kind of imperatives, for they show proper recognition of the imperial status of moral obligations. This imperative is an intuitive, immediate, and absolute injunction that all rational agents understand by virtue of their rationality.

Moral duty must be done solely for its own sake ("duty for duty's sake"). Some people conform to moral law because they deem it in their own enlightened self-interest to be moral, but they are not moral, because they do not act for the sake of the moral law. For example, a businessman may believe that honesty is the best policy. That is, he may judge that it is conducive to good business to give his customers correct change and good-quality products; but unless he does these acts *because* they are his duty, he is not acting morally, even though his acts are the same as they would be if he were acting morally.

The kind of imperative that fits Kant's scheme as a product of reason is one that universalizes principles of conduct. He names it the *categorical imperative*. "Act only on that maxim whereby thou canst at the same time will that it would become a universal law." This is given as the criterion, or second-order principle, by which to judge all other principles.

By *maxim*, Kant means the general rule in accordance with which the agent intends to act, and by *law*, he means an objective principle, a maxim that passes the test of universalization. The categorical imperative is the way to apply the universalization test. It enables us to stand outside our personal maxims and impartially and impersonally estimate whether they are suitable as principles for all of us to live by. If you could consistently will that everyone would do some type of action, then an application of the categorical imperative enjoins that type of action. If you cannot consistently will that everyone would do some type of action, that type of action is morally wrong. The maxim must be rejected as self-defeated. The formula looks like this:

Maxim (*M*)

|

Second-Order Principle (*CI*) → Rejected Maxims

|

First-Order Principle (P)

To take one of Kant's examples, suppose I need some money and consider whether it would be moral to borrow the money from you and promise to repay it without intending ever to do so.

M: Whenever I need money, I should make a lying promise while borrowing the money.

Can I universalize the maxim of my act?

P: Whenever anyone needs money, that person should make a lying promise while borrowing the money.

But something has gone wrong, for if I universalize this principle of making promises without intending to keep them, I would be involved in a contradiction. The resulting state of affairs would be self-defeating, for no one in his right mind would take promises as promises unless there was the expectation of fulfillment. So the maxim of the lying promise fails the *universalizability* criterion. Hence, it is immoral. Now I universalize the opposite:

M_1: Whenever I need money, I should make a sincere promise while borrowing it.

Can I universalize this maxim?

P_1: Whenever anyone needs money, he or she should make a sincere promise while borrowing it.

Yes, I can universalize M_1, for there is nothing self-defeating or contradictory in this. So it follows that making sincere promises is moral. We can make the maxim of promise keeping into a universal law.

Some of Kant's illustrations do not fare as well as the duty to keep promises. For instance, he argues that the categorical imperative would prohibit suicide, for the principle

P: Whenever it looks like one will experience more pain than pleasure, one ought to kill himself

is, according to Kant, a self-contradiction in that it would go against the very *principle of survival* on which it is based. But whatever the merit of the form of this argument, we could modify the principle to read

P_1: Whenever the pain or suffering or existence erodes the quality of life in such a way as to

make nonexistence a preference to suffering existence, one is permitted to commit suicide.

Why couldn't this (or something close to it) be universalized? It would not oppose the general principle of survival itself but would cover rare instances where no hope is in sight for terminally ill patients and victims of torture or deep depression. It would not cover the normal kinds of suffering and depression that most of us experience in the normal course of life. Kant seems unduly absolutist in his prohibition of suicide.

Kant's other two examples of the application of the categorical imperative are also questionable. In his third example, he claims that we cannot universalize a maxim to refrain from developing our talents. But again, could we not qualify this and stipulate that under certain circumstances it is permissible not to develop our talents? Perhaps Kant is correct: If everyone refrained from developing any talent, society would soon degenerate into anarchy. But couldn't one universalize the following maxim?

M_2: *Whenever I am not inclined to develop a talent and this refraining will not seriously undermine the social order, I may so refrain.*

Kant's fourth example of the way the categorical imperative functions regards the situation of not coming to the aid of others whenever I am secure and independent. He claims that I cannot universalize this maxim because I never know whether I will need the help of others at some future time. It seems that Kant is wrong again. I could universalize that people who are completely independent never help those who are less well-off just as long as their own independence is not threatened by the less well-off. Perhaps it would be selfish and cruel to make this into a universal law, but I don't see anything contradictory or self-defeating in the principle itself. The problems with universalizing selfishness are the same ones that we encountered in analyzing egoism, but it's dubious whether Kant's categorical impera-

tive captures what is wrong with egoism. Perhaps he has other weapons that capture that. We will return to this shortly.

Kant thought that he could generate an entire moral law from his categorical imperative. It seems to work with such principles as promise keeping, truth telling, and a few other maxims, but it doesn't seem to give us all that Kant wanted. It has been objected that Kant's categorical imperative is both *too wide* and *too unqualified,* leading to horrendous possibilities.

The charge that it is too wide is based on the perception that it seems to justify some actions that we would think trivial and even immoral. Consider, for example, principle *P:*

P: Everyone should always tie one's right shoe before one's left shoe.

Can we universalize *P* without contradiction? Why not? Just as we universalize that people should drive cars on the right side of the street rather than the left, we could make it a law that everyone must tie the right shoe before the left. It seems obvious that there would be no point to such a law; it would be trivial. It is justified, however, by the categorical imperative.

It may be objected that the only thing this counterexample shows is that it may be permissible to live by the principle of tying the right shoe before the left, for we could also universalize the opposite maxim (tying the left before the right) without contradiction. That seems correct.

A more serious objection is the charge that the categorical imperative seems to justify acts that we judge to be horrendously immoral. Consider P_1:

P_1: *Always kill blue-eyed children.*

Is there anything contradictory in this injunction? Could we make it into a universal law? Why not? Blue-eyed children might not like it (and might even be required to cooperate or commit suicide), but there is no logical contradiction involved in such a principle. Had I been a blue-eyed child when this command was in effect, I would not be around to write this book, but the world would have survived my loss without too much inconvenience.

Of course, it would be possible to universalize the opposite: no one should kill innocent people, but that only shows that either type of action is permissible.

It may be objected that Kant presupposed that only rational acts could be universalized, but this won't work, for the categorical imperative is supposed to be the criterion for rational action. Perhaps when we come to Kant's second formulation of the categorical imperative, he will have more ammunition with which to defeat P_1.

Finally, Kant thought that the categorical imperative yielded unqualified absolutes. The rules that the categorical imperative generates are universal and without exception. He illustrates this point with regard to truth telling. Suppose that an innocent man comes to your door, begging for asylum, because a group of gangsters is hunting him down to kill him. You take the man in and hide him in your third-floor attic. Moments later the gangsters arrive and inquire about the innocent man. "Is he in your house?" they ask. What should you do? Kant's advice is to tell them the truth: "Yes, he's in my house."[11]

What is Kant's reasoning here? It is simply that moral law is sacrosanct and without exception. It is your duty to obey its commands, not to reason about the likely consequences. You have done your duty: hidden an innocent man and told the truth when asked a straightforward question. You are absolved of any responsibility for the harm that comes to the innocent man. It's not your fault that there are gangsters in the world.

To many of us, this kind of absolutism seems counterintuitive. There are two ways in which we might alter Kant here. First, simply add qualifications to the universal principles, changing the sweeping generalization "Never lie" to the more modest "Never lie except to save an innocent person's life." The trouble with this way of solving the problem is that there seem to be no limits on the qualifications that would

have to be attached to the original generalization: for example, "Never lie *except* to save an innocent person's life (except when trying to save the innocent person's life will undermine the entire social fabric)" or "Never lie unless lying will spare people great anguish (e.g., don't tell a cancer patient the truth about her condition)." And so on. The process seems infinite and time-consuming, and thus impractical.

A second way of qualifying the counterintuitive results of the Kantian program is to follow W. D. Ross and distinguish between *actual* and *prima facie* duties. As noted earlier, a *prima facie* duty that wins out in the comparison is called the *actual duty* or the *all-things-considered duty*. We can apply this distinction to Kant's innocent man example. First, we have the principle *L: Never lie.*

Next, we ask whether any other principle is relevant in this situation, and we discover that principle *P: Always protect innocent life,* also applies. But we cannot obey both *L* and *P* (we assume for the moment that silence will be a giveaway). We have two general principles, but neither is seen as absolute or non-overridable, but rather as *prima facie*. We have to decide which of the two overrides the other, which has greater moral force. This is left up to our considered judgment (or the considered judgment of the reflective moral community). Presumably, we will opt for *P* over *L,* so lying to the gangsters becomes our actual duty.

Will this maneuver save the Kantian system? Well, it changes it in a way that Kant might not have liked, but it seems to make sense. It transforms Kant's absolutism into an objectivist system, but now we need to have a separate criterion to adjudicate the conflict between two objective principles.

I conclude that the categorical imperative is then an important criterion for evaluating moral principles, but it needs supplementation. In itself it is purely formal and leaves out any understanding about the content or material aspect of morality. The categorical imperative, with its universalizability test, constitutes a necessary condition for being a valid moral principle, but it does not provide us with a sufficiency criterion. That is, any principle, if it is to count as rational or moral, must be universalizable. It must apply to everyone and every case that is relevantly similar. If I believe that it's wrong for others to cheat on exams, it is also wrong for me to cheat on exams unless I can find a reason to believe that I am relevantly different from others. If premarital heterosexual coitus is prohibited for women, it must also be prohibited for men (otherwise, with whom would the unmarried men have sex? other men's wives?). However, this formal consistency does not tell us whether cheating itself is right or wrong or whether premarital sex is right or wrong. That has to do with the substantive content of morality, on which other considerations must help us decide.

KANT'S SECOND FORMULATION OF THE CATEGORICAL IMPERATIVE

Kant offered a second formulation of the categorical imperative, which has been referred to as the principle of ends: "So act as to treat humanity, whether in your own person or in that of any other, in every case as an end and never as merely a means only." Each person qua rational being, has dignity and profound worth, entailing that he or she must never be exploited, manipulated, or merely used as a means to our idea of what is for the general good or to any other end.

What is Kant's argument for viewing rational beings as having ultimate value? It goes like this: In valuing anything, I endow it with value. It has no value apart from someone's valuing it. As a valued object, it has *conditional* worth, derived from my valuation. On the other hand, the person who values the object is the ultimate source of the object's value and, as such, belongs to a different sphere of beings. We, as valuers, must conceive of ourselves as having *unconditioned* worth. We cannot think of our personhood as a mere thing, for then we would have to judge it to be without any value except

that given to it by the estimation of other people. Then that person would be the source of value, and there is no reason to suppose that one person should have unconditional worth but not another who is relevantly similar. Therefore, we are not mere objects. We have unconditional worth and so must treat all such value givers as valuable in themselves, as ends, not merely means. I leave it to you to evaluate the validity of this argument, but most of us do hold that there is something exceedingly valuable about human life.

Kant thought that this formulation, the principle of ends, was substantively identical with his first formulation of the categorical imperative, but most scholars disagree with him. It seems better to treat this principle as a supplement to the first, adding content to the purely formal categorical imperative. In this way, Kant would limit the kinds of maxims that would be universalized. Egoism and principle P_1, enjoining the killing of blue-eyed children, would be ruled out at the very outset since they involve a violation of the dignity of rational persons. The process would be as follows:

1. Maxim (M) formulated.
2. Ends test (Does the maxim involve violating the dignity of rational beings?)
3. Categorical imperative (Can the maxim be universalized?)
4. Successful moral principles survive both tests.

Does the principle of treating persons as ends in themselves fare better than the original version of the categorical imperative? Three problems soon emerge. The first has to do with Kant's setting such a high value on rationality. Why does reason and only reason have intrinsic worth? Who gives this value to rational beings, and how do we know that they have this value? What if we believe that reason has only instrumental value?

Kant's notion of the high inherent value of reason is more plausible to those who believe that humans are made in the image of God and interpret that, as does the mainstream of the Judeo-Christian tradition, as entailing that our rational capabilities are the essence of being created in God's image. We have value because God created us with worth, that is, with reason. Kant doesn't use such an argument. Instead, he thinks that we must necessarily value rational nature, since we, qua rational beings, must value ourselves—and so, by the principle of consistency, anyone rational like us.

Kant seems to many to be correct in valuing rationality (the essence of our rational nature). It does enable us to engage in deliberate and moral reasoning and lift us above lower animals. Where he is more controversial is in neglecting other values or states of being that may have moral significance. For example, he believed that we have no obligations to animals since they are not rational. Many of us believe (with Jeremy Bentham and Peter Singer) that the fact that animals can suffer should constrain us in our behavior toward them. We should not cause unnecessary harm. Perhaps Kantians can supplement their system to accommodate this objection.

This brings us to our second problem with Kant's formulation. If we agree that reason (or rational nature) is an intrinsic value, does it not follow that those who have more of this quality should be respected and honored more than those who have less? Doesn't more mean better here?

Following Kant's logic, we should treat people in exact proportion to their ability to reason. Thus, geniuses and intellectuals should be given privileged status in society (as Plato and Aristotle might argue). Kant could deny the second premise and argue that rationality is a threshold quality, that anyone having a sufficient quantity of it grants one equal worth. The question is whether Kant or Kantians have good (nonreligious) reasons to accept the egalitarian premise that all those who have rational nature have equal worth. I leave this question for you to discuss and come to your own conclusion.

The third problem with Kant's view of the dignity of rational beings is that even if we should respect them and treat them as ends, this does not tell us very much. It may tell us not to enslave them or act cruelly toward them without a good reason, but it doesn't tell us what to do in conflict situations. For example, what does it tell us to do about a terminally ill patient who wants us to help her die? What does it tell us to do in a war when we are about to aim our gun at an enemy soldier? Aren't we treating the soldier merely as a means?

Furthermore, what does it mean to treat this rational being as an end? What does it tell us to do with regard to the innocent victim and the gangsters who have just asked us about the whereabouts of the victim? What does it tell us about whether we should steal from the pharmacy, procuring medicine that we can't afford to buy in order to bring healing to a loved one?

Conclusion

In this chapter, we have discussed two classical ethical theories. Teleological ethics instructs us to produce the best consequences, using rules as mere tools to this end. Deontological ethics instructs us to follow the correct rules regardless of the consequences. We also noted that rule-utilitarianism took rules more seriously than act-utilitarianism. There are several other varieties of these theories. Some philosophers, call them *Mixed-Deontologists,* would combine deontological ethics with consequentialism, holding that we ought to follow the rules in general, since they have strong presumptive force, but override them with the principle of beneficence where great good can be accomplished. A mixed-deontologist may hold that although we ought not normally do utilitarian calculations in deciding what to do, in extreme circumstances we should do so. For example, such a philosopher might adhere to the combatant/noncombatant distinction in war and yet justify dropping the atom bomb on Hiroshima to save a million lives and shorten the war. Both deontological and consequentialist ethics have important insights. The question is, how do we best incorporate these insights into a unified ethical theory?

Study Questions

1. Consider Jeremy Bentham's and John Stuart Mill's versions of utilitarianism. Evaluate the strengths and weaknesses of each. Then evaluate the main criticism of utilitarianism.

2. One criticism of utilitarianism is that it fails to protect people's rights. Consider five excitable sadists getting a total of 100 hedons while torturing an innocent victim who is suffering 10 dolores (units of pain). On a utilitarian calculus, this would result in a total of 90 hedons. If no other act would result in as many or more hedons, the utilitarian would have to endorse this act and argue that the victim had a duty to submit to the torture and that the sadists had a duty to torture the victim. What do you think of this sort of reasoning? How much does it count against utilitarianism?

3. Consider the case, discussed in the text, of the doctor who needs organs for five needy patients, all of whom are in danger of dying unless he gets suitable organs within the day. One needs a heart transplant, two need kidneys, one needs a lung, and another needs a liver. A bachelor who has no family walks into the hospital for minor care (a flu shot). By killing him and using his organs for the five, the doctor could save five persons, restoring them to health. If he doesn't kill the man, is he negatively responsible for the death of the five patients? Explain your answer.

4. Rawls's false-analogy argument: John Rawls argues that utilitarianism errs in applying to society the principle of personal choice. That is, we all would agree that an individual has a right to forgo a present pleasure for a future good. I have a right to go without a new suit so that I can save the money for my college education or so that I can give it to my favorite charity. Utilitarianism, however, prescribes that you must forgo a new suit for someone else's college education or for the overall good of the community—whether or not you like it or agree to it. That is, it takes the futuristic notion of agent-utility maximization and extends it to cover society in a way that violates the individual's rights. Is this a fair criticism?

5. Do you think that the Kantian argument that combines the categorical imperative with the notion of the kingdom of ends is successful? Is the notion of treating persons as ends clear enough to be a significant guiding action? Does it cover some intelligent animals but not severely retarded people? What about fetuses and infants? Are they included in it? Why, or why not?

6. Note the comments of the anti-Kantian Richard Taylor:

   > If I were ever to find, as I luckily never have, a man who assured me that he really *believed* Kant's metaphysical morals, and that he modeled his own conduct and his relations with others after those principles, then my incredulity and distrust of him as a human being could not be greater than if he told me he regularly drowned children just to see them squirm.[12]

   He and others have criticized Kant for being too rigid. Many people use the idea of moral duty to keep themselves and others from enjoying life and showing mercy. Do you think that there is a basis for this criticism?

7. Kant has been criticized for stifling spontaneous moral feelings in favor of the deliberate will; the person who successfully exercises the will in overcoming a temptation is superior to one who isn't tempted at all but acts rightly spontaneously. For example, the person who just barely resists the temptation to shoplift through a strenuous act of the will would be, judged by this criterion, morally superior to one who isn't tempted to shoplift at all. Based on your analysis of Kant, do you consider this a fair interpretation of Kant, and if so, does it undermine his ethics?

8. Here is a question similar to the one above. Kant holds that we must act from a motive centered on doing the morally right act simply because it is right, not because we are altruistic or benevolent or have good moral habits. He has been criticized for emphasizing the will too much and for rejecting the place of character and feelings in moral actions. Are these criticisms valid?

9. Many people besides Taylor have a negative reaction to Kant's moral theory. Evaluate the following quotation from Oliver Wendell Holmes, Jr.:

> From this it is easy to proceed to the Kantian injunction to regard every human being as an end in himself and not as a means. I confess that I rebel at once. If we want conscripts, we march them up to the front with bayonets in their rear to die for a cause in which perhaps they do not believe. The enemy we treat not even as a means but as an obstacle to be abolished, if so it may be. I feel no pangs of conscience over either step, and naturally am slow to accept a theory the seems to be contradicted by practices that I approve.[13]

10. One might be a determinist and still accept utilitarianism, since what matters is the maximization for utility. However, Kant's moral theory seems to depend on a libertarian view of freedom of the will. Can the rational nature of humanity have the dignity or high worth it does without the notion of radical free will? Most people who believe in free will deny that animals have such a capacity. Do you agree? Should that make a difference in how we regard them? Explain you answer.

Endnotes

1. Jeremy Bentham, *An Introduction to the Principles of Morals and Legislation* (1789), ch. 1.

2. Ibid., ch. 17.

3. John Stuart Mill, *Utilitarianism* (1863), ch. 2.

4. See Anthony Quinton, *Utilitarian Ethics* (listed in chapter 1, "For Further Reading"), 49f., for a good discussion of this and other similar points.

5. Arthur Koestler, *Darkness at Noon* (New York: Macmillan, 1941), 80.

6. This example and the trolley car example are found in Judith Jarvis Thomson's "The Trolley Problem" in her *Rights, Restitution and Risk* (Cambridge, MA: Harvard University Press, 1986): 94–116.

7. Dietrich von Nieheim, Bishop of Verden, *De Schismate Librii*, iii, ad 1411, quoted in Koestler, op. cit., 76.

8. Thomson, op. cit.

9. Soren Kierkegaard, *Either/Or*, vol. 2, trans. Walter Lowrie (New York: Anchor Books, 1959), 271.

10. Immanuel Kant, *Fundamental Principles of the Metaphysics of Morals*, trans. T. K. Abbott (1873), sect. 1.

11. Immanuel Kant, *On a Supposed Right to Lie from Altruistic Motives* (1797) in *Immanuel Kant: Critique of Practical Reason and Other Writings in Moral Philosophy*, ed. Lewis White Beck (New York: Garland, 1976).

12. Richard Taylor, *Good and Evil* (Buffalo: Prometheus, Books, 1984), xii.

13. Oliver Wendell Holmes, Jr., *Collected Legal Papers*, (New York: Harcourt Brace Jovanovich, 1920), 340.

Chapter 5

The Sanctity of Life versus the Quality of Life

The fundamental fact of human awareness is this: "I am life that wants to live in the midst of other life that wants to live." A thinking man feels compelled to approach all life with the same reverence he has for his own.

ALBERT SCHWEITZER[1]

Sanctity of life is not just a vague theological precept. It is the foundation of a free society.

NORMAN CANTOR[2]

Imagine that we invented a mighty Convenience Machine that would make our lives wonderfully more enjoyable and enable us to reach more of our goals. Unfortunately, using the machine would cost us about 50,000 lives each year. Would you use the machine? Should we allow it to be sold on the market? When I have asked audiences this question, there is virtually universal agreement that we should not, for no amount of comfort equals the value of a single life. Human life is of absolute value. "Life is sacred."

We are often told that we ought not to take life because it is sacred. This statement is frequently used as the major premise in arguments opposing abortion, suicide, euthanasia, war, and the death penalty. Sometimes it is used to promote animal rights or vegetarianism. With the onset of sophisticated medical technology, which can keep a person in a persistent vegetative state alive indefinitely, the question of the sanctity of life becomes especially urgent. Does a physician have an absolute duty to sustain indefinitely the life of an irreversibly comatose patient by means of expensive life support systems while resources are denied poor families? Must defective newborns, no matter how degrading or painful their condition, be kept alive and cared for? Should all fetuses, no matter how burdensome for the mother, the family, or society, be given an absolute right to life, so that abortion is equated with murder?

Life is wonderful! The sprouting of a plant, the blooming of a flower, the emergence of a chick from an egg, the birth of a baby—who could not stand in wonder at these miracles? The mystery of life is the ultimate miracle, one that must have amazed the caveman millennia ago as much as it does us today. Even those with little religious feeling stand in awe of the birthing process and are likely to believe that birth is a gift of God and that only God should be able to end one's life. Murder is universally condemned as the worst crime of all.

There is a primordial tendency to treat life as sacred, to surround life with a mystic aura and set high value to it. Edward Shils suggests that it is a universal, self-evident intuition that even predates organized religion. It is the "proto-religious" feeling. Thus it is not surprising that virtually every major religion has espoused a version of the sanctity of life. Indeed, the idea of the sanctity of life is essentially a religious one. Its roots are in a religious world view. Animists believe that all things have souls and are to be revered. Vitalists believe that all biologic life contains a dynamic force that cannot be reduced to the elements of chemistry or physics. Hindus and Jains believe all animals have a divine soul; Jews and Christians believe only humans have sacred souls. Each person is endowed with an immortal soul that is of infinite value. It is our true self and that which gives us whatever worth we have. Questions do remain of whether such a thing as a soul exists, of what evidence is available for the existence of such an entity, and who, if anyone, possesses a soul.

We will examine two versions of the Sanctity of Life principle in this chapter: the vitalist version and the humanist version. The vitalist version says that all living things are sacred and to be revered. The humanist version says that human life is special and only human life is infinitely valuable.

Vitalism

Albert Schweitzer (1875–1965), the famous missionary doctor and nobel Peace Prize winner, combined Christian and animist views of life in advocating a vitalism that he called "Reverence for Life." While serving as a doctor in French Equatorial Africa, Schweitzer's personal goal was to discover a universal ethical principle. One day in 1915 while wearily trekking along an island set in the middle of a wide river, he spotted four hippopotamuses and their young plodding along on the other side of the island. "Just then, in my great tiredness and discouragement, the phrase 'Reverence for Life' struck me like a flash. As far as I knew, it was a phrase I had never heard nor ever read. I realized at once that it carried within itself the solution to the problem that had been torturing me." In a passage that has become a classic expression of the Sanctity of Life principle, Schweitzer explains what he means by the "Reverence of Life":

I am life which wills to live, and I exist in the midst of life which wills to live. . . . A living world—and life view, informing all the facts of life, gushes forth from it continually, as from an eternal spring. A mystically ethical oneness with existence grows forth from it unceasingly. . . . Ethics thus consists in this, that I experience the necessity of practising the same reverence for life toward all will-to-live, as toward my own. Therein [lies] the fundamental principle of morality. It is *good* to maintain and cherish life; it is *evil* to destroy and to check life. A man is really ethical only when he obeys the constraint laid on him to help all life which he is able to succour, and when he goes out of his way to avoid injuring anything living. He does not ask how far this or that life deserves sympathy as valuable in itself, nor how far it is capable of feeling. To him life as such is sacred. He shatters no ice crystal that sparkles in the sun, tears no leaf from its tree, breaks off no flower, and is careful not to crush any insect as he walks. If he works by lamplight on a summer evening, he prefers to keep that window shut and to breathe stifling air, rather than to see insect after insect fall on his table with singed and sinking wings. . . . Should he pass by an insect which has fallen into a pool, he spares the time to reach it a leaf or stalk on which it may clamber and save itself.

Ethics is in its unqualified form extended responsibility with regard to everything that has life.[3]

Schweitzer ordered his life according to this principle. Instead of choosing the comfort of a cool breeze in his rooms in hot Equatorial Africa, he kept the windows shut so as not to attract insects and flies who would otherwise have immolated themselves against the kerosene lamps or hot light bulbs.

Schweitzer's Reverence for Life principle has been heralded as the essence of morality, a recognition of our symbiotic relationship with nature, a benevolence to all living things, a harbinger of heaven. Is it true?

In this passage Schweitzer has gone beyond the idea that all life is sacred to include inanimate things such as ice crystals as part of the moral domain. But ignoring this problem and concentrating on his vitalism, one wonders if he ever weeded his garden or exterminated termites. Did he ever use bacteria-killing antibiotics to help cure his sick patients? According to Schweitzer's principle, all of life is equally sacred, so we may not choose between saving the life of a phytoplankton or a mosquito, on the one hand, and saving that of a human being, on the other. If life is the only relevant consideration and questions of quality do not enter in, two cockroaches are worth more than one human being. The more living things, the better, regardless of levels of sentience or consciousness.

Note that adherents of the Sanctity of Life principle may display apparent inconsistency in their behavior. An animist may pull weeds from his or her garden or cut down a tree to build a house, a Hindu may kill an animal to save a human life. Even Schweitzer performed operations in which millions of live bacteria were sacrificed for the health of one human.

Many will find this leveling of life forms highly implausible. Since the vitalist does not offer an argument for this absolute position but only an intuition, it is left to anyone who fails to have that intuition to reject such absolutism. We may agree that life is valuable without agreeing that it is the one and only absolute value.

Sacred Humanism

The *sacred* is a religious idea. God (or the gods) is holy, and whatever else is holy derives its holiness from God. While religious vitalists like Schweitzer believe that all life is holy, Jews and Christians believe that only humans have sacred souls. Since God created humans in His own image, all humans are equally and essentially valuable, though they may lose merit through sin and acquire merit by improving the character of their souls. But, even as a bent and corroded coin bears the king's image, so the most distorted and degraded human life still bears the sacred image of the King of kings.

"Thou has made man a little lower than the angels, as little gods," the Psalmist writes. "According to Jewish law," writes Rabbi Byron Sherwin, "life is to be preserved, even at great cost. Each moment of human life is considered intrinsically sacred. Preserving life supersedes living the 'good life'. The sacredness of life and the uniqueness of the individual require that every possible action be taken to preserve life."[4] The eminent Protestant ethicist Paul Ramsey expresses the Christian perspective this way.

> The value of a human life is ultimately grounded in the value God is placing on it. . . . Man is a sacredness *in* human biological processes no less than he is a sacredness in the human social or political order. . . . Every human being is a unique, unrepeatable opportunity to praise God. His life is entirely an ordination, a loan, and a stewardship. His essence is his existence before God and to God, as it is from Him. His dignity is 'an alien dignity,' an evaluation that is not of him but placed upon him by the divine decree.[5]

We must ask two central questions with regard to the doctrine of the sanctity of life. The first is: What are the implications of the doctrine? If all human life is equally sacred, would it mean that we should become vegetarians and even forgo using antibiotics? The second question is: What is the evidence for the Sanctity of Human Life principle? If you give up the religious basis of the doctrine, can you continue to maintain the doctrine on some other grounds?

Let us turn to the first question. The doctrine of the sanctity of human life seems to provide a basis for the pro-life movement. If all *Homo sapiens* are possessed with eternal and sacred

souls and if fetuses are *Homo sapiens,* then abortion is murder. Likewise, all humans, whether severely deformed, retarded, or in agony have something sacred within, so it would be immoral to shorten their lives.

Rabbi Moshe Tendler puts it this way: "Human life is of infinite value. This in turn means that a piece of infinity is also infinity and a person who has but a few moments to live is no less of value than a person who has 60 years to live . . . a handicapped individual is a perfect specimen when viewed in an ethical context. The value is an absolute value. It is not relative to life expectancy, to state of health, or to usefulness to society."[6]

As an example of how radical the Sanctity of Human Life principle is, note the following case described by Anthony Shaw:

> A baby was born with Down's syndrome (mongolism), intestinal obstruction, and a congenital heart condition. The mother, believing that the retarded infant would be impossible for her to care for adequately, refused to consent to surgery to remove the intestinal obstruction. Without surgery, of course, the baby would soon die. Thereupon a local child-welfare agency, invoking a state child-abuse statute, obtained a court order directing that surgery be performed. After a complicated course of surgery and thousands of dollars worth of medical care, the infant was returned to her mother. In addition to the mental retardation, the baby's physical growth and development remained markedly retarded because of her severe cardiac disease. A follow up enquiry eighteen months after the baby's birth revealed that the mother felt more than ever that she had been done an injustice.[7]

Many of us would object to this treatment. It seems unjust to force an infant with such low quality of life expectations on a family, but those holding to the Sanctity of Life principle would reply that we are not to play God in deciding who is to live.

As Paul Ramsey says in rejecting the possibility of abortion in the case of a fetus with Tay-

Sachs disease, "There is no reason for saying that [6 months in the life of a baby born with the invariable fatal Tay-Sachs disease] are a life span of lesser worth to God than living seventy years before the onset of irreversible degeneration. . . . All our days and years are of equal worth whatever the consequences; death is not more a tragedy at one time than another."[8]

Quality of life considerations are irrelevant to theologians like Tendler and Ramsey, as they were to the Department of Health and human services in inaugurating "Baby Doe" regulations. "Considerations such as anticipated or actual limited potential of an individual . . . are irrelevant and must not determine the decisions concerning medical care."[9]

The question is, why don't those who treat human life as an absolute stop driving cars? If you drive a car, your behavior shows that you don't value human life as absolute. Indeed, the Convenience Machine in our earlier thought experiment is the car. We know with high probability that each year over 50,000 people will lose their lives in automobile accidents in the United States alone. Cars also cause harmful air pollution, which shortens life. As I write these words the United States is engaged in a destructive war in the Middle East over oil, 40 percent of which is consumed by automobiles. Anyone who believes that human life really is of absolute value should be against the use of automobiles! Yet the staunchest right-to-lifer drives to the antiabortion protest without blinking a eye over the inconsistency, and the most militant pacifist and abolitionist (with regard to capital punishment) has not the slightest conscience qualm when it comes to gunning his or her Cadillac, Ford, or Nissan.

Of course, we could reinterpret the notion of the sanctity of life in such a way as to make it less radical, a nonabsolute. We could interpret it as offering a presumption in favor of preserving life wherever possible unless a strong moral reason overrode it. But then the principle would lose much of its force as quality of life considerations become relevant.

Here the most pressing question arises: Is the Sanctity of Life principle true? As we saw earlier, the principle rests on a religious foundation and different religions generate different conclusions as to the nature of this sanctity idea. So one problem for us to settle is whether any religion is the true religion. Does any religion possess credentials to claim our rational allegiance? This is not a question we can take up here, except to say that liberal versions of Judaism and Christianity do allow for quality of life considerations.

One thing more should be said. The notion of a separate soul inhabiting a body, so important for the absolutist view of the Sanctity of Life doctrine, has lost much of its credibility in the light of neuroscience. According to neuroscience, the brain, not a separate soul, is the center of mental activity, the locus of memories, and the place where consciousness, an emergent property of the nervous system, resides. If this is so, we can suppose that when the brain dies, the person dies.

This is no proof that there is no soul, but neuroscience puts the matter in doubt. Furthermore, those who doubt whether there is a God will doubt even more whether animals or humans have godlike souls.

Can the Sanctity of Life principle survive without a religious basis? How could it? If no transcendent dimension ("the holy") exists, how can individual things be sacred? The doctrine loses its essential support.

The Quality of Life

The doctrine of the sanctity of life is opposed by the doctrine of the quality of life. The Quality of Life principle states that the values a life contains are more important than mere living. Some kinds of life are more worth living than others. Socrates said, "The unexamined life is not worth living," suggesting that a life of reflection and moral deliberation is a worthwhile life. Although life is the foundation of values, without these other values life is not worth living. Life by itself has only *potential value,* depending on these other features.

We may represent the difference between the sanctity of life view and the quality of life view this way: whereas the sanctity of life view looks at nonbeing as a negative and at even the worst human existence as a positive (small though it may be), the quality of life view looks at nonbeing as neutral and regards some lives as having positive value and others as having negative value. Deeply moral people, productive geniuses who advance our knowledge, such as Newton and Einstein, and decent people all have varying degrees of positive worth, whereas evil people or people whose lives are plagued with suffering and unremitting agonizing pain may have negative worth. We may represent the scorecard this way:

	Quality of Life Position	Sanctity of Life Position
The optimally good life	+1	+1
Nonbeing (not being born)	0	−1
The maximal bad life	−1	+0.01 (or $n > 0$)

The two positions differ radically on the status of not being born (or more accurately, never having become conscious) and being born to a bad life. For those who hold a sanctity of life view, not to live is tragic—the more life the better. It's as though souls are waiting to be born and will not inhabit heaven unless we do our duty to procreate as much and as often as possible. The quality of life view holds that we cannot give any value to what never even exists. Likewise, for the sanctity of life view even a horrible life with gratuitous suffering is good, whereas for the quality of life view some lives have negative value.

The truth is that Judaism and Christianity are ambiguous on this issue. They sometimes speak as though life were an absolute or near absolute value. But they also contain quality of life aspects that qualify the high value of life. Quality counts to some degree. Even Jesus, usually seen as the paragon of respect for life, said of Judas, "It were better that he were never born" (Matt 26:24), suggesting that nonexistence is preferable to an evil existence. An evil life has negative worth; it is bad. Evil is associated with causing gratuitous suffering and pain, with doing things harmful to others. Hence, we might conclude that even from a Christian perspective, death is preferable to excruciating pain without the expectation of remission. Furthermore, if life were an absolute, then God would have no right to call on believers to risk their lives for their religion.

There is further evidence that the Judeo-Christian position has never really regarded life as an absolute value. Risks of life are often worth the goals of enhancing the quality of life for others. The martyr, the missionary to hostile territory, the settler, the witness to the truth all value something higher than their own life. If biologic lives were all-important, we should not wash ourselves or brush our teeth, for in doing so we unnecessarily kill millions of human cells with the exact genetic information of a single-cell zygote!

Just how the Quality of Life principle operates is a controversial matter. Let's look at how typical representatives of the three ethical theories discussed in the last chapter view the matter. Take first the classic deontologist, Immanuel Kant (1724–1804), himself a liberal Christian. Kant reinterpreted the idea of the sanctity of human life in such a way as to make it dependent on a determinate quality: rationality. It is our ability to engage in rational deliberation that gives us worth. Kant wrote,

> Now I say, man, and in general every rational being exists as an end in himself and not merely as a means to be arbitrarily used by this or that will. . . . Act so that you treat humanity, whether in your own person or in that of

another, always as an end and never as a means only. Human beings qua rational have an inherent dignity and so ought to treat each other as ends and never merely as means.[10]

We are to respect human beings and all rational beings simply because they are *persons* (a technical term, standing for the possession of the requisite value-endowing properties) capable of moral self-determination. Social status, wealth, talents, education, intelligence, occupation, and other qualities are unimportant.

Kant's position has frequently been analyzed to mean that rational self-consciousness is the distinguishing feature of human worth. As such, the severely retarded, senile, and insane are not really persons since they do not possess self-conscious rationality. On this criterion fetuses and infants are also nonpersons, though they are potential persons. On the other hand, adult chimpanzees, dolphins, whales, and other animals probably are persons, since they manifest behavior similar to that of self-conscious humans.

There are many ways of interpreting Kant's notion of the kingdom of ends. One interpretation leads us to do whatever we can to preserve all rational creatures, so that suicide and driving automobiles would be morally forbidden. Another way of interpreting Kant is to emphasize the rational independence of persons, their *autonomy*. Never exploit or impose your values on other persons, since they, qua rational, must be left to decide for themselves on how they should live their lives. In this case, Kant's principle would justify suicide when life irretrievably loses its meaning.

Kant's idea that reason gives us worth can be questioned. Some have called it the idealization of reason. If following rules and exercising deductive reasoning count, computers can reason and robots may have artificial intelligence, but there is nothing intrinsically valuable about them. It's not wrong to discard your old computer when you can get a better one, but it is wrong to discard your aging parent or spouse even when you can find a more rational one.

Another problem in Kant's formula of rationality is that it seems to lead not to equal human worth but to unequal worth, for if rational self-consciousness gives us our value, then the fact that some people are more self-aware and rational should lead us to conclude that these people are worth more than those who are less self-aware or rational. Kant and his followers would reply that rational self-consciousness is a threshold concept. As long as you have some of that property, you are of equal value. But this is just pious bootstrapping, a desperate move to save a secular faith in equality. A convincing explanation for equal human worth based on unequal rationality has yet to be offered. The appeal to reason as the criterion of intrinsic value is essentially inegalitarian.

The idea of what makes humans valuable is problematic. Kant's insight that the locus of human value is rational self-consciousness is persuasive because it enables us to have plans and projects, to project our wishes into the future, to discipline ourselves so that we sacrifice immediate pleasure for future good, and to develop language and communicate with one another.

Reason alone is not enough to give us a right to life, since computers can think. What gives our reason a special worth is the fact that we are persons who can feel pains and emotions, that we have a sense of identity that computers lack (at least up until now). That is, we have the combination of self-consciousness and rationality that makes us intrinsically valuable and grants us a right to life.

The defective neonate described above by Anthony Shaw would be allowed to die in a Kantian view, but a normal fetus would not be allowed to be aborted, since it would likely develop into a rational child.

Utilitarians such as Jeremy Bentham (1748–1832), John Stuart Mill (1806–1873), and Peter Singer find quality of life in the notion of happiness, including the minimization of suffering. Pleasure or happiness is equated with the good, and pain and suffering with evil. The aim of utilitarianism is to maximize happiness and minimize suffering and pain. The ability to enjoy things and to suffer—not reason—grants every sentient being, animals and humans, moral consideration. So when our life becomes too fraught with pain or suffering, we have reason to take our life.

Utilitarians would encourage the death of the defective neonate (where a quality of life is extremely unlikely) as a means to alleviate suffering in others. Utilitarians are inclined to support pro-choice organizations such as Planned Parenthood and the National Abortion Rights Action League since therapeutic abortions can be justified on utilitarian grounds.

The accusation that utilitarians sometimes play God and take life into their own hands is a charge that they must answer. On the one hand, they point out that all medical decisions of whether to treat sick people (thus thwarting *natural* processes) are in a sense playing God. On the other hand, when innocents may be sacrificed for the good of the whole, their thinking tends to become more complicated and qualified. Some utilitarians, called *rule-utilitarians,* urge only that we devise a set of rules that would result in the greatest good for society. These thinkers would reject most proposals for sacrificing innocent lives for the good of the whole.

Finally, contractualists such as Thomas Hobbes (1588–1679) argue that the notion of intrinsic human worth is a mistake. Since all value is a function of human desires, the only value a person has is his or her market value, how much he or she is valued by others. My children have a value because I desire that they live and prosper.

According to this kind of contractualist, we don't need a notion of inherent human value to live moral lives, for all morality consists in agreements that we make with others or with society as a whole. We all accept a mutual nonaggression pact, agree to keep contracts, submit to the law, and the like. If we examine the situation carefully and choose to allow abortions or voluntary euthanasia, nothing more can be said.

Many regard contractual ethics as having a serious weakness in being willing to undermine "minority rights." If the social contract we embrace fails to include certain powerless people, the contractualists on their principles are guilty of no mistake. Deontologists and most utilitarians object, but they must explain why contractualism is wrong. If we give up the religious notion of the sanctity of human life, are we left with nothing more than a degrading contractualism?

Some people argue that if we give up the idea of the sanctity of human life, we will be on the slippery slope to Auschwitz. Let us see how slippery-slope arguments might be used to support the notion that human life is of absolute value, never to be taken under any circumstances (except possibly to save one's own life). The argument is that once we admit that human life may be taken, issues other than the value of human life can be considered to override a right to life. The danger is that utilitarian considerations will outweigh the right to life so that a situation such as developed in Nazi Germany could arise. Witness these excerpts from letters sent by the German chemical company I. G. Farben to the commander at Auschwitz during the Second World War.

> In contemplation of experiments with a new soporific drug, we would appreciate your procuring for us a number of women. . . . We received your answer but consider the price of 200 marks a woman excessive. We propose to pay not more than 170 marks a head. If agreeable, we will take possession of the women. We need approximately 150.

After the women were received by I. G. Farben and the experiments accomplished, a second letter was sent by the chemical company: "Received the order of 150 women. Despite their emaciated conditions, they were found satisfactory. We shall keep you posted on developments concerning this experiment. . . . The tests were made. All subjects died. We shall contact you shortly on the subject of a new load."[11]

The letters show to what depths of evil people can descend. Yet you do not have to believe in the Sanctity of Life principle, which is an extreme notion, to hold that the Nazi practices of sacrificing humans was reprehensible. If what we have said about the Quality of Life principle is accurate, it is sufficient to prohibit such atrocious conduct. Whether in a deontologic or utilitarian guise, the Quality of Life view is that human beings are valuable by virtue of their rational self-consciousness or capacity for happiness and that their right to life may not be violated. It does not deny that life is important, simply that it is sufficient in itself to procure any positive value.

The Quality of Life principle recognizes that life is a necessary condition for other values and, as such, it recognizes a strong presumption in favor of preserving human life. Biologic human life is not an absolute value, but without it none of the other good things are possible. To prevent a callous disregard of human life, as reflected in the letters of I. G. Farben, this presumption must be emphasized, and locutions such as "the sanctity of life," properly understood, may play a valuable role.

If this is correct, the idea that life is sacred or valuable is, at best, of symbolic value, a shorthand for saying that the good things in life (rational self-consciousness, happiness, knowledge, love, justice, and so forth) should be promoted. The notion by itself needs interpretation. By itself it doesn't inform us on any major moral problem. Even if we agree that rational or human life is more valuable than the life of an ant or a rat, this doesn't deal with the crucial issues of quality. It does tell us not to take innocent life, but it doesn't tell us whether abortion or voluntary euthanasia are sometimes justified. It doesn't tell us whether capital punishment is sometimes valid. Nor does it speak one way or the other on the issues of suicide, vegetarianism, or animal research. It doesn't even tell us whether we should abandon or curtail the use of automobiles and adopt other modes of transportation. In all of these cases, quality of life considerations must enter into our deliberations. This is what we will be doing in examining the life and death issues in the rest of this book.

Study Questions

1. Explain the Sanctity of Life principle. What are its strengths and weaknesses? What are the far-reaching implications of adhering to it?
2. Can you believe in the sanctity of life without believing in a religion? Can a secularist hold the Sanctity of Life view? Why or why not?
3. Discuss Albert Schweitzer's "Reverence for Life" principle.
4. Contrast the Sanctity of Life principle with the Quality of Life principle. What are the key differences?
5. Socrates said, "The unexamined life is not worth living," and Jesus said of his betrayer, "It were better that he were never born." Do these statements support the Quality of Life principle over the Sanctity of Life principle?
6. How do the three major ethical theories view the Quality of Life/Sanctity of Life dispute?

Endnotes

1. Albert Schweitzer, *Civilization and Ethics* (Part II of *The Philosophy of Civilization*), trans. John Naish, (London: Macmillan Publishing Co., 1929), 246.

2. Norman Cantor, "A Patient's Decision to Decline Lifesaving Medical Treatment: Bodily Integrity Versus the Preservation of Life," *Rutgers Law Review* 26 (winter 1973): 228–264.

3. Schweitzer, op. cit., 246–247.

4. Byron Sherwin, "Jewish Views of Euthanasia," in Marvin Kohl's *Beneficent Euthanasia* (Buffalo: Prometheus, 1975), 7.

5. Paul Ramsey, "The Morality of Abortion," in *Moral Problems* ed. James Rachels, (New York: Harper & Row, 1971), 11–13.

6. Moshe Tendler, quoted in Edward Keyserlingk's *Sanctity of Life or Quality of Life* (Law Reform Commission of Canada, 1982), 21. Tendler's logic might prevent us from brushing our teeth or washing, for if each part of a human is holy, each cell should be kept alive.

7. Anthony Shaw, "Dilemmas of 'Informed Consent' in Children," *New England Journal of Medicine* 289 17 (1973).

8. Paul Ramsey, *Ethics at the Edges of Life* (New Haven: Yale University Press, 1978), 191.

9. *The Federal Register* 49 (238), 48160.

10. Immanuel Kant, *Foundations of the Metaphysics of Morals,* Lewis Beck, trans. (Indianapolis: Bobbs-Merrill, 1959), 46.

11. Quoted in Bruno Bettleheim, *The Informed Heart* (London: Macmillan, 1960), ch. 6.

Chapter 6

Death and Dying

Normally we admire and praise the person who reaches his or her goal sooner than others. The first runner to reach the finish line, the climber to reach a mountain peak in the shortest time, the first person to fly the Atlantic Ocean, the first baseball pitcher to win 400 games, the first person to figure out a difficult problem, the youngest person to graduate from college or medical school; these people accomplish worthy feats that challenge us and draw our praise. Generally, the faster we reach our goal or end, the better. The one exception is death. Although it is the end of life, where every human and animal is destined to end up, rare is the person in a hurry to die. All of us will die sooner or later. We are all traveling on different roads to the same destination. All roads lead, not to Rome, but to the grave.

We are all moving nearer to our end. This minute you are closer to death than the last minute, today you are closer to death than yesterday, this year closer than last year, and tomorrow you will be closer to it than today. People impatient for the future puzzle me because they are moving closer to their end. As St. Augustine said, "Any space of time that we live through leaves us with so much less time to live, and the remainder decreases with every passing day; so that the whole of our lifetime is nothing but a race towards death, in which no one is allowed the slightest pause or any slackening of the pace."[1]

I, like many of you, have experienced the psychological equivalent of an earthquake at the death of my loved ones and heros. I remember the deep tremors of death's dance when my parents and two brothers died. Along with many people throughout America and the world, I glimpsed death's grim visage one November afternoon in 1963 when President John F. Kennedy was assassinated, and then when Martin Luther King, Jr. was murdered in April 1968. But the death that shook the foundations of my soul was that of my teenage friend, George, the star of our high school football team. It occurred in the early summer after our sophomore year in high school. George, having been told by his physician that he had a heart murmur that would prevent him from ever again playing football, went up into his attic and hanged himself. The whole town of Cicero, Illinois, was shaken by this repudiation of existence, but no one more than I. For two weeks I walked in a daze—dizzy, disoriented, dumb with pain. My world had collapsed, my happy childhood abruptly ended. I wished that I were dead with George.

Gradually I recovered and became deeply religious as a result of this tragedy, but the sense of loss has followed me throughout life. You don't fully recover from these catastrophes, though they tend to lend life perspective.

Death comes to everyone. It's a dark kingdom from which no visitors return, as Hamlet put it, a solemn mystery that from time immemorial has moved men and women to deep fear. It has inspired people to set up monuments in their memory, beget children as tokens of their immortality, fight holy wars, renounce the normal pleasures of life, leave their families, and give themselves entirely to religion. Pyramids and cathedrals have been erected on the fear of death and hope of immorality.

What should be our attitude toward death?

The Western tradition has had five classic views of death: the Old Testament–Hebrew view, the Platonic–Christian view, the Epicurean view, the Stoic view, and the Existential view. Each one proposes a different response to this uninvited guest. We will better understand the meaning of death and dying if we examine each of these. You, the reader, may be able to combine some of these into a stronger position, or you may have to contribute a sixth position.

Views of Death in Western Society

THE OLD TESTAMENT–HEBREW VIEW: DEATH AS PUNISHMENT

There is no clear notion of immortality in the Hebrew Bible. Death is seen as punishment for sin—namely, the sin of our first parents, Adam and Eve, who were thrown out of the Garden of Eden because of disobedience. As children of fallen parents, all humans must taste death. "For dust thou art, and unto dust shalt thou return" (Gen. 3:19). What is ultimately important for the Hebrews is not the individual but the nation Israel. A person has identity through the nation and through one's progeny or family within that nation, so you will continue to live in the *memory* of the tribe long after you are gone—unless you have been immoral, in which case "may your memory be blotted from the earth." The fate worse than death is to be forgotten by the group.

The lack of a notion of an afterlife in Hebrew thought is paralleled by the ancient Greeks, as reflected by Homer, who said that he would rather be a servant on earth than reign in Hades, the land of the dead, where souls dwelt in a shadowy, passive, sleeplike existence.

It should be added that much of Judaism, especially the Pharisaic Judaism, by the time of Christ had accepted the doctrine of eternal life as do Orthodox Jews today.

THE PLATONIC–CHRISTIAN VIEW: IMMORTALITY AND RESURRECTION

The Greek philosopher Plato (427–347 B.C.E.) and Christian doctrine share a common fundamental idea with Orthodox Judaism, Islam, and Hinduism: Death is not the end of conscious life. Death, as the end of conscious existence, is an illusion. We survive our "deaths" in another world or in another form.

Look at the Platonic view. Some of us were taught the following prayer:

Now I lay me down to sleep,
I pray the Lord my soul to keep,
If I should die before I wake,
I pray the Lord my soul to take.

This prayer is often taught in Sunday School or by parents who thought that it was the Christian view of the matter. But actually, the notion of the soul departing from the body is not Christian in origin. It's a Greek notion, and the prayer expresses a non-Christian view of death and eternal life.

Among the ancient Greeks, Pythagoras (fifth century B.C.E.) and Plato believed that the soul was immortal, having neither beginning nor end. In a previous immortal existence we learned the essential truths about the True, the Good, and the Beautiful. Thus, we have the capacity for knowledge, moral action, and the appreciation of beauty, regardless of how we've been brought up. Depending on how we live this life, we will be reincarnated in a future earthly existence into a bodily form fitting our moral worth in this life. People who live like pigs will become such, people who live nobly will be born with added talents and opportunities. At the end of the pilgrimage of existence, the soul is merged with the GOOD, the essence of God.

For Plato the rational soul was lodged within the body as a tomb and at death was liberated from this clay coffin. Philosophy, for the Greeks, was a process of learning to die, learning to liberate oneself from the sensual, material nature of existence by purifying the soul through rational living. For the philosopher death becomes welcome relief, a rite of passage to a higher existence.

In the Christian view of death, Christ promised eternal life after death in a spiritual world in the presence of God. The support for this claim is Christ's resurrection from the dead, which is viewed as the model of our resurrection to eternal life. For the Christian, death, as the end of conscious life, really doesn't exist. As Paul says "O death, where is thy sting? O grave where is thy victory? The sting of death is sin; and the strength of sin is the law. But thanks be to God, which giveth us the victory through our Lord Jesus Christ." (I Cor. 15:55–57).

Although Christianity does not have a concept of a separate soul that is immortal, the *person* is created with eternity within him or her. We cannot die but will inhabit a godless hell or a God-filled heaven after death. For the believer death really doesn't exist. Eternal blessedness awaits the faithful, though it is not a soul but a transformed glorified body that inherits heaven.

This view is aptly illustrated by Benjamin Franklin, who had the following inscription prepared for his tombstone, which you may see in Philadelphia:

> The Body of Benjamin Franklin in Christ
>   Church cemetery,
> Printer, Like the Cover of an Old Book,
> Its contents torn out,
> And stript of its Lettering and Gilding,
> Lies here, Food for Worms.
> But the work shall not be lost;
> For it will, as he believed,
> Appear once more in a new and more elegant
>   Edition.
> Corrected and Improved by its Author.

This reconstituted self in a glorified body where the essential identity of the person is preserved is the hallmark of the Christian perspective on survival of death.

One of the most moving episodes of life is to witness the death of a believer. When devout Oxford University scientist Charles Coulson, who was terminally ill with cancer, knew he had only a few weeks to live, he made appointments to see all his friends. They came to see him, one by one, spoke of the meaning of their friendship and their lives, and left deeply moved by the wisdom and humor of this saintly man who could stare death in the face and fearlessly smile. As the last guest left the room, Coulson expired in deep peace. His funeral was marked by so much joy and celebration over his life that passersby thought a wedding was taking place.

Of the early Christian martyrs, who were often devoured by lions or burned at the stake, and who died singing praises to God and forgiving their executioners, it was said that their nobility in dying was evidence of the truth of their beliefs. "Behold how they die!" was a common comment on their brave martyrdom in the Roman world, as their blood became the seed of the Church.

THE EPICUREAN VIEW OF DEATH: SECULAR MORTALITY

Epicurus (341–270 B.C.E.) believed that it is irrational to fear death. If there were an afterlife with punishments, you might be justified in having fear; but since there is absolutely no reason to believe that there is an aferlife (especially since we are material beings without souls), it is irrational to worry about future existence.

> Death is nothing to us. It does not concern either the living or the dead; since for the former it is not, and the latter are no more.
>
> Death is not to be feared, for Death and I never meet and no one should fear what he will never meet. We shall never meet, for when and where I am, Death is not; and where and when Death is, I am not. Hence there is nothing to fear from Death.

What we never meet, we have no reason to fear. So it's irrational to fear death. In essence the Epicureans deny death.

Leonardo da Vinci held that just as a day well spent brings happy sleep, so a life well spent should bring a happy death. A happy person is not seriously pained by the thought of death, nor does he or she morbidly dwell on the subject.

The motto, "Eat, drink, and be merry for tomorrow we die," originates with the Epicureans. Put the thought of death out of your mind and enjoy life while it lasts. Contrary to common belief, the Epicurean life was actually quite moderate, not a gourmet or gluttonous, hedonistic life (in the contemporary sense). Epicurus advocated a tranquil, communal existence, "Far from the madding crowd," where cultured friends indulged not in sexual orgies but in refined conversation, literary excursions, and artistic delights—all accompanied by modest amounts of wine and cheese.

THE STOIC VIEW OF DEATH: CREATIVE RESIGNATION

Zeno (335–264 B.C.E), the founder of Stoicism, Cicero (106–43 B.C.E.), and Epictetus (60–138 C.E.) believed that although we could not control our external destiny, we could completely control our internal attitude toward our destiny. They taught that rational persons ought to resign themselves to their destiny and accept the inevitable. "If you can't get what you desire, desire what you get!"

We can overcome the fear of death by thinking about it constantly and in the proper manner. Life is a banquet from which we ought to retire at the proper time, graciously and gratefully—possibly through suicide. Here is how Stoic philosopher Seneca (3–65 C.E.) put it:

> Life has carried some men with the greatest rapidity to the harbor, the harbor they were bound to reach if they tarried on the way, while others it has fretted and harassed. To such a life, as you are aware, one should not always cling. *For mere living is not a good, but living well.* Accordingly, the wise man will live as long as he ought, not as long as he can. He will mark in what place, with whom, and how he is to conduct his existence, and what he is about to do. He always reflects concerning the quality, and not the quantity of his life. As soon as there are many events in his life that give him trouble and disturb his peace of mind, he sets himself free. And this privilege is his, not only when the crisis is upon him, but as soon as Fortune seems to be playing him false; then he looks about carefully and sees whether he ought, or ought not, to end his life on that account . . . He does not regard death with fear, as if it were great loss; for no man can lose very much when but a driblet remains. It is not a question of dying earlier or later, but of dying well or ill. And dying well means escape from the danger of living ill.[2]

Similarly, Shakespeare's Julius Caesar exemplifies Stoic resignation,

> Cowards die many times before their death,
> The valiant never taste of death but once.
> Of all the wonders that I yet have heard,
> It seems to me most strange that men should fear,
> Seeing that death, a necessary end,
> Will come when it will come.[3]

German philosopher Martin Heidegger echoed a Stoic theme when he said that death is our last act, which gives point to life. Dying is the one thing no one can do for you; you must die alone. To shut out the consciousness of death is therefore to refuse your own freedom and individuality; it is to refuse to live authentically. Death is the last chord in the symphony of our lives, which reverberates through all that has gone before, giving it meaning.

Although Stoicism was marked by resignation, it was not a passive resignation, but an active one, committed to making the best of a person's lot. It was a philosophy that emphasized doing one's daily duty as though today were the last day of one's life. That is, the thought of death concentrated one's mind to squeeze all the nectar out of the living fruit of our finite existence. As a second-century Stoic, Roman Emperor Marcus Aurelius said, "Hour by hour resolve to do the tasks of the hour carefully, with unaffected dignity, affectionately, freely and justly. You can avoid distractions that might interfere with such performance if every act is done as though it were the last act of your life. Free yourself from random aims and curb any tendency to let the passions of emotion, hypocrisy, self-love and dissatisfaction with your allotted share cause you to ignore the commands of reason."[4]

The modern equivalent to Marcus Aurelius's credo is a well-known prayer by Reinhold Niebuhr:

> Lord, Give me the courage to change the things which can be changed.
> And give me the patience to accept the things that cannot be changed.
> But most of all, give me the wisdom to know the difference.

Wisdom lies in living a life that knows when to exercise courage and when to exercise resignation. Death is a case in which both are called for. We resign ourselves to the unalterable fact that we will die, but we courageously overcome any useless perturbations over that fact.

Creative resignation learns to live gracefully with the tragedy of death; it lets the thought of death concentrate the mind so that we may more intensely appreciate each moment of life.

THE EXISTENTIAL VIEW OF DEATH: DEATH AS ABSURD

Existentialists hold that death is meaningless and absurd, and that it shows that life is utterly meaningless and absurd. Schopenhauer believed this and advocated grim recognition and resignation. Life—what is left of it—should go on in aesthetic contemplation. Nietzsche taught that the Superman will be constantly aware of death in all its power and will not permit death to seek him out in ambush, or strike him down unawares. The Superman will be constantly aware of death, joyfully and proudly accepting death as the natural end of life. In this, the existentialists are similar to the stoics.

Albert Camus in his essay *The Myth of Sisyphus* asserted that the only interesting philosophic question is, "Why not commit suicide?" Since life is absurd, utterly meaningless, we are hard put to find a reason to continue living. His solution to the problem of absurdity is to rebel, to live defiantly in the midst of absurdity.

Jean-Paul Sartre sees death as an absurdity, proving that life is absurd, that we are *de trop* (superfluous, unnecessary). Humans strive for permanency, to be God or eternal, but death puts an end to such grandiose projects and proves them ridiculous. There is just Nothingness, endless Nothingness, and we are Nothings. In the light of Nihilism, it doesn't matter what we do; yet we're absolutely free, "condemned to freedom," condemned to create our own absurd life projects in spite of their fundamental meaninglessness.

Where is the truth in these matters? The Existentialist view is the most pessimistic. Although some existentialists affirm that the creative use of our freedom produces personal value, this contradicts their idea that there are no objective values, that it really doesn't matter how we live. But Existentialism may give up too easily, for even if there is no afterlife, it doesn't mean that this life cannot be good in its own right. Life need not be absurd. Finite happiness is still happiness, a worthy existence. The Epicurean view is too unreflective, a naive case of self-deception. It's simply sophistry! Perhaps we don't "die" in the Epicurean sense of meeting death, but our consciousness comes to an end, we leave our friends and loved ones forever. And that is sad.

The Platonic–Christian view is the most optimistic. It has a certain logic in its favor, for it has the only chance of being *verified*, while it can't be *disproven*. For if life continues after death, both the disbeliever and the believer will experience it, but if no life occurs after death, then the disbeliever will never be able to prove it to himself or herself or to the believer—because they will both be annihilated.

However, the Platonic–Christian View suffers the handicap of not having much strong evidence in its favor. The doctrine of reincarnation seems flawed because of good evidence that personality is a function of brain states, not some separate soul that transmigrates. In fact the notion of a simple soul unconnected to sense organs and the brain's memories seems like an empty concept. Furthermore, it's hard to see why reincarnation should comfort us. If my soul was once Abraham Lincoln's soul, but I am not Abraham Lincoln, then having inherited someone else's soul is about as comforting as inheriting someone else's genes. My children have inherited half of my genes, but they are not me. Likewise, even if some future person will inherit my soul, that won't be me—but a sort of descendant.

With regard to immortality in general, the problem for many of us who would like to believe in life after death is simply that people don't come back from the dead and describe its geography or climate.

In my philosophy classes I often ask students, "How many here believe that there is life after death?" Usually 99 percent raise their hands—especially at the University of Notre Dame and the University of Mississippi, where I've taught. Then I ask them, "How many of you (as good Jews or Christians) believe that you are going to Heaven when you die?" About the same number of hands go up.

Then I ask, "How many of you believe that Heaven is infinitely more blissful than this corrupt earthly existence?" All hands go up.

"How many of you want to go to this wonderful place, right now?" I ask. Usually no one raises his or her hand. Such is the gap between religious profession and actual belief.

Nevertheless, perhaps there is some indirect evidence for survival after death. James Moody documents several cases of clinically dead persons, who on being revived reported remarkably similar out-of-the-body (or *near-death*) experiences. Moody sets down an idealized report in the following passage:

A man is dying and, as he reaches the point of greatest distress, he hears himself pronounced dead by his doctor. He begins to hear an uncomfortable noise, a loud ringing or buzzing, and at the same time feels himself moving outside of his own physical body from a distance, as though he is a spectator. He watches the resuscitation attempt from this unusual vantage point as in a state of emotional upheaval.

After a while, he collects himself and becomes more accustomed to his odd condition. He notices that he still has a "body," but one of a very different nature and with very different powers from the physical body he has left behind. Soon other things begin to happen. Others come to meet and to help him. He glimpses the spirits of relatives and friends who have already died, and a loving, warm spirit of a kind he has never encountered before—a being of light—appears before him.

This being asks him a question, nonverbally, to make him evaluate his life and helps him along by showing him a panoramic, instantaneous playback of the major events of his life. At some point he finds himself approaching some sort of barrier or border, apparently representing the limit between earthly life and the next life. Yet, he finds that he must go back to the earth, that the time for his death has not yet come. At this point he resists, for by now he is taken up with his experiences in the afterlife and does not want to return. He is overwhelmed by intense feelings of joy, love, and peace. Despite his attitude, though, he somehow reunites with his physical body and lives.[5]

This passage is not meant to represent any one person's report but is a composite of the common elements found in many stories. Moody himself makes no claims for the interpretation that the patients really experienced what they claimed to have experienced. Neurologic causes might account for these experiences, or they could be attributed to wish fulfillment. But these experiences should be included with all of our other thinking on this matter and should be followed up with further research. The reports may allow some of us to live in a rationally based hope of immortality.

Is the fear of death universal? Freud, Ernest Becker and other psychoanalysts thought so, but I doubt it. It seems to occur primarily where heightened self-consciousness arises, where individualism takes root, and individuals value their own existence more than the group's. Primitive human beings, like animals or Adam and Eve in the paradisiacal garden, are unencumbered by the perturbations of mortality. Small children do not seem to fear death, and it is likely that primitive humans who identified with the tribe probably didn't fear death the way modern Europeans or Americans do. Aldous Huxley, in his classic, prophetic novel, *Brave New World,* describes people bred on *soma* and sensuous "feelies," who lack deep self-consciousness and hence the fear of death. You may differ with me here, but then you should work out an alternate account of the fear of death.

Death seems a natural event, not something that has been imposed on us from without as punishment for sin, but it is still perceived as an evil once we understand what it implies. We come to fear it as our sense of self develops. Children between the ages of three and six frequently express horror at the idea of their own future demise. On hearing that a relative died, my three-year old daughter asked me, "Will I die too, Daddy?"

"Yes," I answered.

"But I don't want to. I won't do it!"

Tears filled her eyes and replaced her defiant words as it dawned on her that death wasn't something over which she had any control. It happens whether we like it or not.

Death is an evil. As persons we have desires and projects. When these desires and projects are satisfied, we are usually happy. When they are not, we are frustrated. To the extent that our values are not realized in the world, the world is evil for us. But in death all our desires are finally frustrated, all our projects taken away from us. All that we value is separated from us forever. We are removed permanently from all we value: our loved one, conscious experience, our work, beauty, creativity, pleasure, happiness, and knowledge. We will never again hear the song of birds, smell the fragrance of flowers, or hear the laughing voices of children. Hence death must be seen both as natural and as evil.

Nevertheless, though death is an evil and fear has to do with being confronted by the prospect of such evil, we ought not fear death. Epicurus was the first philosopher to argue that we ought not fear death, since we should not fear things that we will never encounter and death and I will never meet. "For when it is, I am not, and when I am, it is not." Although this argument states our relationship to death in a misleading fashion, there is some truth in its message that it is irrational to fear death. Let me explain.

What distinguishes rational from irrational fear? Rational fear has to do with avoiding what is harmful and can be avoided. The fear of fire causes us to keep our distance from it. The fear of danger causes us to stay out of some neighborhoods at night. The fear of cancer causes some people to stop smoking. The fear of AIDS causes people to restrain their sexual proclivities. Rational fear is purposive and instrumental to reaching worthy goals such as good health.

But irrational fear is not instrumental in this way. A fear of water (hydrophobia) keeps you from enjoying some good things, such as swimming and boating. A fear of people, sex, or love is disastrous to our personal growth. Some people suffer irrational anxiety for no apparent reason or go through life as guilt gluttons, feeling remorse for what they could in no way have prevented. This is the truth of Epicurus's dictum that we ought not to fear death since the two of us will never meet. It is not that we never meet, but that the meeting is unavoidable and what is unavoidable ought to be met with resignation and courage, as the Stoics counsel us.

Deeply engrained within our psyche as it is, thanophobia (fear of death) can be conquered, if not altogether, then to a great extent. We can learn to smile at the Grim Reaper. We may have to go through a mental practice, such as yoga, Stoic resignation, prayer, or meditation on the nature of things, but we can become wise regarding this inevitable event. Of course, we will still have an aversion to death and try to prolong life with happiness as long as possible, and we will still fear an agonizing or demeaning death with loss of dignity. But death itself is not to be feared; that fear can be conquered through reason and the will. We can live like a Stoic, letting the thought of death concentrate the mind to get the most out of life.

In the ancient Greek myth, Sisyphus is condemned by the gods to roll a huge stone up the side of a mountain until it reaches the top, whereupon the stone rolls down to the bottom and Sisyphus must follow its course and retrieve it. He goes through the process again and again, for all eternity. Tedious, boring, meaningless, such is the process of this neverending toil. But Sisyphus, if he is sufficiently resourceful, can find meaning in his toil. As Camus recognizes, "The struggle towards the heights [in life] is enough to fill a person's heart. One must imagine Sisyphus happy."[6]

And so it is with us. We can find meaning to life in the midst of our labors, even though we, unlike Sisyphus, will die. A wise person accepts the inevitability that all good things come to an end, including life, treating life as a glorious banquet. Having enjoyed life to the full but now coming to the end, he or she retires gracefully, grateful for all the good things experienced. Death becomes an occasion for saying thank you.

Study Questions

1. What are the five classic views of death in Western society? Which one, if any, do you believe in, and why?
2. Discuss James Moody's description of out-of-body experiences. Does the evidence available support the view that there is life after death?
3. Is death an evil? Is the fear of death rational? If it is irrational, can such fear be overcome? Explain.
4. How does the fact that you will die affect your value system? The way you live? Does the fact of death help us understand the meaning of life?
5. If there is no God and no life after death, does it make any difference how we live? Is life absurd?

Endnotes

1. St. Augustine, *City of God*, ch. 13.
2. Seneca, "On Suicide," *Epistula Morales*, vol. 2, trans. R. M. Gumere (Cambridge: Harvard University Press, 1920), 54.
3. William Shakespeare, *Julius Caesar*, Act II, Scene II.
4. Marcus Aurelius, *Meditations*, Book Ten.
5. James Moody, *Life after Life* (New York: Bantam Books, 1976), 21f.
6. Albert Camus, *The Myth of Sisyphus*, trans. Justin O'Brien (New York: Vintage Books, 1960), 91.

Chapter 7

Suicide

Chapter 7

Suicide

A few years ago I was on a fellowship at a major medical center. The following situation arose on the intensive care unit and was discussed at a case conference. A Korean woman, Mrs. C, who was on a ventilator and being fed through a nasogastric tube, asked to have the ventilator removed so that she could die. Mrs. C had married an American soldier in Korea against the wishes of her parents and, hence, had been disowned by them. She came to America, got a divorce, remarried, and had a son. But guilt and shame haunted her throughout her life. She felt a total failure and was often deeply depressed. She attempted suicide eight times, failing each time. On her eighth attempt, she put a gun to her head and pulled the trigger. The pistol jolted, and instead of going through her head, the bullet went through her neck, paralyzing her from the neck down. She was a quadriplegic. Now she wanted to be left to die.

Mrs. C's husband and ten-year-old son were called in. Both loved her and wanted her to live, but they also respected her wishes and were willing to let go and allow her to die, if that was her wish.

The physicians, psychiatrists, therapists, nurses, and hospital administrators argued the case out. About half of those involved believed that the woman should be allowed to die, the other half holding that she should be kept alive and given extensive psychological counseling. What was the right thing to do? How are the patient's wishes in such cases to be balanced by the principle of preserving conscious life? Doctors have been trained to save life, above all "to do no harm." Are we now calling on them to change their basic philosophy of medicine?

Mrs. C's case forces us to reconsider our views on suicide, as well as euthanasia. When, if ever, does a person have a right to take his or her own life? Is suicide ever morally permissible? Since the most controversial kinds of euthanasia are extensions of the notion of suicide, let us first be clear on the ethical status of suicide before we turn to the problem of euthanasia.

Suicide is a taboo subject in our society. Whereas our ancestors spoke openly of death, including suicide, and were silent on sex, we are garrulous on sex, but silent on death, especially suicide. Bring it up at the next party to which you're invited and you won't have to worry about party clothes for a long time.

Earlier I spoke of the experience of losing a loved one as the psychological equivalent of an earthquake. The earthquake in the case of suicide registers around 10 on the Richter scale—its force is compounded by the horror of its cosmic irreverence. Suicide shakes the foundations of the entire structure of our values. In one fell swoop, all that we take for granted in daily life has been put in question. Here is someone who has refused to "suffer the slings and arrows of outrageous fortune" and has taken arms against them, as Hamlet once contemplated.

Can one ever make a rational decision to kill oneself? Is it ever moral to commit suicide?

Suicide can be defined as an action in which a person intentionally brings about his or her own death in circumstances in which others do not coerce that person to act. That is, (1) death is intended by the agent, (2) it is caused by the agent, and (3) no one else is forcing the agent to this killing of self. We also distinguish between (a) self-regarding and (b) altruistic suicides, the former being done to eliminate suffering of the self while the latter eliminates suffering or even the death of others.

The first condition, intentionality, rules out "slow-motion suicides," such as that discussed by the sociologist Ronald Maris[1]: "Suicide occurs when an individual engages in a lifestyle that he knows might kill him . . . and it does [kill him]. This is an omnibus definition of suicide, which includes various forms of self-destruction, such as risk-taking and many so-called 'accidents.'" Ian Martin identifies overdrinking and smoking with attempted suicide.[2] But by this omnibus definition we could get the strange situation of a woman who is murdered while walking through a dangerous neighborhood in order to get home. The murderer pleads, "Ms. Jones committed suicide knowing, as she did, the danger of our neighborhood. I can't be tried for murder—only for assisting in a suicide." The omnibus definition is too "omni-"; it takes purpose out of the act.

There is a question about whether the agent must have strictly intended his or her death or simply voluntarily caused it. Consider the following news release:

> The American soldier who threw himself on an exploding grenade to save his comrades during a fierce fight in Viet Nam was identified as Daniel Fernandez of Los Lunas, N.M. Under intense enemy pressure the unit fell back carrying their wounded with them, but the Viet Cong followed up with rifle and grenade fire. Fernandez was reported to have jumped on a Viet Cong grenade and covered it with his body to shield other members of his unit from the explosive blast which killed him. "He sacrificed himself to save us," one of his buddies said. (Associated Press Report, February 1966)

Fernandez seems to have voluntarily caused his own death but did he commit suicide? If you think that *voluntarily and knowingly* causing one's own death is sufficient to constitute a suicide, you will say that Fernandez committed suicide. If you take *intended* more strictly, you will say that he did not commit suicide, for he didn't jump on the enemy grenade to die, but to save his fellows.

A borderline case is that of the sickly Captain Oates, who walked out of Scott's tent on the Antarctic expedition to save the expeditionary party. Did Oates commit suicide? Ethicists have debated this back and forth. Roy Holland argues that he did not commit suicide because he merely intended to relieve his party of his presence. "The blizzard killed him. Had Oates taken out a revolver and shot himself I should have agreed he was a suicide."[3] In such cases as these, there seems to be a fine line between knowing the certain consequences of your actions and intending that those consequences take place.

In one sense, it doesn't matter what we call these cases as long as we agree on the moral status of the acts. We can say that they were suicides, but morally good—altruistic—acts, so it turns out that some suicides are justified or permitted. Or we can say that Fernandez's and Oates's acts were not suicides, but acts of voluntarily causing their own death. I'm inclined to say that Fernandez's act was not a suicide. In the spontaneity of the moment, his thought may only have been to protect his comrades. The distinct intention of dying was lacking. The fact that Oates premeditated on his act and voluntarily took steps to ensure his death puts his act closer to what we would call a suicide.

But what about the Buddhist monk who immolates himself to protest a tyrannical government? Or Sidney Carton in Dickens's *Tale of Two Cities,* who takes the place of his friend and goes to the guillotine? Here an intention to die is present, so we should agree that the monk and Carton both committed suicide.

Interestingly, early Christian theologians Tertullian (150–220 C.E.) and Origin (182–254 C.E.) believed that Jesus committed suicide, intending to die for the world's salvation by voluntarily giving up the ghost. If they are correct, the crucifixion was an altruistic suicide.

Suicide need not be an overt act. As long as the intention is present, allowing oneself to die is sufficient. Sidney Carton voluntarily walked to the guillotine, but he did not pull the blade down on his neck. If I wish to die and hire you to pull the plug on my ventilator, in a sense I've committed suicide and you've committed allocide (assisting in a suicide). Likewise, if someone accidentally cuts me with a knife so that I bleed, and I deliberately do not stanch the flow of blood, I have (passively) committed self-slaughter.

Whether they are called "suicide" or "voluntary self-slaughter," society has always praised altruistic or other-regarding suicides. But self-regarding suicide has suffered just the opposite judgment. It is the paradigm of cowardly or selfish action, of taking fate into one's own hands, a sin against God. Wittgenstein expresses a widespread sense of horror at such self-demise. "If suicide is allowed then everything is allowed. If anything is not allowed then suicide is not allowed. This throws a light on the nature of ethics, for suicide is, so to speak, the elementary sin."[4]

Yet until the sixth century Christianity not only tolerated suicide but also praised a form of martyrdom that bordered on suicide. There is no word against suicide in the Old Testament, where four suicides are recorded without adverse comment, or in the New Testament, where Judas Iscariot hanged himself. At Masada (72 C.E.) Eleazar led some 900 Jews in a mass suicide rather than be captured by the Romans. As I mentioned earlier, leading Christian theologians Tertullian and Origin regarded Jesus' death as a suicide, noting that he voluntarily "gave up the ghost." Early Christians often embraced martyrdom willingly, sometimes paying strangers to kill them so they might enter Heaven immediately. Virgins killed themselves to prevent being raped. "Let me enjoy those beasts," exclaimed Christian martyr Ignatius in the second century, "whom I wish more cruel than they are; for if they will not attack me, I will provoke and draw them by force." Gibbon tells us that one Christian sect, the Donatists, "frequently stopped travellers on the public highways and obliged them to inflict the stroke of martyrdom by promise of a reward if they consented—and by the threat of instant death if they refused to grant so very singular a favor."[5]

It was Augustine, Bishop of Hippo (354–430), who in response to the growing loss of Christians in his domain through voluntary martyrdom, first proclaimed that it was sinful, a violation of the Sixth Commandment, "Thou shalt not kill." Suicide was first condemned by the Church at the Council of Braga in 562, at which time people who committed suicide were denied funeral rites. In the next century those who attempted suicide were excommunicated from the Church and later referred to as "martyrs for Satan." Thomas Aquinas (1225–1274) set forth the position of the Catholic Church, arguing that it was a mortal sin against God because it was against nature and charity, an offense against society, and a destruction of God's gift.

Since the sixth century suicide has been generally condemned in Western society and Aquinas's arguments have won widespread acceptance. Traditionally, Jews and Christians have condemned self-regarding suicide as an affront to God, because only God can give and take innocent life. Our lives are gifts of God. They are not owned by us but are God's property. We are stewards of His property. As Kant put it, "Human beings are sentinels on earth and may not leave their posts until relieved by another beneficent hand."[6]

This argument, which has been effective throughout Western history, has two drawbacks. First, if someone doesn't believe in God (or a God who keeps our lives as His property), the argument fails. Second, God is made into a monster, who forces us to endure torture and suffering. If the property–steward view of life were to hold, one would suppose God to take better care of His or Her possessions and to ameliorate the agony of existence more than God does. What kind of sentinel is the terminally ill cancer patient, lying in anguish with only two days to live? God has given us reason to use medicines to alleviate suffering in ourselves and others, and that could include the option of ending our existence when it becomes a burden to us or our loved ones.

The second main argument against suicide is the argument from nature: It is natural to want to live and to promote life. This argument is simply confused. Nature both brings to life and kills. To kill and avoid pain and suffering are natural tendencies. What is unnatural about suicide? As David Hume says, "It would be no crime in me to divert the Nile or Danube from its course, were I able to effect such purposes. Where then is the crime of turning a few ounces of blood from their natural channel?"[7]

To want to live as long as life is pleasurable seems natural. Life itself, I have argued in Chapter 2, is not an absolute value.

If the property argument or the argument from nature were taken seriously, it would mean that we could not morally sacrifice our lives for others—for is it not playing God by going against nature to intervene in the death of others? Daniel Fernandez would be forbidden to fall on the bomb that would have killed his comrades, and Sidney Carton would be forbidden to give his life for his friend. Altruistic suicides, accepted by the Catholic Church, as well as self-regarding suicides would be condemned as immoral.

Suicide and the Meaning of Life

Albert Camus in his gem, *The Myth of Sisyphus,* calls suicide the "one truly philosophical problem."[8] Why not commit suicide? he asks. Consider his grim picture of absurd existence, the kind that, according to Camus, all of us live in one way or another.

On Monday morning a man or woman gets up at 6:30, goes to the toilet, washes, dresses, and eats breakfast. Another hour is spent mindlessly commuting to a job whose work when looked at with a lucid eye is ultimately purposeless. If it weren't for the grim need to earn wages, no sane person would do this kind of thing. Then, return: a mindless commute to a mindless evening before a mindless entertainment box, and then to bed. The saga is repeated Tuesday, Wednesday, Thursday, and Friday for over forty years until the person retires, too old to discover a better way of life. Saturdays he or she spends recovering from the exhaustion of the other five days, and on Sunday he or she is bored at the home of relatives or else, if not very sensitive, he or she enjoys inconsequential gossip about the food, weather, or football game. Occasionally the person gets drunk or soothes his or her raging hormones in an act of lust.

The person's goal is to make enough money to feed and educate his or her children so that they can grow up to repeat this silly game, making enough money to feed and educate their children in order that they can play it too, and so on.

Camus asks us to discover some enduring value in this person's life. One day the person may wake up and discover that there isn't any.

Outraged at this analysis, you might protest, "Life is made meaningful by ameliorating the suffering in society, or bringing about revolution or reform." Perhaps. John Stuart Mill once thought the same. In his *Autobiography,*[9] Mill describes the crisis of meaning that took place in his twenty-second year of life. Following Jeremy Bentham, Mill's whole life had been dedicated to social reform, and as long as he could see the world improving, he felt satisfaction and even happiness. But a crisis arose in 1826. He was in a "dull state of nerves, such as everybody is occasionally liable to," when the following question occurred to him: " 'Suppose that all your objects in life were realized; that all the changes in institutions and opinions which you are looking forward to, could be completely effected at this very instant: would this be a great joy and happiness to you?' An irrepressible self consciousness distinctly answered, 'No!' At this my heart sank within me: the whole foundation on which my life was constructed fell down. All my happiness was to have been founded in the continual pursuit of this end. The end had ceased to charm, and how could there ever again be any interest in the means? I seemed to have nothing left to live for." Mill went through a deep depression that lasted several months, during which he came close to suicide. Ask yourself the same question he did.

Note, in this regard, how much "good work" is simply the negating of social negativities.[10] Some of the highest paid and most prestigious professions involve little more than ameliorating evils rather than creating good. Physicians are parasites on disease, without which they would be extraneous. Doctors don't produce any positive value but merely help negate illness. Lawyers spend their time prosecuting or defending people accused of evil transactions. In executing wills they become partial heirs to estates to which they have no fundamental relation, or, like cisterns, they transfer wealth in costly litigation from one party to another, becoming leaky pipes, siphoning off large doses of the principal. In malpractice suits attorneys may receive between 30 and 40 percent of the award. If people were honest, would we need lawyers to write up wills? If people were moral, where would criminal lawyers be? If people's word were bond, would we need legal contracts? If people lived decently and rationally, how much litigation would there be? Of course, we need lawyers in a society filled with avarice and distrust, but the point is according to this negative analysis, most of the lawyers' functions and earnings are based on human weakness and misery. Without human negativities, a lawyer's lot would be a poor one. Attorneys are negators of negativities.

So much of life is merely negating the negative to keep the status quo. It's as though we are in the middle of the ocean on a boat with numerous leaks and our primary task is to bail out water so that we can simply stay afloat and sail in circles. Would we think a person who decided to call the whole game quits and jump into the ocean stupid or immoral? Certainly not stupid, for the game wasn't worth the bucket.

So why don't we commit suicide?

The answer has to do with what is valuable, what makes life worth living. Although life itself may be neither good nor bad, it is the necessary condition for whatever is good or bad. And there are good things in life: living in loving relationships with spouse, friends, and children; learning about the world—both the external world of physics, chemistry, biology, and so on and the internal world of self and other; creating works of art and music; writing a sonnet or

planning a dinner; becoming an ideal person, a spiritual work of art; becoming accomplished at a complex skill or interesting activity; enjoying simple and profound pleasures. Alleviating suffering and pain also gives life meaning. Although these negatings of negatives are not sufficient to make life positively worthwhile, the hope in pursuing social justice is that when injustice and suffering are removed, victims will find positive meaning. That makes negating the negations worthwhile.

What happens when these values are irretrievably lost? What happens when health, so important for the attainment of most of the other values, is going or is gone? When human relations are hopelessly destroyed? When our minds lose their acuity so that we not only cease to learn the new but also forget the old? When the pain becomes too great to bear? What happens when we have committed a grave evil and cannot make restitution, or when we find that evil uncontrollably manifests itself in destroying others?

When life has lost the values that give it value, when its sum total is in the red, why is it wrong to put a stop to the misery, if one so desires?

Under some conditions suicide appears morally permissible. We have seen that altruistic ones are, for they are supererogatory acts aiming to help others. But other instances of suicide may also be justified if life becomes unbearable and no hope for remission is in sight. As Epictetus put it, "If the room is smoky, if only moderately, I will stay; if there is too much smoke, I will go. Remember this, keep a firm hold on it, the door is always open."

The right to die seems a corollary of our right to life itself, for what is a right if it cannot be waived? A right that cannot be waived is not a right, but a duty. But a good argument against all forms of rational suicide has yet to be given, so there is no reason to suppose that all rational suicide is wrong. The only question is, what are the conditions for rational or morally permissible suicide? I suggest the following:

1. The person has made a realistic assessment of the situation and judges suicide to be the best course of action for him or her.

2. A reasonable time has elapsed for review of the situation.

3. The harm likely to be done to others resulting from the suicide is not likely to outweigh the amount of evil avoided to the person himself or herself.

Let us apply this to some cases. Take the case of a man dying of cancer, who is unable to find relief for his pain, who has settled his accounts, and now has only the prospect of further suffering and huge medical bills. He has fulfilled all three conditions. He knows that there is no hope of remission, a reasonable time of reflection about his case has transpired, and no great harm is likely to be done to others; indeed, he will be sparing them huge medical expenses if he kills himself. Why isn't this man justified in committing suicide? He has every right to do so, according to my criteria.

On the other hand, take the following cases of teen suicide. My friend George, mentioned at the beginning of the previous chapter, committed suicide on being told that his heart murmur would prevent him from playing football again, and two sixteen-year-olds, call them Len and Lisa, who when prevented by their parents from living together asphyxiated themselves to death in a car in the garage of Len's parents.

The tragedy of these kinds of suicides is matched only by their foolishness. None of the conditions mentioned above have been fulfilled. The teenager is usually in no position to make a realistic assessment of his or her situation. If only George had had the patience to wait a few months, he would have found new goals in life to replace football. If only Len and Lisa had waited a year or two, they would have grown out of their love or found a way to get married. Teenage suicides still fill us with horror because we see these young people throwing away their lives before they are lived. They are rejecting the goods that we feel sure are worth the trouble. Moreover, regarding the third condition, they are causing incalculable suffering to family, friends, and community, who have strong emotional investments in them.

Given these conditions, suicide prevention and intervention programs should certainly be instituted to restrain and restore temporarily people who precipitously attempt suicide. The truth is, we all become depressed and in that state may lose lucidity. Philosopher Richard Brandt sums it up nicely:

> Depression, like any severe emotional experience, tends to primitivize one's intellectual process. It restricts the range of one's survey of the possibilities. One thing that a rational person would do is compare the world-course containing his suicide with his best alternative. But his best alternative is precisely a possibility he may overlook if, in a depressed mood, he thinks only of how badly off he is and cannot imagine any way of improving his situation.[11]

Evidence shows that a large percentage of attempted suicides are done in moments of high stress or in order to communicate with others.[12] Intervention is justified in these cases and counseling should commence.

However, when it comes to elderly people who are losing their faculties, or terminally ill patients, or when rational adults have lost all that makes life worthwhile for them, their autonomy should be respected. Although we regret these deaths, we do not feel the same sense of tragedy as we do with teenage suicides, where full autonomy is missing.

Janet Adkins had every right, after counseling, to take her life when the wine was running dry and she could look forward only to semi-consciousness. The same is correct about Mrs. C, the Korean woman mentioned at the beginning of this chapter.

When Dr. and Mrs. Henry Van Dusen, the former President of Union Theological Seminary and his wife, committed suicide together in their eighties, it was done as an act of worship culminating two lives lived in the service of God and humanity. They had lived life to the fullest and decided to depart before their failing powers reduced them to shadows of their former selves and a burden on their children. Perhaps they should have consulted with their children, perhaps their suicides were premature, but we can understand the Van Dusens' concern about their failing powers and their being a burden to themselves and their children.

When it becomes clear beyond reasonable doubt that the nullity of death will be preferable to the negative value of a suffering life, the rational thing to do is act with dispatch.

Gradually, our society is coming to accept a limited version of this argument for morally permissible suicide. While we rightly deplore teenage suicides as unjustified because none of the relevant conditions have been fulfilled, we sympathize with terminally ill patients who have no prospect for a happy life. We judge the elderly and terminally ill less severely.

Note that Barney Clark, the sixty-one-year-old retired dentist and the first human being to receive a permanent artificial heart, was given a key that he could use to turn off the compressor if he should wish at any time to cease living attached to the machine.

> "If the man suffers and feels it isn't worth it any more, he has a key that he can apply," said Dr. Willem Kolff, head of the University of Utah's Artificial Organs Division, inventor of the artificial kidney, and founder of the artificial heart program.
>
> "I think it is entirely legitimate that this man whose life has been extended should have the right to cut it off if he doesn't want it, if life ceases to be enjoyable," he added.
>
> "The operation won't be a success unless he is happy. That has always been our criteria—to restore happiness."[13]

This sounds close to the Stoic doctrine of leaving the smoky room. "If the room is smoky, if only moderately, I will stay; if there is too much smoke, I will go. Remember this, keep a firm hold on it, the door is always open" (Epictetus).

Study Questions

1. Is suicide always immoral, or is it sometimes morally permissible? If it is sometimes morally permissible, under what circumstances?
2. Is self-destructive behavior such as heavy smoking, overdrinking of alcoholic beverages, or drug abuse a form of indirect suicide? Explain.
3. Some people believe that suicide is wrong because it violates natural law. It simply goes against our natural tendency to want to live. Do you agree? What, if any, is the relationship between something being unnatural and its being immoral? Go back and look at David Hume's comment on this. Is Hume correct in comparing the suicide's opening of his or her blood vessel with the opening of a dam?
4. Why does Camus call suicide the only truly philosophical problem? Is he correct?
5. Under what circumstances should we engage in suicide prevention and under what circumstances, if any, should we refrain from interfering?

Endnotes

1. Ronald Maris, "Sociology," in *A Handbook for the Study of Suicide* ed. S. Perlin (Oxford: Oxford University Press, 1975): 100.

2. Ian Martin, "Slow Motion Suicide," *New Society* (October 1974).

3. Roy Holland, "Suicide," in *Moral Problems,* J. Rachels ed. (New York: Harper and Row, 1973).

4. Ludwig Wittgenstein, *Notebooks 1914–1916,* G. H. von Wright and G. E. M. Anscombe, eds. (Oxford: Basil Blackwell, 1961), 91.

5. Edward Gibbon, *The Decline and Fall of the Roman Empire* (1776), vol. 3, 401.

6. Immanuel Kant, *Lectures on Ethics,* trans. Louis Infield (New York: Harper & Row, 1963), 154.

7. David Hume, "Of Suicide," *Essays; Moral, Political and Literary* (Oxford: Oxford University Press, 1963): 585–596.

8. Albert Camus, *The Myth of Sisyphus* (New York: Vintage Books, 1960), 3.

9. John Stuart Mill, *Autobiography,* (Oxford: Oxford University Press, 1873), 94.

10. In the next two paragraphs, I am reflecting the existentialist perspective; it is not necessarily my own, although I think there is truth in it.

11. Richard Brandt, "The Morality and Rationality of Suicide," in *A Handbook for the Study of Suicide* ed. Seymour Perlin, (Oxford: Oxford University Press, 1975).

12. David Greenberg, "Interference with a Suicide Attempt," *New York University Law Review* 49 (May–June 1974): 227–269.

12. Quoted in James Rachels, *The End of Life* (Oxford: Oxford University Press, 1986) 79.

CHAPTER 8

Euthanasia

The intentional termination of the life of one human being by another—mercy killing—is contrary to that for which the medical profession stands and is contrary to the policy of the American Medical Association.

The cessation of the employment of extraordinary means to prolong the life of the body when there is irrefutable evidence that biological death is imminent is the decision of the patient and/or his immediate family. The advice and judgment of the physician should be freely available to the patient and/or his immediate family.

AMERICAN MEDICAL ASSOCIATION POLICY STATEMENT ON VOLUNTARY EUTHANASIA

On April 14, 1975, Karen Ann Quinlan, a twenty-one-year-old woman, lapsed into a coma from which she never emerged. Thus began the most famous case in the history of American medical ethics. The combination of Valium, aspirin, and three gin and tonics at a party may have deprived her brain of oxygen, causing extensive brain damage and a state of persistent vegetation that was to last ten years, while the family, the hospital, and the courts angrily fought over her body. The national media caught every breath and blow in the action.

After months of watching their adopted daughter's body curled up in a fetal position and maintained by life supports, Joseph and Julia Quinlan despaired of hope, and with the approval of their priest they asked the physicians at St. Clare's Hospital in Danville, New Jersey, to disconnect the ventilator. Dr. Robert Morse, attending physician, agreed and had the Quinlans sign a form absolving him of liability. A few days later, Morse, perhaps fearing a malpractice suit, changed his mind and refused to disconnect the ventilator, telling the Quinlans that since Karen was twenty-one, they needed a court order appointing Mr. Quinlan as Karen's legal guardian before the ventilator could be switched off. Karen was not brain dead under New Jersey law. There was some electroencephalographic activity, though neurologists agreed that her comatose condition was irreversible. Meanwhile Medicare was paying the medical costs of $450 per day.

The Quinlans' lawyer, Paul Armstrong, first argued that since Karen was brain dead, she should be unhooked from life-support systems. When Judge Muir pointed out that Karen had not met the criteria for brain death under New Jersey law, Armstrong amended his brief, arguing for a right to die based on three grounds: religious freedom, cruel and unusual punishment, and the right to privacy. The first ground claimed that Karen's wish to die was based on her religious beliefs. The second compared the physicians at the hospital to prison guards who were punishing prisoners. The third, the "right to privacy," appealed to the 1973 *Rowe v. Wade* abortion decision of the Supreme Court which spoke of an individual's right to make personal decisions. The New Jersey Attorney General opposed pulling the plug, arguing that to do so "would open the door to euthanasia." Morse's lawyer, Ralph Porzio, argued that to allow Karen to die would start a slippery slope leading to the killing of people who lived a poor quality of life. "And fresh in our minds are the Nazi atrocities. Fresh in our minds are the human experimentations. Fresh in our minds are the Nuremberg Codes."[1] Judge Muir accepted Porzio's arguments and proclaimed that the family's anguish over their comatose daughter was clouding their judgment.

Vatican theologian, Gino Concetti, condemned the act of removing Karen from life supports. "A right to death does not exist. Love for life, even a life reduced to a ruin, drives one to protect life with every possible care."[2]

The case was appealed, and on January 26, 1976, the New Jersey Supreme Court overruled Judge Muir. It set aside all criminal liability in removing Karen from a respirator. St. Clare's Hospital, fearing bad publicity in allowing Karen's death, stalled and even added a second machine to aid in controlling Karen's body temperature. Finally, after several weeks of waiting, Karen was weaned off the ventilator. St. Clare's asked that she be transferred to another institution, but that proved difficult. Twenty hospitals and nursing homes refused to accept Karen before the Morris View Nursing Home took her in on June 9, 1976, some five and a half months after the court's decision to allow her to die.

For nine years, Karen Ann Quinlan lay in a permanently vegetative state (PVS) on a waterbed in Morris View Nursing Home, artificially fed via a feeding tube. Each day her father rose at 4:30 A.M. for a 40-mile drive to the nursing home, where he talked to Karen, massaged her back, and even sang to her. His comatose daughter was still a person to him. On June 11, 1985, Karen died.

A recent comprehensive study in *Lancet* estimated that between 10,000 and 25,000 adults and between 4,000 and 10,000 children were in PVS, the yearly costs per patient ranging between $24,000 and $120,000. The record case is that of Rita Greene, who became comatose in 1952, at age twenty-four, and died in D.C. General Hospital in the District of Columbia in 1991.[3] The next famous case after Quinlan was that of Nancy Cruzan, who lay in a PVS for almost eight years between January 1983 and December 1990, when she was removed from a feeding tube and pronounced dead. In July 1990, the United States Supreme Court decided that unless there is a prior, clear proof of intent, the matter of allowing patients in a persistent vegetative state to die should be left up to individual states.[4]

The term *euthanasia* comes from the Greek and means "good death." *Webster's Dictionary* defines it as "a quiet and easy death" or "the action of inducing a quiet and easy death." Euthanasia can refer to inducing death either *passively* or *actively,* that is, either by withdrawing treatment or by actively putting to death or hastening death. It can also be divided into two types of patient intentions, the first when the patient has given consent, the second when the patient is not able to do so, that is, *voluntarily* and *involuntarily* (or nonvoluntarily). If we combine these categories, we end up with four distinct types of euthanasia (see the table below).

Active euthanasia is illegal throughout the United States, though under considerable debate. Passive euthanasia has long been practiced. Its application under modern conditions is accepted in some contexts, such as withdrawing life support from the terminally ill, and under debate in other conditions, such as allowing newborns to starve to death when a decision has been made not to operate on Down's syndrome babies with intestinal obstructions.

The official American Medical Association position, quoted at the beginning of this chapter, condemns active euthanasia but permits passive euthanasia, especially the withholding of extraordinary means or heroic measures from the patient. I will criticize the logic of this distinction and the AMA position later, but first we should look at some cases that illustrate the various positions.

Cases of voluntary passive euthanasia happen every day. When a doctor respects the wishes of a Jehovah's Witness or Christian Science practitioner and refrains from administrating a life saving blood transfusion, the doctor is practicing passive voluntary euthanasia. When the doctor withdraws life-support equipment from a patient in a persistent vegetative state or from a seriously defective neonate, or refuses to use extraordinary means to prolong these patients' lives, he or she is practicing involuntary passive euthanasia. In the case of the Korean woman described in Chapter 7, the doctors finally acceded to her wishes and removed the life support system, so that she could die. In the case of permanently vegetative patients, such as Karen Ann Quinlan and Nancy Cruzan, lawyers and doctors argued whether it was right to practice passive involuntary euthanasia and withdraw the life-support system.

A most interesting case regarding voluntary passive euthanasia is the famous 1973 "Texas

	Voluntary	Involuntary

Passive	Refusal of treatment
	No extraordinary means or heroic
	  treatment
		Withdrawing of treatment primarily on
		  defective neonates, incompetent patients,
		  and those in a persistent vegetative state

Active	Inducing death with consent Allocide or mercy killing of hopeless cases	Inducing death without consent mercy Killing of incompetent patients or deformed neonates

burn case," in which a young, athletic man, known in the literature as Donald C., suffered terrible burns when a gas line exploded, leaving 68 percent of his body burned. Crippled, blind, and without fingers, he was kept alive in the hospital, against his will, for two years by a series of painful treatments. Donald continually demanded to be left alone to die, but his doctors refused. A psychiatrist examined him and found him perfectly rational.

Should Donald C. have been allowed to die? Donald, whose real name is Dax Cowart, survived the treatment and is alive today. Since his recovery he has earned a law degree and is living a happy life. Yet he believes that his right to die was violated:

> Freedom, true freedom, not only gives us the right to make the correct choices; it also has to give us the right sometimes to make the wrong choices. In my case, however, it was a moot point whether I was wrong as far as my quality of life went, because that was a secondary issue. The immediate issue, the urgent issue, was that my pain was not being taken care of. That was why I wanted to die.
>
> Today I'm happy; in fact I even feel that I'm happier than most people. I'm more active physically than I thought I ever would be. I've taken karate for a couple of years, I've climbed a 50-foot utility pole with the assistance of a belay line on the ropes course. I do other mental things, like write poetry and practice law. That is not to say, though, that the doctors were right. To say that would reflect a mentality that says, all's well that ends well, or the ends justify the means—whatever means necessary to achieve the results are okay to use. That totally ignores the pain that I had to go through. . . . [i]f the same thing were to happen today under identical circumstances, would I still want the freedom? Knowing what I know now, would I still want the freedom to refuse treatment and die? And the answer is always yes, a resounding yes. If I think about having to go through that kind of pain again, I know that it's not something I would want.[4]

Is Dax Cowart right? Can life become so burdensome, so filled with pain and suffering, that it loses all meaning and value? Should the sufferer be given the right to decide?

Cases of active euthanasia are even more controversial than those of passive euthanasia, for they involve doing something positive to induce death.

In March 1983 Johanna Florian of Fort Lauderdale, Florida, was suffering from irreversible Alzheimer's disease, along with thyroid problems, which would eventually make her senile and helpless. Her husband, Hans, couldn't stand to see his wife suffer and degenerate, so one Friday the seventy-nine-year-old Hans lifted Johanna from her hospital bed, wheeled her into the stairwell, and fatally shot her in the head. When the nurse rushed in and saw what had happened, she ordered Hans back into his wife's room. "The old man meekly obeyed." He was later charged with first-degree murder.[5]

Hans Florian had broken the law and murdered his wife, but had he done anything morally wrong? The Florida grand jury refused to indict him.

R. M. Hare tells the story of a truck driver whose truck had turned over and who lay pinned under the cabin while the truck was on fire. The driver, who was slowly roasting away, begged onlookers to hit him on the head so that he would not experience the pain of roasting to death. Should they have done so as they watched the man slowly die in agony?[6]

Celebrated journalist Stewart Alsop relates an incident that took place in the early 1970s while he was a patient in the solid tumor ward of the cancer clinic of the National Institutes of Health in Bethesda, Maryland. His roommate was a twenty-eight-year-old man he called Jack. Jack had a malignant tumor in his stomach about the size of a softball, which had metastasized and was beyond control.

Jack was in constant pain. His doctors prescribed an intravenous shot of a synthetic opiate every four hours, but it was impossible to control the pain that long. After a few hours Jack would begin to moan or whimper, "then he would begin to howl like a dog." A nurse would come. Codeine would then be given, but it usually did little good, and Jack continued in agony.

"The third night of this routine," Alsop writes, "the terrible thought occurred to me, 'If Jack were a dog . . . what would be done with him?' The answer was obvious: the pound and chloroform. No human being with a spark of pity could let a living thing suffer so, to no good end."[7]

Arguments Against Voluntary Active Euthanasia

There are essentially four arguments against voluntary active euthanasia. Probably the oldest is the argument from Natural Law. Active euthanasia violates Natural Law. We have a natural inclination to preserve life, which is trespassed in this act. We have already commented on this argument in discussing suicide. The notion of Natural Law can't be used to argue against either suicide or euthanasia. Medicine itself would be prohibited if we followed only the natural course of things. Certainly we wouldn't build airplanes or dams. Just as we use a dam to divert a river from its course to prevent the flooding of a city, so it seems natural to use a knife to divert a few pints of blood from reaching the brain to release a terminally ill patient from a period of hopeless suffering.

The second argument is that voluntary active euthanasia is "playing God" and violates the sanctity of life. Only God is allowed to take an innocent life. Our right to life cannot be waived.

The use of the term "playing God" is just a pejorative way of emoting against autonomous action. To use medicine to keep a sick person from dying is playing God, if playing God means affecting the prospects of death. To employ antibiotics to kill harmful bacteria is to play God. Defending oneself from a rapist by killing him is

playing God. Using birth control devices is playing God, as is feeding those starving during a "naturally caused" famine. All difficult moral decisions involve the kind of reasoning and action that might be labeled "playing God."

If playing God simply means doing what will affect the chances of life and death, a lot of responsible social action does that. If, on the other hand, the term means unwarrantedly affecting the life chances of someone, the question boils down to what is morally correct behavior in dealing with the dying process. We need to know which types of playing God are morally correct and which are not.

Sometimes the argument against playing God can be reduced to the property argument discussed in the previous chapter. We are stewards of God's property, so we may not mishandle it or throw it away by killing it. Of course, we are also responsible for using our reason in handling God's property. We do take lives in self-defense, so why not in self-defense against torture or great and irreversible suffering? The best way to exercise stewardship with God's property is to use the best reasons available in deciding how to use that property. Sometimes that means dispensing with it, especially when it is doing great harm.

The third argument against voluntary active euthanasia is the Slippery Slope argument—if we allow active euthanasia, it will lead to terrible abuses. Here is how former President Ronald Reagan's speech writer, Patrick Buchanan, put it:

> Once we embrace this utilitarian ethic—that Man has the sovereign right to decide who is entitled to life and who is not—we have boarded a passenger train on which there are no scheduled stops between here and Birkenau.
>
> Once we accept that there are certain classes—i.e. unwanted unborn children, unwanted infants who are retarded or handicapped, etc.—whose lives are unworthy of legal protection, upon what moral high ground do we stand to decry when Dr. Himmler slaps us on the back, and asks us if he can include Gypsies and Jews?[8]

The Slippery Slope argument is weak. Although the sentiments expressed in Patrick Buchanan's passage are to be taken seriously, the argument is invalid. The fact that a practice *can be abused* does not mean that it shouldn't be used at all. Salt and sugar can be abused and harm us, but that doesn't mean that they shouldn't be used at all—even for legitimate purposes. Knives, cars, and drugs can be abused, but that doesn't mean that they should be outlawed.

We can well imagine serious abuses of the right to die. Imagine Aunt Ann, dying of cancer. She is running up large hospital and doctor bills, depleting her savings. Now Nephew Ned, who figures to collect handsomely from Aunt Ann's estate, is certain that Aunt Ann would be better off dead than alive. He encourages Aunt Ann to come to the same conclusion before her estate becomes bankrupt. We would want to take measures to prevent such manipulation, but if we became convinced that we could not control them, we might well concede that voluntary active euthanasia, while in principle moral, should not become legal.

Difficult as it may be, we can safeguard terminally ill patients from most manipulative practices, so the slippery slope argument isn't obviously valid here. The lesson of the argument is to put in place measures that will protect patients from abuse, while still respecting patient autonomy.

Finally, those opposed to active euthanasia often appeal to the *difference between killing and letting die,* so that while passive euthanasia may be sometimes be justified, it doesn't follow that active euthanasia is. A fundamental difference exists between *doing* something and *allowing* something to happen. This is a standard attack on voluntary active euthanasia. It is the argument included in the AMA statement cited at the beginning of this chapter.

Is there really is a fundamental difference between killing and letting die, between active and passive euthanasia? First of all, it isn't clear that *letting* something bad happen is always worse (or more morally culpable) than *doing* something bad.

Recall Judith Jarvis Thomson's counterexample to this dogma. John is a trolley driver who suddenly realizes that his breaks have failed. He is heading toward a group of workers on the track ahead of him and will certainly kill them if something isn't done immediately. Fortunately, there is a side track to the right onto which John can turn the trolley. Unfortunately, on that track is one worker, who will be killed if John turns the trolley.

Now if the passive–active distinction holds, John should do nothing but simply allow the trolley to take its toll of the five men on the track before him. But that seems terrible. Surely, by turning quickly and causing the trolley to move onto the right track John will be saving a total of four lives. Most of us think that he should turn the trolley to the right and actively cause the death of one man rather than passively allow the death of the five. John is caught in a situation in which he cannot help doing or allowing harm, but he can act so that the lesser of the evils obtains—rather than the greater of the evils. Sometimes we have a duty to cause evil actively rather than permit a greater evil. This may be part of the justification of a just war. Better to enter the war against the Nazi regime, thus causing the death of many people, than allow it to triumph over innocent people.

This shows that the passive–active distinction doesn't always have the moral significance that it seems to have at first glance. Actively harming is not always worse than passively allowing harm. Consider the following illustration offered by James Rachels:

> Smith stands to gain a large inheritance if anything should happen to his six-year-old cousin. One evening while the child is taking his bath, Smith sneaks into the bathroom and drowns the child, and then arranges things so that it will look like an accident. No one is the wiser, and Smith gets his inheritance.

Jones also stands to gain if anything should happen to his six-year-old cousin. Like Smith, Jones sneaks in planning to drown the child in his bath. However, just as he enters the bathroom Jones sees the child slip, hit his head, and fall face-down in the water. Jones is delighted; he stands by, ready to push the child's head back under if necessary, but it is not necessary. With only a little thrashing about, the child drowns all by himself, 'accidentally', as Jones watches and does nothing. No one is the wiser, and Jones gets his inheritance.[9]

Is there really any difference between the moral culpability of Smith and Jones? Is Jones's behavior less reprehensible than Smith's? From a legal point of view, Smith is guilty of first-degree murder, whereas Jones is not, but from a moral point of view these acts seem identical. Both acted from identical motives (personal greed), and both had the same end in view (the death of a child). The result is also the same: the child, whom Smith and Jones were responsible for saving, died.

Philosophers such as Rachels use this argument to show that there is no morally significant difference between killing and letting die. What counts is our motives in doing what we do and the kind of deliberation that goes into our acts. If Rachels is correct, the AMA policy, *that while passive euthanasia is permissible, active euthanasia is always forbidden,* is itself incoherent.

Some people object that arguments like Rachels's against the passive–active distinction miss the point of the AMA guideline. According to ethicists Paul Ramsey and Thomas Sullivan, what is crucial in the AMA statement is the difference between employing ordinary and extraordinary means of preserving life. Here is how Ramsey puts it:

Ordinary means of preserving life are all medicines, treatments, and operations, which offer a reasonable hope of benefit for the patient and which can be obtained and used without excessive expense, pain and other inconveniences.

Extra-ordinary means of preserving life are all those medicines, treatments, and operations which cannot be obtained without excessive expense, pain, or other inconveniences, or which, if used, would not offer a reasonable hope of benefit.[10]

The idea is that we don't have to keep people alive at all costs. This is correct, but it ignores the question of whether a terminally ill person has a right to die and to be assisted to die.

Another distinction is embedded in this argument: the difference between intending to kill someone and foreseeing that he or she will die. A woman who is attacked and raped as she walks through a dangerous neighborhood at night to get home doesn't intend to be raped, though she foresees the possibility and takes her chances. A pilot who drops bombs on enemy installations foresees that innocent people will be killed by his bombs but doesn't intend for them to die. Likewise, a doctor who refuses to employ high-level technology to save a terminally ill patient's life merely foresees that the patient will die. He doesn't intend for the patient to die.

This argument misses the point, confusing intention with action. An act may be morally correct but brought about by a bad intention, or it may be immoral but brought about by a good intention. For example, Jones and Smith both give $1,000 to a worthy cause, but whereas Jones is concerned for the welfare of the people who will be helped by his donation, Smith gives to gain a good reputation. The same act, but two different intentions. Or conversely, Jones and Smith give the donation to help a terrorist cause. Jones gives because he is misguided (culpably, let us say), whereas Smith gives simply for the prestige he will gain by so giving. In this case the same wrong act is accompanied by a good motive (Jones) and a bad one (Smith).

The point is that an act is good or bad independent of whether the motive or intention is good or bad. The intention speaks eloquently of the person's character, but it doesn't touch on the value of the act in question.

If this is correct, then the intention-foresight distinction is largely irrelevant to problems of euthanasia. What is primarily at issue is not the intention of the physician (hopefully that will be good) but the objective rightness of terminating a life when there are good reasons to do so.

Arguments in Favor of Active Euthanasia

It is not enough to see that the arguments against euthanasia are weak. We want to see what can be said in its favor. Three arguments support it: the Right-to-Life argument, the Golden Rule argument, and the Combined argument from Freedom and the Prevention of Cruelty.

1. THE RIGHT TO LIFE INCLUDES THE RIGHT TO DIE.

If I have a right to live my life as I see fit, then so long as I am not harming others I can do what I like with my life, including waive that right and put myself to death. If I cannot put myself to death without another's help, then the other person has a duty to assist in my death. This assisted death is called *allocide* (from the Greek *allo*—"other"—and the Latin *cide*—"death"). When it involves a terminally ill patient, we designate it active euthanasia. If I need help, my right to live may entail a right to be helped by another to die.

This argument is partially correct. If I have any right at all, it is the right to do with my own life what I see fit, including ending my life, so long as I do not unjustly violate any other person's rights. The argument is too strong, however, in asserting that my right to die entails that other people have a duty to assist me in my death. Just as a right to drive a car does not entail that my neighbors have to buy me a car if I can't afford one, so a right to die does not entail that others have a duty to assist me in my death. Whether they have a weak duty may depend on our relationship, expectations, and promises as well as on their feelings about suicide. This right to life / right to die argument

grants one only the right to take one's own life. It doesn't by itself entail allocide or euthanasia.

2. THE GOLDEN RULE ARGUMENT.

The Golden Rule states that we should do unto others as we would have others do unto us (if we were in their shoes). If I were the driver under the burning truck, I would want someone to knock me unconscious so that I would not experience roasting to death. So I should assist the truck driver by putting him out of his pain. Of course, this sense of duty could be overridden by the thought that I may go to jail for several years for voluntary manslaughter. But if we waive that threat, the Golden Rule seems to advise us to kill people who are being tortured by pain and who have no hope of remission.

3. THE COMBINED ARGUMENT FROM FREEDOM AND THE PREVENTION OF CRUELTY.

Two of the basic values of a civilized society are freedom and the elimination of cruelty or unnecessary suffering. Maximal freedom or autonomy consistent with the freedom of others is a desideratum, a fundamental value. Likewise, if civilized people abhor anything, it is cruelty. Sadists or torturers call up our deepest disdain and condemnation. But suffering people, such as Jack (in Stewart Alsop's story), the immolated truck driver (in R. M. Hare's story), or Mrs. C, the Korean woman (in my story), are being tortured by nature. Freedom dictates that we allow them to choose whether they want to die sooner and without pain, and the principle of preventing cruelty dictates that we do whatever necessary to help them die.

You must decide whether these arguments are convincing. If they are correct, society's present thinking about suicide and euthanasia is superstitious or, at least, confused. Even if you agree that euthanasia is morally permissible, this in itself does not entail that it should be legally permissible. Not every moral principle should be incorporated into law (for example, principles forbidding lying and bad intentions couldn't effectively be enforced). The consequences of legalizing euthanasia could be sufficiently bad as to prevent us from making the act legal. One could imagine Nephew Ned, who stands to inherit a largesse from Aunt Ann, encouraging his dear old aunt to leave this life "for the greater good" of all concerned. "Aunty, you seem to be losing your health and energy. Life must be a burden for you."

On the other hand, in general the laws should reflect these moral concerns. Safeguards should be built into the law to prevent the abuse of a legitimate but potentially dangerous practice.

In light of these concerns, each person should have a living will to insure that he or she will not be kept alive (receive extraordinary measures) against his or her will. A typical living will looks like this:

A Living Will

Death is as much a reality as maturity and old age—it is one certainty of life. If the time comes when I, _____, can no longer take part in decisions for my own future, let this statement stand as an expression of my wishes, while I am still of sound mind.

If the situation should arise in which there is no reasonable expectation of my recovery from physical or mental disability, I request that I be allowed to die and not be kept alive by artificial means or "heroic measures." I do not fear death itself as much as the indignities of deterioration, dependence, and hopeless pain. I therefore ask that medication be mercifully administered to me to alleviate suffering even though this may hasten the moment of death.

This request is made after careful consideration. I hope you who care for me will feel morally bound to follow its mandate. I recognize that this appears to place a heavy responsibility upon you, but it is with the intention of relieving you of such responsibility and of placing it upon myself in accordance with my strong conviction, that this statement is made.[11]

In 1995, following the Supreme Court rule that allowed states to devise their own guidelines regarding assisted suicide, the state of Oregon put forth the following death with dignity act:

The Death with Dignity Act

1. The patient must be at least 18, terminally ill (having less than 6 months to live), and an Oregon resident.

2. The patient must voluntarily make an oral request to the attending medical/osteopathic physician for a prescription for medication to end his or her life. A 15-day waiting period then begins.

3. The attending physician ensures the patient understands the diagnosis and prognosis. The patient is informed of all options, including pain control, hospice care, and comfort care, as well as the risks and expected result of taking the medication.

4. The attending physician (a) determines whether the patient is capable of making health care decisions and is acting voluntarily; (b) encourages the patient to notify his or her next of kin; (c) informs the patient that he or she can withdraw the request for medication at any time and in any manner; and (d) refers the patient to a consulting physician who is asked to confirm the attending physician's diagnosis and prognosis.

5. The consulting physician also decides whether the patient is capable of making the decision and is acting voluntarily. If either or both physicians believe that the patient is suffering from a psychiatric illness or depression that causes impaired judgment, the patient will be referred for counseling.

6. Once the preceding steps have been satisfied, the patient voluntarily signs a written request witnessed by two people. At least one witness cannot be a relative or an heir of the patient.

7. The patient then makes a second oral request to the attending physician for medication to end his or her life.

8. The attending physician again informs the patient that he or she can withdraw the request for medication at any time and in any manner.

9. No sooner that 15 days after the first oral request and 48 hours after the written request, the patient may receive a prescription for medicine to end his or her life. The attending physician again verifies at this time that the patient is making an informed decision.

Study Questions

1. Outline the differences between the four forms of euthanasia. Which types do you think are morally permissible? Which are not?
2. Discuss the case of Janet Adkins (from the Introduction to this book). Was she right in wanting to end her life? Was Dr. Kevorkian morally justified in assisting her? How could the situation have been dealt with differently?
3. Discuss the case of Karen Ann Quinlan. With what decisions, if any, do you disagree? Why?
4. Discuss the AMA position (quoted at the beginning of this chapter) regarding passive and active euthanasia. Does Rachels' counterexample undermine that distinction? Does the trolley car example show that something is wrong with the distinction?
5. Do you think that the right to life entails a right to die under certain circumstances? Explain.
6. Should the laws be changed to grant a universal right to voluntary active euthanasia (assisted suicide)?

Endnotes

1. Gregory Pence, *Classic Cases in Medical Ethics* (New York: McGraw-Hill, 1990), 11.

2. Ibid., 13.

3. See Pence, op. cit. ch 1.

4. "U.S.A.: Right to Live, or Right to Die?" *Lancet,* vol. 337, January 12, 1991, quoted in Gregory Pence, *Classic Cases in Medical Ethics,* 2nd ed.,(McGraw-Hill, 1995), 25.

4. "Confronting Death: Who Chooses, Who Controls?" A Dialogue between Dax Cowart and Robert Burt, *Hastings Center Report,* vol. 28:1 (January-February, 1998): 17–18.

5. Knight-Ridder Newspapers, 19 March 1983.

6. R. M. Hare, *Philosophic Exchange,* vol. II (Summer 1975), 45. Hare continues: "Now will you please all ask yourselves, as I have many times asked myself, what you wish that men should do to you if you were in the situation of the driver. I cannot believe that anybody who considered the matter seriously, as if he himself were going to be in that situation and had now to give instructions as to what rule the bystanders should follow, would say that the rule should be one ruling out euthanasia absolutely."

7. Stewart Alsop, "The Right to Die with Dignity," *Good Housekeeping,* (August 1974): 130.

8. Patrick Buchanan, *Birmingham News,* 16 November 1983, 11a; quoted in James Rachels, *The End of Life* (Oxford: Oxford University Press, 1986), 63.

9. Rachels, op.cit., 112.

10. Paul Ramsey, *The Patient as Person,* quoted in Thomas Sullivan, "Active and Passive Euthanasia: An Impertinent Distinction?" *Human Life Review,* vol. 3, no. 3 (summer 1977), 44.

11. Copies and information are available from The Society for the Right to Die, 250 W. 57th St, New York, NY 10107.

Chapter 9

What Is Death?
The Crisis of Criteria

A woman in New York is beaten by a man until she is unconscious. She is put on a ventilator until physicians decide that she is irreversibly comatose. The ventilator is then detached, and she dies. Later in court the lawyer for the man accused of beating her to death argues that the doctors, not the accused, killed the woman. Had the doctors not removed the respirator, the woman would still be alive.

In Kansas a man on a ventilator was declared brain dead, but when he was transported across the border to be buried in his home state, Oklahoma, he was declared alive again, since the definitions of death in the two states differed.

In a famous case in Kentucky, *Grey v. Swayer* 91952), a court had to decide which of two individuals, a man and a woman, would inherit a large sum of money. The will stated that the person who survived the other would inherit the money. Both parties were killed in an automobile accident, but while the man soon lost his pulse, the woman, who had been decapitated, continued to spurt blood for a short time after the accident. Physicians testified that "a body is not dead so long as there is a heartbeat and that may be evidenced by the gushing of blood in spurts."[1] The court ruled on the basis of this cardiovascular definition of death that the woman survived the man—even though she had been decapitated before he died.

On May 24, 1968, a worker in Virginia named Bruce Tucker fell, sustaining a severe head injury. When the ambulance delivered him to the emergency department of the Medical College of Virginia Hospital, he was found to be bleeding within his brain. He was put on a ventilator and an operation was performed to relieve the pressure on the brain. It was unsuccessful, and Tucker was described by the physician in charge as "mechanically alive . . . [his] prognosis for recovery is nil and death imminent."

At the same time a patient named Joseph Klett was in a ward waiting for a donor heart. When the electroencephalogram attached to Tucker showed a flat line, the doctors concluded that he was "brain dead." They operated and transplanted his heart to Klett. Tucker's kidneys were also removed for transplantation.

Although Tucker's wallet contained his brother's business card, including a phone number and address only fifteen blocks away from the hospital, no attempt was made to contact him. William Tucker, the brother, brought suit against the doctors who performed the operation, but the doctors were exonerated in court, even though Virginia law defined death as total cessation of all bodily functions. William Tucker, disappointed with the verdict, exclaimed, "There's nothing they can say to make me believe they didn't kill [my brother]."[2]

When is someone dead? Until the mid-twentieth century this was seldom a serious question. If someone failed to have a pulse and stopped breathing, this clearly determined that he or she was dead. But in the middle of this century biomedical technology developed ways to keep the body alive almost indefinitely, causing us to reflect anew on the meaning of death. Moreover, this same technology can transplant organs from one patient to another, so we need a definition of death to guide us as to when to remove the organs from the person declared dead.

Several physicians, philosophers, and medical ethicists, including Henry Beecher, Robert M. Veatch, Tristram Engelhardt, Jr., and Roland Puccetti, have called for a redefinition of death in terms of brain functioning, "brain death." Others, like Paul Ramsey and Hans Jonas, have opposed this move.

What Is Death?

Four definitions of death appear in the literature: (1) the departure of the soul from the body; (2) the irreversible loss of the flow of vital fluids or the irreversible cessation of cardiovascular pulmonary function; (3) whole brain death; and (4) neocortical brain death.

THE LOSS OF SOUL

The first major philosopher to hold that death occurred with the departure of the soul was Plato, but this view is found in the Hindu, Orthodox Jewish, and Christian traditions and in the writings of René Descartes (1596–1650), who believed that the soul resided in the pineal gland and left the body at death. The sign of the departure was the cessation of breathing. Orthodox Jews believe that a person is dead only when the last breath is drawn.[3] Note that the Hebrew word for spirit, *Ruach,* is the same word used for breath, and the Greek word *pneuma* has the same double meaning.

There are problems with this view. First, it is difficult to know what the soul is, let alone whether we are endowed with one (or more). Second, neurologic science can explain much of human behavior by an appeal to brain functioning, so the notion of a separate spiritual entity seems irrelevant. Third, if a soul is in us and if it leaves us only after we have breathed our last, we are left with the belief that medical technology can keep the soul in the body for scores of years after the brain has ceased to function and, as far as we can tell, all consciousness has long disappeared. Unless we are really convinced that God has revealed this doctrine to us, we should dismiss it as unsupported by the best evidence available.

THE CARDIOPULMONARY VIEW

When the heart and lungs stop functioning, the person is dead. This has been the traditional medical definition. *Black's Law Dictionary* puts it this way: "The cessation of life: the ceasing to exist; defined by physicians as a total stoppage of the circulation of the blood, and a cessation of the animal and vital functions consequent thereupon, such as respiration, pulsation, etc." In *Thomas v. Anderson,* a California District Court in 1950 quoted *Black's* and added, "Death occurs precisely when life ceases and does not occur until the heart stops beating and respira-

tion ends. Death is not a continuous event and is an event that takes place at a precise time."[4]

This standard definition is problematic in that it goes against the intuitions of many of us that irreversibly comatose patients such as Karen Ann Quinlan or Nancy Cruzan are not alive at all. Bodily functioning alone does not constitute human life. We need to be sentient and self-conscious.

THE WHOLE BRAIN VIEW

As Roland Puccetti puts it, "Where the brain goes, there the person goes."[5] In the same year that Bruce Tucker had his heart and kidneys removed, the Ad Hoc Committee of the Harvard Medical School, under the chairmanship of Dr. Henry K. Beecher, met to decide on criteria for declaring a person dead. The study was a response to the growing confusion over the uses of biomedical technology in being able to keep physical life going for an indefinite period of time after consciousness has been irretrievably lost. It also was a response to the desire to obtain organs from "donors" who were diagnosed with minimal or no brain function, but whose organs were undamaged—because of the ability of technology to keep the vital fluids flowing.

The committee came up with four criteria that together would enable the examiner to pronounce a person dead; (1) unreceptivity and unresponsivity (i.e., no response to externally applied stimuli); (2) no movement or breathing without the use of artificial mechanisms; (3) no reflexes—the pupils are fixed and dilated and will not respond to bright lights; (4) a flat electroencephalogram, which indicates that there is no cerebral activity. The tests must be repeated at least twenty-four hours later to rule out rare false-positives. In addition, these tests must be conducted with the body temperature in a normal range and without the presence of response-altering drugs.

The Harvard committee's criteria have been widely accepted as a safe set, allowing medical practitioners to detach patients from artificial respirators and to transfer organs to needy recipients. Of thousands of patients tested, no one has regained consciousness who has met the criteria.

Critics have objected that the Harvard criteria are too conservative. By its norms, patients who are permanently comatose or in persistent vegetative states, such as Karen Ann Quinlan and Nancy Cruzan, would be considered alive, since their lower brainstems continue to function. Indeed, people have been recorded as living as long as thirty-seven years in such an unconscious state. Since by these criteria they are alive and can be fed intravenously, or via gastric feeding tubes, we have an obligation to continue to maintain them. The worry is that hospitals and nursing homes could turn into mausoleums for the comatose. So a fourth view of death has arisen.

NEOCORTICAL BRAIN DEATH

What is vital to human existence? Henry Beecher, head of the Harvard Ad Hoc Committee, says "consciousness." Robert Veatch, a prominent medical ethicist, says it is our capacity for social interaction, involving the powers of thought, speech, and consciousness. These higher functions are located in the neocortex of the cerebrum or upper brain, so when a sufficient part of this section of our brain is destroyed, the patient is dead. As Tristram Engelhardt, Jr. says, "if the cerebrum is dead, the person is dead"[6] An electroencephalogram can determine when the cerebrum has ceased to function.

Beecher, Veatch, and Engelhardt see human death as the loss of what is significant for human life. Veatch defines death this way: "Death means a complete change in the status of a living entity characterized by the irreversible loss of those characteristics that are essentially significant to it."[7]

Where does the truth lie? To understand what is going on in this debate, we should note the relevant physiologic and neurophysiologic as-

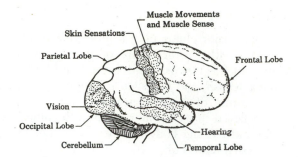

Figure 9–1 *The right cerebral hemisphere, seen from the side, showing the four lobes and the localized areas concerned with special functions. Association areas are unshaded. "Skin sensations" lie in the parietal lobe; "muscle movements," in the frontal lobe.*

pects. The brain has three basic anatomic parts (Fig. 9–1): (1) the cerebrum, with its outer layer, the cortex; (2) the cerebellum; and (3) the brainstem, including the midbrain, pons, and medulla oblongata. Although the cerebrum is the locus of thought, memory, and feelings, consciousness itself remains a mystery. Many believe it to result from complex interrelations between the brainstem and cortex. Circulating blood carries oxygen and glucose keeping the brain alive. If it is deprived of oxygen for more than a few minutes, it sustains permanent damage. After four or five minutes of deprivation, it usually dies.

Respiration, on the other hand, is controlled in the medulla of the brainstem (Fig. 9–2) When the medulla is destroyed, the body is unable to breath and normally dies unless placed on an artificial respirator. When the respiratory system is destroyed, the heart is deprived of vital oxygen and dies. Unlike the respiratory system, the heart can pump blood without instructions from the brain, though the brain may control the heart rate. When the heart's function ceases, it cannot pump oxygen to the brain, so the brain dies.

We see the possible combinations:

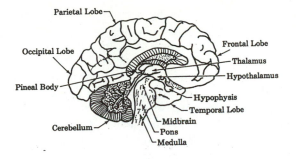

Figure 9–2   *The brain as seen in a vertical midline section.*

1. Normal respiration ceases but artificial respirator keeps heart and brain oxygenated.

2. Heart ceases but artificial heart pumps blood to brain and lungs.

3. Cerebrum destroyed but heart and lungs still function (persistent vegetative state). Neocortical death.

4. Both brainstem and cerebrum destroyed but heart still beats and lungs oxygenate body via artificial respirator. Whole brain death.

5. Brainstem, cerebrum, and heart all destroyed.

Biomedical technology has allowed these possibilities to arise. We are looking at the issue as a problem, but in a sense, the problem is simply the downside of an enormous blessing. We should be grateful for such lifesaving mechanisms. Without the ventilator, many living people would be dead. Because of the ventilator, we can keep organs fresh to transplant them to needy recipients.

Still, the new wonders have brought with them new responsibilities and conceptual confusion about the meaning and nature of death.

The move to alter our definition of death is well motivated. First, we desire to alleviate the agony and financial burdens of relatives waiting for their comatose loved ones to die. How long

must the relatives maintain irreversibly unconscious patients? Karen Ann Quinlan was kept alive in a nursing home for ten years, and others have been maintained even longer. If we can agree to a view of death that includes the cessation of consciousness or neocortical functioning, we can mitigate the emotional suffering and financial hardship of loved ones.

Second, a redefinition of death would enable us to transplant organs from biologically viable human bodies to needy recipients. By temporarily keeping the body alive but pronouncing the person dead, we can justifiably transfer fresh organs to waiting patients.

There is a growing tendency to accept this logic. How absurd to care for bodies without minds! Keeping Karen Ann Quinlan in a nursing home for ten years seems irrational. When the cerebral cortex dies, so does the human being. All that is valuable comes to an end with the end of conscious life. To be permanently comatose is to be dead.

However, this argument has a problem that must be addressed before its conclusion is accepted. The questionable move involves substituting a value for a fact or deriving a factual definition from our moral values. Veatch is guilty of this when he defines life as containing "those characteristics that are essentially significant to it" and death as the irreversible loss of those characteristics. The key phrase is "essentially significant," that is, *valuable.*

This redefinition muddies the waters. A comatose human whose lower brainstem is still functioning, whose heart is beating, and whose respiratory system is intact is still a living organism. Thus, something like the second view of death is correct. Death is an event, not a process, in which the biological organism ceases to function. The vital fluids cease to flow, and the heart and lungs cease forever.

David Mayo and Daniel Wikler make this point with regard to the dying process by distinguishing four possible states of the human organism. Beginning with death proper, the stages are:

Stage 4. All principal life systems of the organism (cardiovascular, central nervous, and pulmonary) irreversibly cease functioning. The organism as a whole permanently ceases to function. This is death proper.

Stage 3. The patient is irreversibly comatose because the entire brain ceases functioning, but cardiovascular and pulmonary functions continue because they are maintained by artificial life support systems.

Stage 2. The patient is irreversibly comatose because the cerebral cortex has ceased functioning but the brainstem is still active, so that the cardiovascular and pulmonary functions continue.

Stage 1. The dying patient is conscious and in pain and desires to be in Stage 4.[8]

Here Mayo and Wikler separate the biological from the valuational or moral dimension. That persons in Stages 1 to 3 are alive is a biological fact. But whether we should keep them alive is a value question. Only Stage 4 constitutes death, properly understood, but our respect for the patient's autonomy should place the burden of proof on those who would paternalistically intervene in preventing the patient from going from Stage 1 to Stage 4. In Stage 2, the case of irreversible coma, we are absolved of any duty to preserve life since it has lost what is valuable about humanity. The same goes for Stage 3. The patient should be detached from the artificial systems and biological death allowed to occur.

So what should we do about the tragic blessing of biomedical technology, with its ability to keep the organism, but not the mind, alive indefinitely? If Mayo and Wikler are right, we should give up our notion of the sanctity of biological life and recognize that some lives are not worth living, including life as an organism in a persistent vegetative state. Although an irreversibly comatose being is biologically alive, it is no longer a life possessing any quality. If we see that personhood involves being self-conscious, we may say in these cases that although the body is alive, the *person* is dead. Not only should the body be detached from expensive life-prolonging machines, but also its organs should be removed for use in the living. Organs are a precious medical resource that can be used to enable people to live longer and better.

Indeed, you might conclude that this reasoning entails a presumption of organ removal in irreversibly comatose patients, to be overridden only by the expressed wishes of the person when he or she was alive. That is, given suitable public education, we should realize that the organs of the irretrievably comatose or dead should be used to help the living.

Just as the United States Supreme Court has ruled that a dying person can give advance notice that should he or she become irreversibly comatose, all life-support systems should be removed, so our living wills should have provisions in them directing that our organs be removed for transplantation while we are in such a state. In this case, the immediate cause of death should be recorded as the donation of vital organs rather than the removal of life support. This should be the next step in the attempt to make moral use of our technological wonders. Eventually, a presumption in favor of transplanting organs from brain dead and neocortically dead patients should be recognized.

The response of the definitional reformers to all of this is that the term *death* already has value connotations with the public, so when we include the permanent loss of consciousness in the definition of death, we are preserving what is practically valuable about the concept.

This response needs careful consideration. It may, in the end, be the right way to go. Nonetheless, clarity of thought inclines us to separate the biological fact of death from the valuation and admit that a body with a dead cerebrum but a living brainstem is still biologically alive. Perhaps we need two locutions, "biological death" and "person death," to preserve the integrity of meaning. So long as we see the issue clearly, the names don't matter.

Finally, let's look back on the problem cases mentioned at the beginning of this chapter. In the case of the New York woman who was beaten until she was irreversibly comatose, the assailant robbed her of all that was valuable to her as a person. This is just as evil as if he had killed her. We need a new concept for rendering a person permanently comatose, but the punishment should be equal to that given to a murderer.

Likewise, in *Grey v. Swayer* the law must recognize irreversible loss of consciousness as tantamount to death. If it had to decide between the two parties, it should have made the opposite award, for a body without a head cannot be conscious.

In Bruce Tucker's case, due process was violated. His family should have been notified, and the electroencephalogram reapplied several hours later. Even though the doctors were correct in wanting to transplant Tucker's heart and kidneys, the laws in place would have given his brother William the right to veto that desire. Doubtless the hospital was unwise in permitting the procedure.

Whether people like William Tucker, who believe that a brain-dead body breathing via a life-support system is still a person, should be allowed to veto what society's experts deem to be rational procedure, is a difficult issue. Given our commitment to democratic processes, it is hard to see how we could justly override these vetoes, at least until a consensus is formed in society for such an override. That is one of the challenges of our time—to educate the public to the importance of quality concerns without destroying a basic commitment to the preservation of life. On one hand, we need to reject the absolutism of the Sanctity of Life principle. On the other hand, we need to respect a basic presumption in favor of life as the basis of all other values. This is not an easy set of distinctions, but that's just why the process of coming to a clearer understanding is a challenge.

Study Questions

1. Discuss the four definitions of death. Which seems nearest to the truth? Why?
2. Discuss Mayo and Wikler's four stages of the human organism and their implications for our view of death. How cogent is their argument?
3. Since body organs are a scarce natural resource, should our policy be changed to allow the automatic removal of the organs from a patient as soon as he or she dies (or while the dying person is unconscious or brain dead)? What are the arguments for and against this policy?
4. Should relatives be allowed to veto a person's advance instructions written in a living will?
5. Do you have a living will with advance instructions? Have you discussed your wishes with your family?

Endnotes

1. Cited in H. Tristram Engelhardt, Jr., *The Foundations of Bioethics* (Oxford: Oxford University Press, 1986), 209f.

2. Cited in Robert M. Veatch, *Death, Dying, and the Biological Revolution* (New Haven: Yale, 1976), 21–24.

3. Immanuel Jakobovitz, *Jewish Medical Ethics* (Philadelphia: Block, 1959), 277.

4. Quoted in Thomas Beauchamp and Seymour Perlin, eds., *Ethical Issues in Death and Dying* (Englewood Cliffs, N.J.: Prentice Hall, 1978), 14.

5. Roland Puccetti, "Brain Transplantation and Personal Identity," *Analysis* 29 (1969): 65. Engelhardt restates Puccetti's motto, "If the cerebrum is dead, the person is dead." (Engelhardt, op. cit., 211).

6. Engelhardt, op. cit., 211.

7. Engelhardt, op. cit., 53.

8. David J. Mayo and Daniel Wikler, "Euthanasia and the Transition from Life to Death," in Thomas Mappes and Jane Zembaty, eds., *Biomedical Ethics* (New York: McGraw Hill, 1986), 400–408.

Interlude:

On the Use and Abuse of Slippery Slope Arguments in Moral Arguments

Legal scholar Yale Kamisar echoes the fears of many people when he argues that we ought not to permit voluntary euthanasia of terminally ill patients since such a practice may bring us closer to involuntary euthanasia.[1] Moral theologian Joseph V. Sullivan puts it this way:[2]

> To permit in a single instance the direct killing of an innocent person would be to admit a most dangerous wedge that might eventually put all life in a precarious condition. Once a man is permitted on his own authority to kill an innocent person directly, there is no way of stopping the advancement of that wedge. There exists no longer any rational grounds for saying that the wedge can advance so far and no further. Once the exception has been made it is too late; hence the grave reason why no exception may be allowed. That is why euthanasia under any circumstances must be condemned.
>
> If voluntary euthanasia were legalized, there is good reason to believe that at a later date another bill for compulsory euthanasia would be legalized. Once respect for human life is so low that an innocent person may be killed directly even at his own request, compulsory euthanasia will necessarily be very near. This could lead easily to killing all incurable charity patients, the aged who are a public care, wounded soldiers, all deformed children, the mentally afflicted, and so on. Before long the danger would be at the door of every citizen.

Others have argued that if we legalize abortion (except possibly to save the mother's life), we will embark on a course leading to infanticide and, eventually, the killing of small children and unwanted elderly.

Robert Wright argues in a similar vein on behalf of animal rights. "Once you buy the premise that animals can experience pain and pleasure, and that their welfare therefore deserves *some* consideration, you're on the road to comparing yourself with a lobster. There may be some exit ramps along the way—plausible places to separate welfare from rights—but I can't find any."[3]

Perhaps nowhere is the Slippery Slope argument used more effectively than in the abortion debate. Opponents of abortion, such as John Noonan, argue that since there is no nonarbitrary cutoff point between conception of the single-cell zygote and the full adult, where we can say, "Here we do not have a human being and here we do," to draw the line anywhere but at conception is to justify infanticide, the killing of small children, and the unwanted elderly.[4]

Where do you draw a nonarbitrary line in these social practices? Slippery Slope arguments, sometimes called "Edge of the Wedge" arguments, have been used as the trump card of traditionalists opposed to social change. Give innovation an inch and it will take a mile. The first step to Auschwitz begins with a seemingly innocent concession to those who would promote social considerations over the sanctity of life.

Let's examine these kinds of arguments. But first I want to prove to you that no poor people exist in the world. You will agree that having a single penny does not make the difference between being wealthy or poor, won't you? Perhaps having a penny will make the difference in purchasing something, but that in itself doesn't constitute the difference between poverty and wealth. Then I hope that you'll agree that possessing a billion dollars constitutes being wealthy (it used to be only a million dollars, but such is inflation and the sliding notion of comparative wealth). Now take a penny away from our billionaire. Does the loss of one cent make him poor? Of course not. We've already agreed that the gain or loss of one penny doesn't make a difference with regard to whether someone is poor or wealthy. Now take another penny from him and another and another until he is worth only $1.25, the price of the Sunday *New York Times*. He's homeless and can't afford even a half-gallon of milk, but by our argument, he's not poor, for all we did was subtract pennies from him one by one, and such small increments can't make a difference.

Of course, we could work the argument the other way around and prove that no one is rich—that everyone is poor. We'll agree to the same crucial premise that a penny doesn't make a difference between wealth and poverty. Then we'll agree that possessing only a penny makes no one rich. Then we'll add pennies to our poor man, one by one, until he possesses a hundred billion pennies or a billion dollars.

Or consider this argument: no one is really bald, for taking a single hair from anyone with a complete head of hair cannot produce baldness, so we begin to take hairs from your head, one by one, until you have no hair at all on your head. At what point were you really bald? Surely having one piece of hair is being bald, and adding a second makes no difference to the designation of being bald. So we can go from baldness to a full head of hair without ever finding a cutoff point where baldness ends and hairiness begins. Yet we are sure that there is a difference between baldness and a full scalp.

When does an accumulation of sand, soil, and rock become a mountain? A piece of sand, a speck of soil, and a tiny stone do not constitute a mountain, but if we keep adding sand, soil, and rocks long enough we'll eventually end up with a structure larger than Mt. Everest!

You get the point. Concepts are clear. Their application in reality is unclear. Slippery Slope arguments trade on this vagueness. The fallacy of the Slippery Slope argument is to suppose that because there is no distinct cutoff point in reality where concepts change (rich to poor etc.), there is no real difference between state A and state B. But there is. We know the difference between wealth and poverty even though we cannot define it in absolute monetary terms. We know the difference between a full head of hair and baldness even though we cannot say exactly where baldness begins. We know the difference between a hill and a mountain even though there is a grey area in between where we're not sure what to call it.

The lesson of vagueness is to remind us, transposing Hegel's dictum, that "while concepts are green life is grey." We ought to be careful in making social policy, and we ought to

guard against abuse. Where there is doubt, we ought to err on the side of protecting life.

Now apply this point to the moral dilemmas discussed in this book. There may be grounds for permitting abortion at early stages of development, whereas we want to protect self-conscious human life. Even though we do not know where the line is drawn (no line may exist), it doesn't mean that no difference exists. The lesson of the Slippery Slope kind of reasoning is to play it safe, to err on the side of life. Since there is no definite cutoff point where mere biological life ends and self-conscious life begins, we'll pick a safe place within the grey area.

Likewise with euthanasia. We should set safeguards for the innocent so that ruthless relatives hoping to gain an early inheritance can't exploit Aunt Ann by granting her a blessed exit into the beyond.

And likewise with our animal rights argument. Just because we recognize an animal's ability to experience pleasure and pain as morally significant doesn't mean that we are forbidden to call the exterminator when termites are devouring our houses, or that we can't eat animals or experiment on animals for human good. We must be able to justify our practices in impartial ways. As far as we know chickens, termites, and experimental mice do not have a notion of self and do not reason in self-conscious ways, so killing them is not violating their right to carry out personal projects in the same way as if we killed our fellow humans or self-conscious chimpanzees.

Where and how to draw the line is a difficult problem, and we may err, but part of the human condition is to be called upon to make difficult decisions and take responsibility for the consequences. This is the essence of moral reasoning—to reason impartially, to change your mind as the evidence refutes you, and to take responsibility for your actions. This is dangerous, but it's also challenging, and it calls on the best that is in us.

One more point must be made. The Reverse Slippery Slope argument can be maintained to justify social change: If we don't act justly in this small issue, we may be hardened so that we won't act justly in a large issue. Unless we grant women the right to abortion and terminally ill people the right to die, all of our rights may be in jeopardy.

The Reverse Slippery Slope argument, while an exaggeration, is as good as the basic version of the argument.

Endnotes

1. Yale Kamisar, "Euthanasia Legislation: Some Nonreligious Objections," *Minnesota Law Review* 42, no. 6 (1958).

2. Joseph V. Sullivan, "The Immortality of Euthanasia," in *Beneficent Euthanasia* ed. Marvin Kohl, (Buffalo: Prometheus, 1965), 24.

3. Robert Wright, "Are Animals People Too?" *New Republic* (March 12, 1990).

4. John T. Noonan, "An Almost Absolute Value in History," reprinted in *The Problem of Abortion,* ed. Joel Feinberg, (Belmont, CA: Wadsworth, 1984).

CHAPTER 10

Abortion

The Greatest Moral Problem of Our Generation

Every unborn child must be regarded as a human person with all the rights of a human person, from the moment of conception.

ETHICAL AND RELIGIOUS DIRECTIVES FOR CATHOLIC HOSPITALS

[Abortion] during the first two or three months of gestation [is morally equivalent] to removal of a piece of tissue from the woman's body.

THOMAS SZASZ, "The Ethics of Abortion," *Humanist*, 1966

With reference to [abortion] the world is upside down. When a criminal is sentenced to death, the whole world is dismayed because it goes against human rights. But when an unborn baby is sentenced to death, the world approves of it because the "rights" of the mother take precedence over the rights of an innocent human life. But how is this different from the Nazi holocaust where Mother Germany sent twelve million innocent lives to the gas chamber. Haven't we sent over 30 million innocent lives to their death?

LOIS HOPE WALKER

Introduction: Genocide or
Expression of Autonomy?

The major social issue that divides our society as no other issue does is the moral and legal status of the human fetus and the corresponding question of the moral permissibility of abortion. On the one hand, such organizations as the Roman Catholic Church and the Right-to-Life movement, appalled by the more than 1.5 million abortions that take place in the United States each year, have exerted significant political pressure toward introducing a constitutional amendment that would grant full legal rights to fetuses. These movements have made abortion the single issue in recent political campaigns. On the other hand, pro-choice groups, such as the National Organization of Women (NOW), the National Abortion Rights Action League (NARAL), and other feminist organizations have exerted enormous pressure on politicians to support the proabortion legislation. The Republican and Democratic political platforms of the last four presidential elections (1984 through 1996) took diametrically opposite sides on this issue.

Let's look at the argument of Lois Hope Walker. Imagine we're in Nazi Germany in 1943. Millions of Jews, Romanies (gypsies), people with mental disabilities, and protestors are being sent to the gas chambers. Are we doing the same today to millions of innocent fetuses? And are those who countenance today's abortions similar to those who looked the other way as the Jews were led to Auschwitz, Dachau, Bergen-Belsen, Birchenau, and Treblinka? This is how antiabortionists regard our present practice of abortion.

Note that the same arguments used to justify abortion could be used to justify the holocaust: (1) A woman has an absolute right to do what she wants with her own body = Mother Germany has an absolute right to do what she likes with her body, the German people. (2) Fetuses are not fully human = Jews and people with mental disabilities are not fully human. (3) If we don't make abortion legal, women will seek abortions anyway and risk their lives = If we don't make destroying the Jews legal, people will take the law into their own hands and risk their lives in eliminating the Jews.

In the 1992 Presidential Debate Bill Clinton argued that a woman has an absolute right to have an abortion because she has an absolute right to her own body. President Bush responded that because a fetus is a human being, abortion is an act of murder. This also makes the doctor who performs an abortion a murderer. I will examine each of these arguments in a moment. Your decision on the abortion issue has wide-ranging effects, including a whole host of other political, legal, and moral questions.

Why is abortion a moral issue? Take a fertilized egg, a zygote, a tiny sphere of cells. It is hard to see what is so important about such an inconspicuous piece of matter. It is virtually indistinguishable from other clusters of cells or zygotes of other animals. On the other hand, take an adult human being, a class of beings that we all intuitively feel to be worthy of high respect, having rights, including the right to life. To kill an innocent human being is an act of murder and universally condemned. However, no obvious line of division separates that single-cell zygote from the adult it will become. Whence, the problem of abortion.

I shall begin my examination by sketching the three main positions on abortion. I shall draw the implications from the major arguments on the two ends of the spectrum and then turn to the middle position, which seeks to make a compromise between the concerns of the other positions. The *conservative* position states that because fetuses are full human beings, abortion is never justified, except perhaps to save the mother's life. Perhaps the most well-known version of the conservative position is that of the Roman Catholic Church, which allows abortion only in cases of ectopic pregnancy—when the embryo is lodged in the fallopian tube—and a cancerous uterus, when the death of the fetus is *foreseen* but not *intended*.

John Noonan formulates the conservative argument this way:[1]

1. We ought never to kill innocent human beings (except in self-defense, when our lives are threatened).
2. Fetuses are innocent human beings.
3. Therefore we ought never to kill fetuses, that is, have abortions (except when the mother's life is threatened because of the pregnancy).

The *liberal* position is that, since the fetus is not a human being but has the same status as a vestigial organ, abortion is justified any time a woman desires to have one.

Thomas Szasz's view that abortion during "the first two or three months of gestation [is morally equivalent] to removal of a piece of tissue from the woman's body," seems extreme, but it is frank and accurate. For the liberal, a fetus has no more moral status than an appendix.

Moderates argue that a fetus does not have a full right to life, but as a potential person it has some rights, and abortion may be justified only in the earliest stages of pregnancy, when the fetus promises to be seriously defective, or when the pregnancy constitutes a danger to the mother's health or life.

The debate usually starts with the question, when does the fetus become a full human being, a person with a right to life? Liberals traditionally say that a cutoff point occurs somewhere. Let us look at the proposed candidates for such a cutoff point.

1. QUICKENING

People used to maintain that the soul entered the body at quickening, and some theologians countenanced abortion during the first weeks of pregnancy on the basis that the fetus had not yet been ensouled. Few still hold this view, since quickening is merely the first time the mother feels the fetus move.

2. VIABILITY

The United States Supreme Court in the *Roe v. Wade* (1973) decision came close to espousing viability as the cutoff point between not having a right to life and having one. The court held that the state has a legitimate interest in protecting potential life and that this interest becomes compelling at viability "because the fetus then presumably has the capability of meaningful life, outside the mother's womb." But the judgment lacks clear argument. It doesn't tell us why the life of a six-month-old fetus is more meaningful outside the womb than inside, nor why the viable fetus has more potential human life than the not-yet-viable fetus. One would think that the potentiality was relatively similar.

Another criticism is that the viability criterion makes humanness dependent on the state of technology. Thirty years ago, little Johnny, who is a six-month-old fetus, would have been a nonperson, but today, thanks to technology, he is judged a full person. It seems odd to base the metaphysical issue of personhood on the whims and caprice of technology. A fetus either has intrinsic value or it doesn't. Something external, such as medical technology, doesn't affect that value. Personhood is more than a matter of luck.

3. EXPERIENCE

A being with a right to life must be able to perceive, suffer, and remember. A fetus cannot do any of these things, so it is not a full human being. This argument seems dubious for three reasons. First, the criterion, strictly interpreted, would exclude infants from being persons since they do not perceive in the strong sense of that term, nor do they remember. Second, in the weak sense of experience, there is some evidence that fetuses can suffer pain and pleasure, "experience" sensations, and so forth. Furthermore, the criterion could be used to give animals (including insects) equal rights to life, for they also experience.

4. BIRTH

Many people hold that birth is the decisive cutoff point between nonpersonhood and personhood. But this seems an arbitrary distinction. There is no reason to suppose that a fetus's status one second before birth is miraculously transformed one second after birth. A prematurely born infant may actually be less developed than a fetus near the end of a normal pregnancy. Birth is simply the time when a baby is detached from its mother's body and becomes a visible social being. It has no intrinsic significance. If children stayed attached to the mother's placenta or large mechanical incubators (perish the thought) until they were ten years old, they wouldn't suddenly become human beings upon being detached.

The conclusion is that quickening, viability, experience, and birth are arbitrary cutoff points between nonhumanness and humanness. There doesn't seem to be a cutoff point between conception and infancy. If there is not, either single-cell zygotes are full human beings with a right to life or infants are not full human beings with a right to life. Since most liberals and moderates are horrified by the thought of viewing infanticide as morally acceptable, they are defeated. Conservatives win the debate.

However, conservatives must pay a high price for victory. If all forms of human life are equally valuable and grant the being, whether a fetus or an adult, an equal right to life, radical consequences follow. In particular, there is no reason to prefer the mother's life to the fetus's when the two are in conflict. In fact, there is reason to save the fetus instead of the mother. Three arguments support this thesis.

1. THE FAIRNESS ARGUMENT

If biological life is the highest value, we ought to sacrifice the mother for the fetus because the mother has already enjoyed a number of years but the fetus hasn't. It should be given its turn.

2. THE SELF-DEFENSE ARGUMENT

You may counter that the mother has a right to defend herself against the fetus, for we have a right to defend our lives against those who threaten us even if those who threaten us are innocent. That may be, but then isn't the doctor, who performs the abortion, acting as an accomplice in a killing? By what right does he take sides? Wouldn't the doctor be at least as justified in preferring the life of the fetus? If the fetus is a full human, doesn't it deserve legal representation?

3. THE INVITED GUEST ARGUMENT

Assuming that the fetus was conceived in a voluntary act of sexual intercourse, isn't its presence similar to that of an invited guest in your home? When your roof begins to cave in, aren't you obligated to do everything in your power to save the guest even if it means risking your own life?

So if the conservative is correct in asserting that the fetus is a full human being, he cannot prefer the mother's life to the fetus's life when the two are in conflict.

Another implication of the conservative thesis is that rape is not a grounds for abortion. If all human life is of equal value, then no amount of mental suffering on the part of a teenager who has been brutally raped can justify the killing of her fetus. How grimly ironic and grossly illogical that people who are against capital punishment for the criminal, the rapist, would advocate it for one of the innocent victims, the fetus.

The conservative position leaves many of us in a dilemma, for it tells us that our intuitions about preferring the mother's life to the fetus's and about permitting abortion in the case of rape are mistaken. Sometimes we must give up our intuitions for our principles, but sometimes our intuitions are signals that our principles are too rigid or unqualified. In any case, before we jettison those intuitions, we should take a look at the liberal and moderate positions on abortion.

The Liberal Position

The liberal position asserts that it is always or almost always morally permissible for a woman to have an abortion. It allows abortion on demand. Four arguments for this position have been offered:

1. Subjectivism: radical relativism
2. The Absolute Right to Privacy Argument (reproductive freedom)
3. The Quality of Life Argument (in cases of the probability of defective neonates)
4. The Personhood Argument

1. SUBJECTIVISM: RADICAL RELATIVISM

Abortion is a private matter into which the law should not enter. No one should be forced to have children. H. Schur in his book *Crimes without Victims* calls abortion a victimless crime. Unfortunately, he supplies no argument for his view that fetuses are nonpersons. Schur assumes that morality is merely a matter of individual choice. Who are we to judge?

Subjectivism is a dubious doctrine. If fetuses are persons, then isn't what we're doing tantamount to killing innocent people? Aren't we all engaged in mass killings? And isn't the killing of innocents to be condemned?

2. THE ABSOLUTE RIGHT TO PRIVACY ARGUMENT

The National Organization of Women and many radical feminists hold that since a woman has an absolute right to her own body, on which a fetus is dependent, she may do whatever is necessary to detach the fetus from her, including putting it to death.

The first problem with this argument is that it is unclear whether we have any *absolute* rights at all. An absolute right is one that always overrides all other considerations. It is doubtful that we have many of these. The only ones I can think of are rights such as the right not to be harmed or tortured unnecessarily. We have no reason to believe that our right to use our own bodies as we wish is an absolute right. Consider 500-lb. Fat Fred, who decides to sit down. Your money-packed wallet happens to be directly on the spot where he sits. You ask him to move so that you can get your wallet, but he refuses, claiming that he has an absolute right to do with his body what he will.

The doctrine of absolute rights to privacy or body use suffers from lack of intelligent support. Since our bodies are public and interact with other people's bodies and property, we need ways of adjudicating possible conflicts, but there is no such thing as an absolute right to do whatever we want with our bodies. A parent of dependent children doesn't have a right to remove his or her body to a different locale, abandoning the children. A man may be morally obligated to take his body to the army recruitment center when his nation is in danger and the draft board picks his number.

Suppose that President Clinton suddenly develops a rare form of liver and bilateral kidney failure, such that he needs to be plugged into a human being's kidneys and liver. That person will have to walk around with the president, sleep in his bed, and eat at his table for nine months. One hundred people with the right kinds of kidneys and livers are rounded up and invited to participate in a lottery. One person, the loser, will be plugged in to the president. Each of the 100 people will win $1,000 for playing the game. You are one of the people invited to play. Would you play?

Most people asked, including myself, say that they would take the risk of playing the lottery. Once we agree to play, we are obligated to accept the inconvenience if we lose. It would be absurd to back out, claiming an absolute right to privacy or bodily use.

The implications of the lottery game for abortion are obvious. When people voluntarily engage in sex, they are engaged in the lottery game. Even if they use birth control devices, pregnancy might result. If a fetus is a person with a right to life, the woman cannot simply dismiss that right by invoking a superior right to privacy. She has suspended that right by engaging in an act that brought the new being into existence.

3. THE QUALITY OF LIFE ARGUMENT

One strategy available to liberals is to deny that life is of absolute value. We have set forth this argument in Chapter 2, arguing against the doctrine of the sanctity of life. The quality of life, not its quantity, is the crucial factor. Some lives are not worth living; they do not have positive value. The severely deformed, retarded, or hydrocephalic child may live a negative existence, in which case abortion may be warranted. Suppose that a pregnant woman is informed that the fetus she is carrying has Tay-Sachs disease or spina bifida and is told that if she aborts, in five months she will be able to conceive a normal child. If it is quality that counts, not only may the woman abort, she has a positive duty to do so.

This argument can be extended to cover cases in which a woman is incapable of providing an adequate upbringing for the child to be born—cases such as pregnant teenagers and families that cannot afford another child. Overpopulation is another consideration arguing for the abortion of unwanted children. No unwanted child should enter the world.

There is merit in the Quality of Life argument—quality does count—but it has weaknesses that must be met. First, the argument against bringing unwanted children into the world may be offset by the availability of adoption. Many childless couples want these children. Nevertheless, not all children are likely to be adopted into loving homes, so abortions would still be permitted in some cases.

A more significant objection is that the Quality of Life argument leaves the status of the fetus untouched. If the fetus is a person, then it makes no more sense to speak of aborting it because you don't think it will have a good quality of life than it does to kill a baby or a ten-year-old or a ninety-year-old because you don't think he or she will have a good quality of life. Quality counts, but we don't have the right to play God in this way with people's lives. It's too dangerous.

So the status of the fetus has to be addressed.

4. THE PERSONHOOD ARGUMENT

Our intuitions generally tell us that a fetus does not have the same moral status as a mother. Antiabortionists often base their conclusions on their religious heritage, but even there the case is ambiguous. The notion of ensoulment argues for the personhood of the fetus, but earlier Biblical ideas lend support for a distinction of status. For example, Exodus (21:22) says that if a man causes a woman to abort, he shall be punished, but if the woman's death follows, those responsible shall give "life for life, eye for eye, tooth for tooth." Furthermore, serious difficulties arise with viewing the single-cell zygote or the conceptus as a person, given the phenomenon of twinning, which can take place up to the third week of pregnancy. If the embryo splits into two (or three, four or more) embryos, does one person (soul) become two (or more)? How can personhood, with its characteristic of complete unity, be divided?

It is not enough for liberals to point out problems in the conservative position. They must go to the heart of the matter and attempt to dismantle the conservative arguments for the fetus's right to life. The central one is that offered by Noonan (above).

1. We ought never to kill innocent human beings.

2. Fetuses are innocent human beings.

3. Therefore we ought never to kill fetuses (that is, have abortions).

Liberals point out that the term *human being* is used ambiguously in the argument. Note that sometimes when we use *human being* we have a biological concept in mind, the species *Homo sapiens,* but at other times we have a psychological–moral concept in mind, someone with the characteristics of humans as we typically find them—characteristics such as rationality, freedom, and self-consciousness, which separate them from other animals. In philosophy we sometimes use the word *person* for this type of being. A *person* is someone who has an intrinsic right to life. If we apply this distinction to Noonan's argument, we see that it trades on this ambiguity.

In the first premise, "human beings" refers to persons, while in the second, it refers to *Homo sapiens.* The argument should read:

1. We ought never to kill innocent persons.

2. Fetuses are innocent *Homo sapiens.*

3. Therefore we ought never to kill fetuses.

This is an invalid argument, since it is not obvious that all *Homo sapiens* are persons.

The question is, by virtue of what characteristics does someone have a right to life? Liberals point out that it is a form of prejudice, similar to racism, sexism, nationalism, religionism, and ethnocentricism, to prefer one species to another simply because it is your species or to grant someone a right simply because he or she is a member of a biological group. Peter Singer, in his work on animal rights, calls this prejudice *speciesism.*

Speciesism, like racism, sexism, and other "isms," violates the first principle of justice: treat equals equally and unequals unequally. Suppose it turned out that one ethnic group or gender usually made better musicians than other groups. It would still be unjust to automatically allow all and only members of that group to enter music school. Individuals have a right to be judged according to their abilities, so we would want to test individuals independently of ethnic group or gender to ascertain their potential for musical performance.

Which characteristics that give beings a right to life are analogous to those that give candidates a right to enter music school? Liberals argue that certain properties that most adult humans have are the proper criteria for this distinction. These properties are intrinsically valuable traits that allow us to view ourselves as selves with plans and projects over time, properties such as self-consciousness and rationality. Both conservatives and liberals agree that these qualities are intrinsically good. Liberals, however, try to draw out their implications: that our ability to make plans, to think rationally, and to have a self over time give us a special right to life.

Although it is difficult to exactly specify the necessary and sufficient conditions for personhood, and liberals have described these conditions differently—some emphasizing desires and interests, others emphasizing agency or the ability to project into the future, others emphasizing the capacity for a notion of the self—they all point to a cluster of characteristics that distinguish children and adults from fetuses, infants, and most animals. Those characteristics enable us to interact and reciprocate on the social playing field of civilized existence. Joel Feinberg describes personhood this way:

> What makes me certain that my parents, siblings and friends are people is that they give evidence of being conscious of the world and of themselves; they have inner emotional lives, just like me; they can understand things and reason about them, make plans, and act; they can communicate with me, argue, negotiate, express themselves, make agreements, honor commitments, and stand in relationships of mutual trust; they have tastes and values of their own; they can be frustrated or fulfilled, pleased or hurt. . . . In the commonsense way

of thinking, persons are those beings who are conscious, have a concept and awareness of themselves, are capable of experiencing emotions, can reason and acquire understanding, can plan ahead, can act on their plans, and can feel pleasure and pain.[2]

A certain vagueness inheres in the specification of these qualities, and individuals possess them to different degrees—life is not neat and tidy—but we have an adequate idea of what they are. Practically, a typical test of whether someone is a person is the ability to reason about or emphatically communicate about interpersonal relations. Studies show that not only humans, but also gorillas, chimpanzees, and dogs have this ability.

I think the phrase *rational self-consciousness* captures what we typically mean by this property. It distinguishes the average adult human from most of the animal kingdom. But not all humans have these qualities. Severely retarded children, anencephalic babies, severely senile adults, and people in persistent vegetative states do not possess them, but dolphins, whales, chimpanzees, apes, and even some dogs and pigs may possess them. The following diagram represents the relationship between humans and animals with regard to personhood.

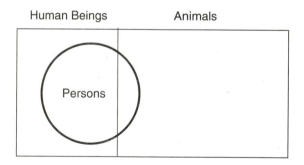

If rational self-consciousness marks the criterion for having a right to life, then fetuses do not have a right to life, since they are neither rational nor self-conscious.

The Conservative Response and the Liberal Counterresponse

How do conservatives respond to this argument? First they point out two counterintuitive implications of the liberal position, and then they point out something missing that changes the liberal's logic.

If the personhood argument were followed, we would be permitted to kill unconscious and severely retarded and senile humans—even normal people when they sleep, for none of these have the required characteristics for personhood. The argument would also sanction infanticide, something that most liberals are loathe to allow. Finally, the argument ignores the fact that a fetus is a potential person, and potentiality for self-consciousness should be seen as granting a being similar rights as an actual person.

Poignant as these objections are, liberals have a response to each of them. Regarding the killing of the retarded and senile, a liberal would point out that most of these people still have an adequate amount of rationality and that it would be dangerous to put into practice a policy of doing away with all but the most obvious cases of loss of selfhood. With regard to those who sleep or are unconscious, they still have the capacity for rational self-consciousness, so we may not kill them.

Here liberals distinguish between a *capacity* and a *potentiality*. Consider a lump of clay. It doesn't have the capacity to hold water, but it has the potentiality for that capacity. Suppose that I mold it into a cup. Now it has the capacity for holding water, even though at present it is not holding any. A fetus only has the potentiality for self-consciousness, whereas the unconscious person has the capacity for it.

Potentiality is not enough, only actuality or capacity for self-consciousness is sufficient for granting someone a right to life. Let me illustrate this with an example from the 1996 presidential campaign. Suppose that during the campaign, Republican Party presidential candidate Bob

Dole had suddenly appeared at the White House with his family and furniture. "I'm moving in here," he announces to an incredulous White House staff.

"You can't. It's unlawful!" objects the staff member.

"You don't know what you're talking about. Don't you Democrats believe that a potential person has all the rights of an actual person? Well, on that same logic, a potential president has the same rights as an actual president. Since I am potentially the president, I'm taking advantage of my rights, so let me in."

Although the fetus may be a potential person, it is not yet one; hence, it does not have the same rights as an actual person. In this regard, Mary Anne Warren offers the following thought experiment:

> Suppose that our space explorer falls into the hands of an alien culture, whose scientists decide to create a few hundred thousand or more human beings, by breaking his body into its component cells, and using these to create fully developed human beings, with, of course, his genetic code. We may imagine that each of these newly created men will have all of the original man's abilities, skills, knowledge, and so on, and also have an individual self-concept, in short that each of them will be a bona fide (though hardly unique) person. Imagine that the whole project will take only seconds, and that its chances of success are extremely high, and that our explorer knows all of this, and also knows that these people will be treated fairly. I maintain that in such a situation he would have every right to escape if he could, and thus to deprive all of these potential people of their potential lives; for his right to life outweighs all of theirs together, in spite of the fact that they are all genetically human, all innocent, and all have a very high probability of becoming people very soon, if only he refrains from acting.[3]

Warren, in a later article, seems to have lost confidence in this argument, conceding that such bizarre situations are inadequate grounds for the refutation of the potentiality principle. But the situation is not as bizarre as we might suppose. We can cast greater doubt on this doctrine, for if someone believes that a single-cell zygote has a right to life, then he or she should refrain from washing and from brushing his or her teeth. Why? Because in doing so, that person is killing thousands of single cells of *exactly the same nature* as the zygote. The only difference between other diploid cells in our body and the zygote is the location. The zygote fortuitously has gotten into the incubator, whereas the others haven't. But that is an irrelevant distinction, having nothing to do with inherent rights or the quality of the cell itself. Given the prospects of cloning, any cell of your body could be developed into a fetus, a baby, and, finally, into an adult. If the zygote is sacred and not to be destroyed, the same goes for every other human cell in the world.

Finally, liberals must respond to the objection that their view permits infanticide. In a sense it does, but it need not. Let me explain.

Liberals can distinguish between a natural right and a social right. A natural right is one that a person has simply by virtue of intrinsic qualities. A social right, on the other hand, is not intrinsic to the being, but something bestowed by society. Society has the privilege and responsibility of protecting things that it deems valuable or useful to its purposes. Just as it can grant a forest or an endangered animal species a protective right, so it can give fetuses or infants such rights if it so desires. The only condition for granting something a social right is that we give a utilitarian reason for doing so. Since the entity at issue doesn't have sufficient intrinsic merit to demand the right, there must be an instrumental reason for doing so.

We are more willing to extend a social right to infants than to fetuses because they are closer to personhood and because they are independent of the mother's body and can be adopted.

If a state decided that there were good reasons to extend the social right to life to fetuses, it would be justified in doing so. But it doesn't have to, and if there were good utilitarian reasons for doing so, the state could remove the social right to life from infants. Because the latter move would cause a revolt, this is unlikely to happen. Nonetheless, on the liberal argument, such a move could not be ruled out as morally unacceptable.

Let me set forth this argument succinctly in seven steps so that you will be able to examine it carefully.

1. All and only actual persons have a moral right to life (that is, potentiality doesn't count).

2. *Persons* may be defined as beings who have the capacity for reason and self-conscious desire ("Reason Capacity")

3. Fetuses and infants do not have Reason Capacities, so they do not have a moral right to life.

4. However, there are social rights (utilitarian rights—including the social right to life) that society may bestow on classes of beings for utilitarian reasons. This includes treating some potential persons as though they had the rights of persons.

5. There are good utilitarian reasons for treating viable fetuses (toward the end of the second trimester) and infants as persons, giving them social rights.

6. Therefore, we ought to bestow social rights on viable fetuses and infants (that is, past a fixed time at which a woman loses her right to abort potential persons, except when they will be seriously defective or when the mother's life or health is endangered).

7. Therefore, we ought to allow abortion only in the earliest stages of pregnancy or when the fetus is known to be seriously defective, or when the mother's life or health is endangered.

The distinction between a deontological right and a social or utilitarian right means that certain rights are largely beyond the authority of society to alter. The basic rights of persons are within this domain. However, optional social rights may be extended or withheld from beings not yet fully human but on the way to becoming so.

Good utilitarian reasons exist for forbidding infanticide, except perhaps when the handicap is so severe as to impede the prospects for a worthwhile life. Anencephalic, severely deformed, and incurably diseased neonates might well be killed at birth to prevent needless suffering. Infants, unlike fetuses, can be taken from their mothers and adopted by others. They also have begun to play a role in society.

The core of the liberal position is the notion that we are not born persons but become such through adequate socialization. Becoming a person is not a biological given, but an interactive process. Studies by Bruno Bettelheim and others of children suffering severe forms of infantile autism (a form of childhood schizophrenia) show that infants abandoned or severely neglected by parents—even intelligent, educated, middle-class parents—fail to learn to speak, and can take on animal characteristics. They eat raw meat, drink by lapping, tear their clothes off and prefer to run around naked, howl, growl at humans, and often bite those who attend them. Reports of feral children, such as Ramalah and Kamalah, two Indian children brought up by wolves, describe children who take on wolflike traits and never attain full human characteristics. They lack language ability, lack a sense of self, and are unable to think abstractly.[4]

If *Homo sapiens* are not born persons but become such through a complex process of socialization, liberals have grounds to permit abortion.

The Moderate Position

Moderates are caught in the middle of this controversy. They are dissatisfied with the arguments on both sides of the fence. Moderates object to the conservative prohibition of abortion because it is one-dimensional, seeing only the abstract right of the fetus, not the complications of life. Moderates contend against the conservative that a mother's psychological and/or physical condition and the quality of life of the fetus must be taken into consideration in decisions about abortion. A victim of rape, a pregnant thirteen-year-old, or a woman with more children than she can care for is probably justified in getting an abortion.

Moderates disagree with the liberal on the issue of abortion on demand. Fetuses are potential persons in a way that other single cells in the body are not. They are already in the process of developing into the kind of beings who will be socialized as self-conscious persons. The closer they come to birth, the more the presumption of life is in their favor.

Even though the following argument is put forward by a conservative, John Noonan, moderates are likely to accept it.

> Consider, for example, the spermatozoa in any normal ejaculate: There are about 200,000,000 in any single ejaculate, of which one has a chance of developing into a zygote. Consider the oocytes which may become ova: there are 100,000 to 1,000,000 oocytes in a female infant, of which a maximum of 390 are ovulated. But once spermatozoa and ovum meet and the conceptus is formed, such studies as have been made show that roughly in only 20 percent of the cases will spontaneous abortion occur. In other words, the chances are about 4 out of 5 that this new being will develop. At this stage in the life of the being there is a sharp shift in probabilities, an immense jump in potentialities. To make a distinction between the rights of spermatozoa and the rights of the fertilized ovum is to respond to an enormous shift in possibilities. For about twenty days after conception the egg may split to form twins or combine with another egg to form a chimera, but the probability of either event happening is very small.[5]

Noonan's argument is one for moderation because he is not arguing that biological probabilities establish essential humanity, but simply that it is commonsensical to suppose that the fetus will develop into a person. Noonan continues, "If the chance is 200,000,000 to 1 that the movement in the bushes into which you shoot is a man's, I doubt if many persons would hold you careless in shooting; but if the chances are 4 out of 5 that the movement is a human being's, few would acquit you of blame."

The argument from probability doesn't give a fetus a clear right to life, but it shows a presumption against aborting. That is, a difference still stands between a potential person and an actual person, but since there is a high probability that the fetus will become a person, we should permit abortion only for compelling reasons: when the mother's health or life is endangered or when the quality of life of the fetus will be seriously compromised.

There you have the three positions and the significant arguments that attach to each one. You have a lot to sort out. If you are to work out a solution from a philosophical perspective, you must provide your reasons for preferring one position over the others. If you believe that an immortal soul inhabits a fetus from conception onward, you will be inclined toward some version of the conservative argument. If you believe that rational self-consciousness makes persons morally significant, you will be inclined toward a version of the liberal position. If you believe that each side has important considerations, you will be inclined toward the moderate perspective. Perhaps at this point you should read over the reasons given in support of each position and weigh the comparative strengths of each major view. The crucial point is that you recognize the difficulty of the issue and use reason, rather than simply emotion, to work out your position.

Study Questions

1. Many people say, "I believe abortion is morally wrong, but I don't believe that there should be a law against it." Is this a coherent position? Is Lois Hope Walker right in comparing the killing of millions of fetuses to the killing of millions of people in Nazi concentration camps?

2. Evaluate the three basic positions: conservative, liberal, and moderate. What are the strengths and weaknesses of each? Which is the most cogent position? Why?

3. John Noonan draws the line between being nonhuman and being human at conception. Do you agree with his argument? Is conception an objectively based, nonarbitrary cutoff point between the two fundamental states?

4. Does the personhood argument that permits abortion also permit infanticide? Why aren't those who are pro-choice on abortion also pro-choice regarding infanticide?

5. Examine the moderate position based on the probability argument that a fetus very likely will develop into a full person. If it were adopted, would it cause us to change our social policy on abortion?

6. What is the relationship between a woman's autonomy and privacy and the responsibility to protect life?

Endnotes

1. John Noonan, "An Almost Absolute Value in History" in *The Morality of Abortion: Legal and Historical Perspectives,* ed. Noonan (Cambridge: Harvard University Press, 1970), reprinted in *The Abortion Controversy* ed. L. Pojman and F. Beckwith (Belmont: Wadsworth, 1998).

2. Joel Feinberg, "Abortion," *Matters of Life and Death: New Introductory Essays in Moral Philosophy,* ed. Tom Regan (New York: Random House, 1980) 189f.

3. Mary Anne Warren, "On the Moral and Legal Status of Abortion," *Monist* 57 (1973), 59–60.

4. See Bruno Bettelheim, "Feral Children and Autistic Children," *The American Journal of Sociology* 64 (March, 1959): 455–67; and *The Empty Fortress: Infantile Autism and the Birth of the Self* (Chicago: University of Chicago Press, 1934). The actual case of Ramalah and Kamalah is controversial, but the phenomenon of feral children has been established.

5. Noonan, op. cit.

Chapter 11

Cloning

My own view is that human cloning would have to raise deep concerns given our most cherished concepts of faith and humanity. Each human life is unique, born of a miracle that reaches beyond laboratory science. I believe we must respect this profound gift and resist the temptation to replicate ourselves. . . .

What this legislation will do is to reaffirm our most cherished belief about the miracle of human life and the God-given individuality each person possesses. It will ensure that we do not fall prey to the temptation to replicate ourselves at the expense of those beliefs. . . . Banning human cloning reflects our humanity. It is the right thing to do. Creating a child through this new method calls into question our most fundamental beliefs.

PRESIDENT WILLIAM CLINTON[1]

At issue are not just benefits and harms, but doubts about the very independence needed to give proper (even retroactive) consent, that is, not just the capacity to choose freely and well. It is not at all clear to what extent a clone will truly be a moral agent.

LEON KASS[2]

119

The Cloning of Dolly and the Implications for Humanity

In Huxley's *Brave New World,* sexuality is divorced from procreation. Sexual intercourse—"feelies"—is recreational, and it occurs promiscuously and daily. Children are genetically manufactured by the "Bokanovsky Process" in state hatcheries according to eugenic principles (Alpha Plus Intellectuals, Beta, Delta workers. . . . Epsilon Minus Morons) to fill various state functions. Individualism, especially personal commitments such as those of family loyalty, were viewed as repugnant, giving way to the social motto "Community, Identity, Stability". This separation of sex from procreation typically struck people as the most implausible feature of Aldous Huxley's 1932 fantasy, but today it is close to a possibility. We have the technological knowledge to be able to produce or manufacture babies with specific genomes. Science fiction may become science.

On February 24, 1997, the front-page story all over the world was about a lamb named "Dolly" that had been cloned at the Roslin Institute in Scotland by a team led by Ian Wilmut. The implications for cloning humans were immediately realized. Within hours thousands of statements condemning that prospect were hurled from leaders throughout the Earth. In New York, legislator John Marchi introduced a bill to make human cloning illegal in his state. An official of the Catholic Bishops Conference of England and Wales urged a ban on human cloning, because "each human being has a right to two biological parents." President Clinton condemned human cloning and set up the National Bioethics Advisory Commission (NBAC) to look into it. After ninety days of study, the NBAC agreed with the president, urging federal legislation to ban human cloning.[3] France's President Jacques Chirac called for the European Commonwealth to ban the technology. On January 12, 1998, nineteen European nations signed an agreement pro-

hibiting the genetic replication of humans. Freelance activist Jeremy Rifkin said, "It's a horrendous crime to make a Xerox of someone. . . . You're putting a human into a genetic straightjacket." He demanded a worldwide ban on human cloning, with penalties for transgressors similar to those for rape and murder.[4] Medical ethicist Daniel Callahan was quoted as saying, "I think we have a right to our own individual genetic identity. . . . I think this could well violate that right."[5] A *Time*/CNN poll conducted a few days after the announcement showed that 93 percent of Americans disapproved of cloning humans.[6] Ian Wilmut himself condemned human cloning.

The day the news of Dolly's cloning broke, I was teaching my medical ethics class at West Point. My first reaction was joy and pride at this tremendous technological breakthrough. We had advanced the horizons of genetic knowledge and now could breed animals for medical purposes. We might help infertile couples and couples with a genetic malady to have children in ways less expensive and cumbersome than in-vitro fertilization (IVF). It might be interesting to clone oneself, one's hero, Einstein, or Mother Teresa. Anyway, now that the genie is out of the bottle, it's not going back in. It's another case of realizing that technology has a life and logic of its own. One can only work to prevent its misuse and abuse—not to prevent its use.

Class discussion was fruitful that day. Some students expressed cautious optimism that we could control the genie. Others offered fearful scenarios such as those in *Boys from Brazil,* a movie in which there is a plot to clone a multitude of little Hitlers, who would take over the world in the name of fascism. Others mentioned *Jurassic Park,* a movie in which dinosaurs retake the world after they are cloned; others that a Frankenstein's monster could be created. The students worried that children produced in this manner would have identity crises, being related—at most—to one parent. Others condemned the possibility as our "playing God" with human life. Sheep and mice were one thing—but cloning humans? Suppose a scientist cloned his father by implanting a nucleus of one of his father's cells into an ovum of the scientist's mother, who then gave birth to the clone of her husband. After the clone grew up, would his mother not have mixed feelings toward her husband–son? Would she tend to treat him as a son or as a lover?

I was waiting for the religious students to ask where and when the soul would enter a cloned cell, for this struck me as the kind of question religious people would have. When I finally raised it, no one had the slightest idea of how souls could enter or accompany such a manufactured being. Is there an answer to this question, or would clones lack souls? Do animals have souls? Does Dolly have one?

Questions came up regarding the selling of one's genes: How much could Michael Jordan or John Elroy get for his genome on the open market? How about Ted Williams or Marilyn Monroe's genes? How much could the owner of a few of their cells make?

How should reflective moral people react to the news of cloning? As noted above, the first reactions of religious leaders, politicians, medical ethicists, and the public at large was overwhelmingly negative. While this should be noted, in itself it should not influence us too much.

One ought to take the initial public reaction to cloning with a grain of salt. Such gut-level reactions are not good reasons to approve or disapprove a policy. In the 1950s it was proposed that we send a man to the moon. People were appalled that we should play God in this way ("If God wanted us to live on the moon, he would have put us there!"), and even eminent philosopher Ludwig Wittgenstein said it was in principle impossible to do this.[7] When the U.S. Supreme Court asserted in *Roe v. Wade* that the constitution supported abortion through the second trimester, a huge public outcry reverberated throughout the land. Only twenty-seven years later most Americans approve of such a permissive policy (though, to be sure, they do not think

it ideal). Similarly, when Louise Brown, the first test-tube baby, was born in England on July 25, 1978, only 15 percent of the public approved. Just twenty-two years later more than 24,000 American children have been conceived this way. The sky hasn't fallen, nor is there evidence that children so created are any worse for it. The procedure has a 70 percent approval rating. Louise seems to be a normal, healthy person, unharmed by the experience.[8] What seems more important than how a baby comes into the world is how he or she is cared for.

A more important question than what the public and the experts think is: What are the moral issues connected with cloning, specifically human cloning? The list our class came up with includes: (1) The question of human dignity. To what extent does natural procreation, leading to a unique genome, endow us with a special dignity? (2) The problem of the misuse and abuse of technology. Science and technology seem to have no limits as to what they could do in creating monsters. Rich people could clone multiple selves and spread their genomes throughout society. (3) The long-range effects of asexual procreation. Is there something fundamentally basic about the heterosexual act in procreation? (4) Eugenics. Should we use genetic information to create more perfect persons (select genomes for longevity, health, intelligence, self-control, and physical prowess)? (5) Commercialization. Should we permit clones to be sold on the open market? Wouldn't this cheapen human life, or do people have a right to sell their genomes?

Following is a closer look at these issues.

What Is Cloning?

Before we attempt a moral assessment of cloning, we should understand what it is. Cloning, or more accurately, nuclear somatic transfer (NST) is a type of asexual reproduction, artificially induced. Related to mammals, it is the process of removing the nucleus of an adult cell and implanting it in an *enucleated* egg (an ovum from which the original nucleus has been removed). Most people, like bioethicist Leon Kass, accept the cloning of nonhuman animals. Currently, the agriculture industry is engaged in nuclear transfer to produce better livestock. Changes in the *phenotype*[9] of livestock are accomplished by bombarding their embryos with genes that will produce livestock with desired traits. Scientists are also engaged in transgenic processes in pigs, in which genetic manipulation of porcine embryos can produce tissue suitable for replacement of human tissue. *Transgenics* involves the exchange of genetic information among plant, animal, and microbial species. In mice embryo experiments, a key gene in the morphological development is knocked out at an early stage. This results in fetuses with no heads. All organs develop normally, except the brain. Hence the resulting mouse cannot live long after birth and has no ability to perceive or act. However, tissue from headless mice may eventually be used for human tissue replacement. The potential uses and abuses of transgenics are enormous.

The Promise of Human Cloning

Here are a few of the positive *possibilities* human cloning offers:

1. Suppose we admired someone—for example, a movie star such as Gregory Peck, Charlton Heston, Audrey Hepburn, or Julie Andrews, or a saintly person such as Gandhi, Mother Teresa, or the Dalai Lama, or an athlete such as Michael Jordan or Mark McGwire, or a scientist sych as Albert Einstein or Stephen Hawking. We could buy that person's genome and clone it, producing an identical twin—only much younger. Of course, environmental differences and personal choices might result in very different kinds of people, so Einstein 2 might became a concert violinist instead of a physicist and the Dalai Lama 2 a stockbroker on Wall Street. Nevertheless, given a suitable environment, societies might one day be able to use cloning to develop a group of outstanding political, scientific, and moral leaders.

2. One spouse might have a genetic disposition toward a serious disease—spina bifida, Tay-Sachs disease, Down's syndrome, cystic fibrosis, or heart disease. We could clone the other spouse's genome. Suppose the husband has the bad genes. We would clone the mother, who would give birth to her own identical twin. She would be both mother and sister to her child. If the man were cloned, he would be both father and brother to the child. Suppose that you, an only child, and your father were killed in an accident. Your mother, deeply distraught at this earth-shaking dual loss, asks her scientist doctor to harvest a cell from your body to clone you, so that you would live on through your clone.

3. A couple could freeze an embryo clone of each of their children, so that should any of the children die, its genetic twin could be developed from the embryo. Applying this process to the example of your being cloned (in possibility 2), one of your cell nuclei would have been transplanted into one of your mother's enucleated ova and frozen in a medical storage plant.

4. We could freeze embryonic clones of an individual so that if the person later needed a bone marrow, liver, or kidney transplant, the clone could be implanted in a gestational surrogate and developed. The tissue match from the clone would be exact, so the vexing problem of tissue rejection would not arise.

5. One could perpetuate not only a family line, but also an exact gene line. Person A might be 90 years old, his or her next twin 50, and the next twin only 5. Suppose it turns out that you are the clone of one of the healthiest, happiest, longest lived people who has inhabited this planet—a person who lived to 110. Given even better nutrition and health standards, you could make it to a happy 150. Would you regret the fact that you were cloned? How would you react to the news? Who would you be if you weren't cloned?

These five positive possibilities may have tremendous financial costs and unknown societal costs attached to them, but in themselves they seem morally acceptable. Let us turn to the arguments against cloning humans.

Arguments Against Human Cloning

The strongest condemnation of human cloning has come from religious leaders, such as the Pope and leaders of the Southern Baptist Church, political leaders such as President Clinton and the leaders of the European Commonwealth, and medical ethicists such as George Annas, Arthur Caplan, Daniel Callahan, and Leon Kass. Kass testified to the NBAC that human cloning was "morally repugnant," so dangerous that the NBAC should act "as if the future of humanity may lie in the balance."[10] He wrote a scathing denunciation of cloning, entitled "The Wisdom of Repugnance", in the June 1997 issue of the *New Republic,* calling for an unequivocal ban on human cloning. "We should declare that human cloning is unethical in itself and dangerous in its likely consequences. In so doing, we shall have the backing of the overwhelming majority of our fellow Americans, and of the human race, and (I believe) of most practicing scientists. Next we should do all that we can to prevent the cloning of human beings. We should do this by means of an international legal ban, at a minimum."[11]

What reasons did Kass give? Essentially, three arguments are set forth. First, there is an appeal to *Natural Law:*

> Cloning turns out to be the perfect embodiment of the ruling opinions of our new age. Thanks to the sexual revolution, we are able to deny in practice, and increasingly in thought, the inherent procreative teleology of sexuality itself. But, if sex has no intrinsic connection to generating babies, babies need have no necessary connection to sex. Thanks to feminism and the gay rights movement, we are increasingly encouraged to treat the natural heterosexual difference and its preeminence as a matter of "cultural construction." But if male and female are not normatively complementary and generatively significant, babies need not come from male and female complementarity. Thanks to the prominence and the acceptability of divorce and out-of-wedlock births, stable, monogamous marriage as the ideal home for procreation is no longer the agreed-upon cultural norm. For this new dispensation, the clone is the ideal emblem: the ultimate "single-parent child."[12]

Kass is arguing that cloning is the logical outcome of our society's repudiation of the traditional natural law doctrine that heterosexuality is the proper process of conceiving and nurturing human beings. Cloning is then unnatural, and as such, an attack on the monogamous family. Those who defend a strong natural law theory, such as Roman Catholics, would accept this argument, but others would reject it. First of all, the notion of *naturalness* is ambiguous. As noted in the discussion of natural law regarding suicide in Chapter 7, naturalness doesn't necessarily mean *good* and unnatural doesn't necessarily signify *bad*. It all depends on what interests are being served. Lightning is natural, but if it kills an innocent child, it has a bad effect; building dams is unnatural, but it can be good if the dams prevent flooding from destroying our property. Birth control devices are artificial, and the Roman Catholic Church condemns their use for that reason, but for most of us, including many Catholics, they seem to serve good ends in morally acceptable ways. Medicine is unnatural, but we think we are justified in using it to kill bacteria and viruses that threaten our lives and health. Eyeglasses are also unnatural, but life would be a lot poorer for many of us without these artificial benefits. For that matter, clothes, money, bicycles, cars, airplanes, houses, churches, and books are all unnatural—nature doesn't produce them by itself. They're artificial products, manufactured goods, but they are, nevertheless, generally good.

Sometimes natural law scholars interpret *naturalness* in a functional way. If an organ has a primary natural function, we shouldn't distort it by using it in a secondary manner. For example, teeth are for eating food, not opening beer bottles; the male sex organ is for emitting semen in the act of propagation, not for penetrating other orifices. But this reasoning seems dubious. Although there are certainly unhealthy or unwise uses of our body parts, there's no reason for us to always adhere to an organ's primary function. The bridge of a nose has the primary function of allowing us to exhale and inhale air, but do we sin if we use it to support our spectacles? And who knows what the primary function of earlobes is, but surely it's not wrong to use them to support earrings. The organs and processes to which we have grown accustomed have evolved over our long history from prehistoric being to modern human being. They have been adequate for survival, but sometimes technology allows us to improve on them. Our eyes tend to weaken with age, but glasses and optical surgery can enhance our sight. Hearing aids improve our hearing. By-pass surgery improves our cardiovascular systems. Kidney dialysis allows people with kidney failure to survive. Transplants replace increasing numbers of our organs. All of these are human artificial interventions in nature. They seem morally justified, if anything does. So why not extend this reasoning to genetic engineering? Why not use genetics to produce a healthy child rather than a sickly one? Even as you would rather be healthy than have cystic fibrosis or Tay-Sachs disease or sickle-cell anemia, why not assume that a future child would too? Why not apply the Golden Rule to the propagation of newborns? Similarly, why not use cloning to produce a child who is likely to lead a happy, constructive life rather than one who will wallow in pain, suffering, and disease? Do not misunderstand me. I believe in stoic acceptance of the

inevitable, of suffering, illness, and death, as much as anyone. But don't we have suffering enough to deal with? Shouldn't we aim at ameliorating it wherever possible?

Many of Kass's opponents believe in an objective moral order as much as he does, but they believe that this moral order leaves more to human reason. Kass has a narrow view of the moral order. It does not accept homosexuality as a morally acceptable sexual orientation, let alone a locus for the family. What I have called a moderate objectivist (see Chapter 2) might respond to Kass's narrower vision by claiming that morality is expansive and embraces many forms of life. More is permitted than traditional culture might lead one to expect. Such a moderate objectivist might respond to Kass's fear about the demise of the family in this way: "I agree with you that monogamous marriage is the best context for producing and nurturing children, but this is a contingent fact, because of how we have evolved and because of the kinds of social history we have experienced. Although monogamous marriage might be the best institution, other institutions may be adequate to the job. The important thing is that children are loved and cared for. All things being equal, it is better for a child to be brought up by a single parent who loves it dearly than by two hateful parents who abuse it. It is better that a child be brought up by a gay or lesbian couple who treat it kindly and decently than by a heterosexual couple who neglect it."

Kass's mistake is to commit the fallacy of false dilemma: either heterosexual family or nothing. I am convinced that there are plenty of places in between. In fact, I think that the heterosexual nuclear family is inadequate for bringing up children today. The community and, especially, the extended family of grandparents and uncles and aunts are needed to supplement and support the immediate family. Sometimes it is better that a gay couple with a supportive community bring up a child than a nuclear family isolated from its roots. The point is, if Kass is really so concerned with the heterosexual family, let him help improve it. At present, evidenced by child abuse statistics and a 50 percent divorce rate, families need a lot of help.

Kass has a second argument against cloning: the *Rootless Narcissism argument*. Here is how he puts it:

> Through cloning, we can work our wants and wills on the very identity of our children, exercising control as never before. Thanks to modern notions of individualism and the rate of cultural change, we see ourselves not as linked to ancestors and defined by traditions, but as projects for our own self-creation, not only as self-made men but also man-made selves; and self-cloning is simply an extension of such rootless and narcissistic self-re-creation.
>
> Unwilling to acknowledge our debt to the past and unwilling to embrace the uncertainties and limitations of the future, we have a false relation to both: cloning personifies our desire fully to control the future, while being subject to no controls ourselves. Enchanted and enslaved by the glamour of technology, we have lost our awe and wonder before the deep mysteries of nature and of life.[13]

This almost sounds like the unabomber manifesto—and like Ted Kaczynski's diatribe, it contains some truth. Technology is a two-edged sword that promises us more power, only to make life more complicated, as well as alienate us from our simpler past. The rate of change in our lives seems mind-boggling and is as discombobulating to us as to the Luddites of the seventeenth century who, traumatized by the changes brought about by technology, went around smashing machines. If Kass were advocating only "Slow down and reflect on what the cost of this new technology will be before we plunge full speed ahead in the pursuit of cloning's wonderful blessings," I would agree with him. A couple of years of reflection over the implications of this technology certainly are in order before we launch our battleships, but remember that we don't even have the technol-

ogy to clone humans yet. Kass might well lower his blood pressure and join in a fuller, calmer discussion of the benefits and liabilities.

Kass judges those who pursue the quest for replication and greater control of the future to be egomaniacs: (1) He is against our wanting to have greater control over the future, and (2) he thinks that those who desire to clone are "rootless and narcissistic." But this seems too sweeping an indictment. Surely other interpretations of the desire to clone are at hand—such as producing healthier, more intelligent children. But I think both parts of this charge are too strong. The desire to have more control of one's future is in itself morally *good*. We call it prudence, a practical wisdom. What's the alternative? Gambling? Russian roulette? If he condemns people for wanting to have significant control over their future, he might as well condemn vaccinations, health insurance, meteorology, flood control projects, the building of dams, education, and birth control. Is not this what wisdom is all about—anticipating and preparing for future contingencies? Besides, we are nowhere near controlling the future. Accidents happen, we die unexpectedly, weather-related, financial, or social upheavals occur. There is every reason to think that a cloned child, like an in-vitro fertilized child, will be surprised by joy, will love to be loved, and will wonder at the "mysteries of nature and of life"—be they in love, death, the human personality, or the universe at large. I don't see cloning having much effect on all of this. Cloned humans are still every bit human, with all the emotions and vulnerability of a human. Your clone is simply a twin younger than you are. It's a delayed twin, not Frankenstein's monster or a manufactured mechanism.

As for the charge of narcissism, there may well be some danger of this, perhaps a bit more than is already the case in wanting to see oneself in one's children. In itself there's nothing wrong in wanting to have *your own* children, rather than someone else's. All praise to those who adopt, nurture, and educate orphans, but it's not the first choice of most of us. Here's where the term *natural* does have a legitimate function. It's natural to want children in your own genetic line (even God created humans in *His* image, not in His rivals'). Cloning oneself is only an extension of this desire, in itself not evil. Granted, the value of monogamous love that yields a being who is the expression of that love, a merging of two souls into one, is a very beautiful ideal. But just because it is the ideal doesn't mean that second best isn't still good.

Suppose a happily married couple wants children, but the wife carries a gene for Alzheimer's disease. They could opt for expensive in-vitro fertilization (IVF) procedures, but why use someone else's donor egg? Why not transplant a cell nucleus of the husband into one of her ova. This way the husband will have his biological child and the wife will carry it to term, nurse it, and be integral to the birthing process. Besides, she will be contributing the mitochondrial element, whose contribution is not fully understood but is thought to be a significant influence on the development of the embryo. Would it be morally wrong to do this?

Kass fears that all of this is an expression of selfishness, of narcissism. Is it necessarily so? As we cash in on our natural love of our own children as projections of our being and our hopes, we might likewise recognize the legitimacy of this attitude and take steps to control it? Forewarned is forearmed. Morality enables us to mitigate the negative aspects of narcissism. Don't we naturally love our children more than we love other people's children partly because we see our image in them. Is it deplorable to want to live on vicariously through the successes and joys and labors of our children? I know no argument that condemns self-interested identification with one's offspring—so long as it does not burgeon into selfishness and injustice, where we are willing to deny other children their legitimate claims to a good life.

Kass concludes in a third argument that a cloned child is not an independent being, for it could not give its consent for the cloning procedure. Call this the *Nonconsent argument*.

> The objection about the impossibility of presuming consent may even go beyond the obvious and sufficient point that a clonant, were he subsequently to be asked, could rightly resent having been made a clone. At issue are not just benefits and harms, but doubts about the very independence needed to give proper (even retroactive) consent, that is, not just the capacity to choose freely and well. It is not at all clear to what extent a clone will truly be a moral agent. For, as we shall see, in the very fact of cloning, and of rearing him as a clone, his makers subvert the cloned child's independence, beginning with that aspect that comes from knowing that one was an unbidden surprise, a gift, to the world, rather than the designed result of someone's artful project.[14]

I think here we have the nub of the anticlone worry. Somehow a child who has been cloned is less than a fully autonomous being. Fundamental independence has been taken from the being. Theologian and bioethicist Nigel Cameron echoes Kass, saying that human cloning "would be perhaps the worst thing we have ever thought of in the maltreatment of our species. It would be a kind of *new slave class*. You would have human beings who were made by other human beings for their purposes."[15] The quotation by Leon Kass above is to the same effect. In a similar vein, Susan Jacoby argues that "No one has the right to jeopardize the precious uniqueness of all members of the human race in order to assuage individual heartbreak and gratify individual desires."[16]

There really are two separate but related arguments here. The first goes like this:

1. If anyone planned your existence, you are not really a free being.

2. If you are not a free being, you are not a full moral agent.

3. Hence because cloned beings were planned, they are not free.

This argument seems to prove too much. Many religious people hold that God planned their being. If that is so, none of us are moral agents. But this seems nonsense. If Kass really wants to convince us that there is a metaphysical difference between being produced by a meandering sperm invading an ovum and the nucleus of a cell being implanted in an ovum—in both cases producing a being with the same number of chromosomes—he has to do better than that. Furthermore, no baby gives his or her consent to be born, whether through simple sex or cloning. A child may not even understand how generation happens, so I don't think consent to being cloned has much to do with whether a person is a moral agent.

Perhaps Kass has something deeper in mind. Perhaps he holds a religious view of humanity, in which case it is a God-endowed soul that makes us moral agents. Somewhere in the act of conception the soul enters into the zygote. Although there are difficulties with the idea of a soul inhabiting our bodies, it is possible. But two questions that cast doubt on Kass's logic: (1) if God can send a soul into a zygote, can't He send one into a clone?, and (2) natural cell division sometimes involves twinning (or quintupling). Does God then send a second soul into the twin (or four new ones into the quintuplets)? I do agree that our ability to clone humans, should it be realized, will cause us to rethink the idea of a separate soul in a body. But I don't think it will undermine the basic idea underlying moral agency: that beings who deliberate about prospective actions are moral agents. In fact, it might be worth cloning just to test this hypothesis.

The related argument by Jacoby—echoed in President Clinton's statement quoted at the beginning of this chapter—is that unless we have a *Unique Genetic Endowment,* we aren't unique. If it were so, no twin (including Siamese twins) or quintuplet would be a unique human being, but they clearly are. It's obvious that twins have separate identities. Eng and Chang, the original

Siamese twins, developed different personalities, one becoming a morose alcoholic, the other a sober, cheerful man. Second, clone twins would be even less identical than "identical" twins, for the host cell's mitochondria contribute some genetic material as well as energy to the clone's development. In utero development will likely also be very different, because of such factors as the clone surrogate mother's nutrition intake, use of drugs, and so forth. Third, it is not only our genes that give us our identity, but also how we are raised, how we relate to others, our unique experiences imbedded in our psyches, and how we *choose* to live our lives. As I said earlier, environmental differences and personal choices might result in very different kinds of people, so Einstein 2 might become a concert violinist instead of a physicist and the Dalai Lama 2 a Wall Street stockbroker. There is no reason to think that clones would be any different in this respect than identical twins or, for that matter, any of the rest of us.

Conclusion

Should we clone humans? This remains a difficult question, for cloning would bring about changes in our ways of looking at life, sex, and procreation itself. I think that sex is too strong an instinct to be endangered by the technology of cloning. Sex, both now and for the foreseeable future, is alive and well. Suppose the cloning of humans becomes feasible in the next decade. I'm hopeful that in the long run a moral society can use the technology for constructive purposes, but I do have deep worries about the short run. Abuses are likely; rich egomaniacs would be tempted use it to spread their genomes through society. And those who see human cloning as humanity's attempt to usurp the role of God will doubtless lash out in acts of terror. Just as the U.S. Supreme Court's decision to recognize a woman's right to kill her fetus has resulted in an angry and powerful anti-abortion movement, which occasionally lashes

out in violence, so the right to artificially produce human life will no doubt result in an angry
and powerful anticloning movement, which will
manifest itself in violence. If our deliberations in
this chapter are sound, there is nothing in principle wrong with human cloning. Thus I end
where I began this chapter—with joy and pride
at the human achievement of a wonderful technology. The question is whether we can use it
for good and not also abuse it.

There was once a man who discovered his
shadow. He became so fascinated by its lithe

movements, its dark shadowing meanderings,
its plasticity and near ubiquitousness, that it became the dominant force in his life. He maneu-
vered in his chair so as to give it pride of place.
He kept the light on at night to preserve its
being. His whole life gradually shifted from
other pursuits to center on his shadow, until at
last he himself became a shadow of his shadow.
The ultimate question is: Who's in control? Will
technology, including human cloning, be put to
moral uses, or will it so dominate us that we in
effect become the shadow of our shadow?[17]

Study Questions

1. Discuss the positive and negative aspects of human cloning. First make a list of them
   and then evaluate them, trying to decide on balance whether cloning should be permitted and under what conditions.
2. Discuss Leon Kass's three arguments against human cloning. How sound are they?
   Evaluate my criticisms of these arguments. How sound are they? How would you
   carry on the debate?
3. Discuss the following case: Suppose Mr. Holmes has a gene for Down's syndrome.
   He and his wife are concerned that their child will not have this disease. Their doctor
   offers them a cloning procedure whereby Mrs. Holmes's genome is cloned in her
   own ovum. Would it be morally acceptable for Mr. and Mrs. Holmes to accept this
   procedure? If so, why? If not, why not? Under what conditions would it not be so?
4. What do you make of the argument that a cloned individual would not be an independent person because he or she would not have a unique genetic identity?

Endnotes

1. President Bill Clinton, in a speech replayed on PBS's *Newshour*, quoted in Patrick Hopkins, "Bad Copies: How Popular Media Represent Cloning as an Ethical Problem," *Hastings Center Report* 28, no. 2 (1998): 9. Clinton went on to announce a ban on cloning. Similarly U.S. Congressman Vernon Ehlers of Michigan urged Congress to pass a law making human cloning a federal crime. He wrote, "Human life is sacred. The good Lord ordained a time-honored method of creating human life, commensurate with substantial responsibility on the part of the parents, the responsibility to raise a child appropriately. Creating life in the laboratory is totally inappropriate and so far removed from the process of marriage and parenting that has been instituted upon this planet that we must rebel against the very concept of human cloning. It is simply wrong to experi-

ment with the creation of human life in this way." Quoted in Gregory E. Pence, *Who's Afraid of Human Cloning?* (Lanham, MD: Rowman & Little-field, 1998), 39. This is the best book on the subject of cloning, and this chapter is indebted to it.

2. Leon Kass, "The Wisdom of Repugnance," *New Republic*, 2 June 1997: 25.

3. Gregory E. Pence, *Who's Afraid of Human Cloning?*, 1.

4. *Time*, 10 March 1997, 70. Quoted in Patrick Hopkins, "Bad Copies: How Popular Media Represent Cloning as an Ethical Problem" *Hastings Center Report* 28, no. 2 (1998): 6–13 and in Pence, op. cit., 27.

5. *Time*, 8 November 1993, 68. Quoted in Hopkins, ibid.

6. Pence, op. cit., 2.

7. Ludwig Wittgenstein, *On Certainty* (New York: Harper & Row, 1969), 108.

8. Pence, op. cit., 4–5.

9. The *phenotype* refers to the properties of an organism that are produced by the interaction of its genetic constitution and the environment.

10. Quoted in Pence, op. cit , p. 5.

11. Leon Kass "The Wisdom of Repugnance," *New Republic,* 2 June 1997, 25.

12. Kass, op. cit., 18.

13. Ibid.

14. Kass, op. cit., 22.

15. Quoted in *USA Today,* 1 April 1997.

16. Susan Jacoby, "Entitled to the Embryo?" *New York Times,* 1 Nov. 1993.

17. I am indebted to Gregory Pence for helpful suggestions for improving this chapter.

Chapter 12

The Death Penalty

Introduction

On August 15, 1990, Angel Diaz, age nineteen, was sentenced in the Bronx for the murder of an Israeli immigrant who had employed one of Diaz's friends. After strangling the man with a shoelace and stabbing him, Diaz and four friends donned Halloween masks to rob, beat, and gang-rape the man's wife and sixteen-year-old daughter. The women were then sexually tortured while the murdered man's three-year-old daughter watched from her crib.

Angel Diaz had been convicted of burglary four times before he was sixteen. His lawyer, Paul Auerbach, said that Diaz was an honest boy forced by poverty to do bad things. Diaz was sentenced to 38⅓ years to life on thirteen counts of murder, robbery, burglary, and conspiracy. His accomplice, Victor Sanchez, twenty-one, who worked for the murdered man and planned the murder, had already been sentenced to 15 years to life.[1]

The National Center of Health Statistics has reported that the homicide rate for young men in the United States is 4 to 73 times the rate of other industrial countries. In 1994, 23,330 murders were committed in the United States. Whereas killings per 100,000 by men fifteen through twenty-four years old in 1987 was 0.3 in Austria and 0.5 in Japan, it was 21.9 in the United States and as high as 232 for African Americans in some states. Scotland had the rate nearest to that of the United States, with a 5.0 homicide rate. In some central city areas it is 732 times the rate of that of men in Austria; in 1994, the rate was 37 per 100,000 men between the ages of fifteen and twenty four.[2] The homicide rate in New York City broke the 2,000 mark in 1990. African American males in Harlem are said to have a lower life expectancy than males in Bangladesh. Escalating crime has caused an erosion in the quality of urban living. It is threatening the fabric of our social life.

Homo sapiens is the only species in which it is common for one member to kill another. In most species when there is a conflict between individuals, the weaker party submits to the stronger through some ritual gesture and is then permitted to depart in peace. Only in captivity, where the defeated animal cannot get away, is it killed. Only human beings deliberately kill other individuals and groups of their own species. Perhaps it is not that we are more aggressive than other species, but that our drives have been made more lethal by the use of weapons. A weapon, allows us to harm or kill without actually making physical contact with our victim. A man with a gun need not even touch his victim. Someone who sends a letter bomb through the mail may have never laid eyes on the victim. The inhibition against killing is undermined by the trigger's power, a point to be kept in mind when discussing gun control legislation. An airplane bomber pilot need not see his victims as he presses the button unleashing his destruction. We are a violent race whose power of destruction has increased in proportion to our technology.

Naturally, the subject of punishment should receive increased attention, as should the social causes of crime. As a radical student activist in the 60s, I once opposed increased police protection for my neighborhood in Morningside Heights, New York City, arguing that we must get to the causes of crime and not deal only with the symptoms. I later realized that this was like refusing fire fighters the use of water hoses to put out fires because they dealt only with the symptoms rather than with the causes of the fire.

The truth is that we do not know the exact nature of what causes crimes of violence. Males commit a disproportionate number of violent crimes in our country, more than 90 percent. Why is this? African American males between the ages of fifteen and twenty-five constitute the group with the greatest tendency toward violent crimes.[3] Why is this? Many people in the United States believe that *poverty causes crime,* but this is false. Poverty is a terrible condition, and surely contributes to crime, but it is not a necessary or sufficient condition for violent crime. The majority of people in India are far poorer than most of the American poor, yet a person, male or female, can walk through the worst slum of Calcutta or New Delhi at any time of the day or night without fearing molestation. As a student, I lived in a very poor neighborhood in a city in England, which was safer than the Midwestern middle-class neighborhood in which I grew up. The use of and traffic in illegal drugs contributes to a great deal of crime, and the turn from heroin to crack as the "drug of choice" has exacerbated the matter, but plenty of crime occurred in our society before drugs became a major problem. We leave the subject of the causes of crime for psychologists and sociologists to solve and turn to the nature of punishment.

The discussion is divided into two parts. In Part One, I discuss the major theories of punishment, preparing the way for a discussion of capital punishment. In Part Two, I argue that a proper understanding of the nature of punishment justifies capital punishment for some crimes. Finally, I examine four objections to capital punishment.

Part One: Punishment

To be responsible for a past act is to be liable to praise or blame. If the act was especially good, we go further than praise. We reward it. If it was especially evil, we go further than blame. We punish it. In this part of the chapter I examine the notion of punishment, and in the next part, capital punishment. First we need to inquire under what conditions, if any, criminal punishment is justified. We will look at three answers to this problem: the Retributivist, the Utilitarian, and the Rehabilitationist.

Even though few of us will ever become criminals nor be indicted on criminal charges, most of us feel very strongly about the matter of criminal punishment. Something about crime touches the deepest nerves of our imagination. Take the following situations, which are based on newspaper reports of the last few years:

1. A drug addict in New York City stabs to death a vibrant, gifted twenty-two-year-old graduate student who has dedicated her life to helping others.

2. A sex-pervert lures little children into his home, sexually abuses them, and then kills them. More than twenty bodies are discovered on his property.

3. A man sends his wife and daughter on an airplane trip, puts a time bomb into their luggage, and takes out a million-dollar insurance policy on them. The money will be used to pay off his gambling debts and for prostitutes.

4. A bomb explodes outside the Federal Building in Oklahoma City, killing more than 160 people and injuring many others.

What is it within us that rises up in indignation at the thought of these atrocities? What should happen to the criminals in these cases? How can the victims (or their loved ones) ever be compensated for these crimes? We feel conflicting emotional judgments of harsh vengeance toward the criminal and, at the same time, concern that we don't ourselves become violent and irrational in our quest for revenge.

THE DEFINITION OF PUNISHMENT

We may define *punishment,* or more precisely *institutional or legal punishment* as *an evil inflicted by a person in a position of authority upon another person who is judged to have violated a rule.*[4] It can be analyzed into five concepts:

1. *An Evil.* To punish is to inflict harm, unpleasantness, or suffering (not necessarily pain). Regarding this concept, the question is: under what conditions is it right to cause harm or inflict suffering?

2. *For a violation of a rule. The violation is either a moral or legal offense.* Should we punish everyone who commits a moral offense? Need the offense already have been committed? Or may we engage in

prophylactic punishment when we have good evidence that the agent will commit a crime?

3. *Done to the offender.* At least the offender must be judged or believed to be guilty of a crime. Does this rule out the possibility of punishing innocent people? What should we call the process of framing the innocent and "punishing" them?

4. *Carried out by a personal agency.*

5. *Imposed by an authority.*

Let us spend a moment examining each of these points and the questions raised about them.

1. Punishment is an evil. It may involve corporal punishment, loss of rights or freedom, or even loss of life. These are things we normally condemn as immoral. How does what is normally morally wrong suddenly become morally right? To quote former Oxford University Professor of Jurisprudence H. L. A. Hart, what is this "mysterious piece of moral alchemy in which the combination of two evils of moral wickedness and suffering are transmuted into good"?[5] Theories of punishment bear the burden of proof to justify why punishment is required. The three classical theories have been Retributivist, Utilitarian Deterrence, and Rehabilitative (or Reform of the Criminal). We shall examine each of these below. These theories attempt not only to justify types of punishment but also to provide guidance on the degrees of punishment to be given for various crimes and persons.

2. Punishment is given for a violation of a rule, but must it be for a violation of a legal statute or may it also be for any moral failure? Although most legal scholars agree that the law should have a moral basis, it is impractical to make laws against every moral wrong. If we had a law against lying, our courts would be cluttered beyond capacity. Also some laws may be immoral (antiabortionists believe that the laws permitting abortion are immoral), but they still are laws, carrying with them coercive measures.

Whether we should punish only offenses already committed or also crimes that are intended is a difficult question. If I know or have good evidence that Smith is about to kill an innocent child (but not which one), and the only way to prevent this is by incarcerating Smith (or killing him), why isn't this morally acceptable? Normally, we don't have certainty about people's intentions, so we can't be certain that Smith really means to kill the child. But what if we do have strong evidence in this case? Nations sometimes launch preemptive strikes when they have strong evidence of an impending attack (e.g., Israel in the Six Day War in 1967 acted on reliable information that Arab nations were going to attack. It launched a preemptive strike that probably saved many Israeli lives). Although preemptive strikes are about defense, not punishment per se, could the analogy carry over? After all, part of the role of punishment is defense against future crimes.

This is a difficult subject, and I can conceive of conditions under which we would incapacitate would-be criminals before they committed their crimes, but the opportunity for abuse is so enormous here that one needs to tread carefully. In general our laws only permit punishing the guilty, relying on the principle every dog may have its first bite—or at least an attempt at a first bite.

3. Punishment is done to the offender. No criminologist justifies punishing the innocent, but classic cases of framing the innocent to maximize utility exist. Sometimes Caiaphus's decision to frame and execute Jesus of Nazareth (John 10:50f) is cited. "It were better that one man should die for a nation than that the whole nation perish." Utilitarians seem to be vulnerable to such practices, but every utilitarian philosopher of law eschews such egregious miscarriages of justice. Why is this? I will discuss this further below.

This stipulation, "done to the offender," also rules out other uses of the word "punish," as when we say that boxer Mike Tyson "punished his opponent with a devastating left to the jaw."

These metaphorical or nonlegal uses of the term are excluded from our analysis. Similarly, we quarantine confirmed or potential disease carriers, but we would not call this imposed suffering "punishment," for our intention is to prevent suffering, not to cause it, and the carrier is innocent of any wrongdoing.

4. Punishment is carried out by a personal agency. Punishment is not the work of natural forces but of people. Lightning may strike and kill a criminal, but only people (or conscious beings) can punish other people.

5. Punishment is imposed by an authority. Punishment is conferred through institutions that maintain laws or social codes. This rules out vigilante executions as punishments. Only a recognized authority, such as the State, can carry out legal punishment for criminal behavior.

We turn now to the leading theories on punishment.

THEORIES OF PUNISHMENT

Retributivist Theories   These theories make the infliction of punishment depend on what the agent deserves as one who has done wrong, rather than on any future social utility that might result from the punishment. That is, rather than focusing on any *future* good that might result from punishment, retributivist theories are *backward* looking, assessing the nature of the misdeed. The most forceful proponents of this view are Immanuel Kant (1724–1804), C. S. Lewis (1898–1963) and Herbert Morris. Following is a classic quotation from Kant, which deserves to be quoted at length:

> Juridical punishment can never be administered merely as a means for promoting another good either with regard to the criminal himself or to civil society, but must in all cases be imposed only because the individual on whom it is inflicted *has committed a crime*. For one man ought never to be dealt with merely as a means subservient to the purpose of another, nor be mixed up with the subjects of real right. Against such treatment his inborn personality

has a right to protect him, even though he may be condemned to lose his civil personality. He must first be found guilty and *punishable* before there can be any thought of drawing from his punishment any benefit for himself or his fellow-citizens.

The principle of punishment is a categorical imperative, and woe to him who creeps through the serpent-windings of utilitarianism to discover some advantage that may discharge him from the justice of punishment, or even reduces its amount by the advantage it promises, in accordance with the Pharisaical maxim, "It is better for *one* man to die than for an entire people to perish" [John 10:51]. For if justice and righteousness perish, there is no longer any value in men's living on the earth . . .

But what kind and what amount of punishment is it that public justice makes its principle and standard? It is the principle of equality, by which the pointer of the scale of justice is made to incline no more to the one side than the other. It may be rendered by saying that the undeserved evil which any one commits on another, is to be regarded as perpetrated on himself. Hence it may be said, "If you slander another, you slander yourself; if you steal from another you steal from yourself; if you strike another, you strike yourself; if you kill another, you kill yourself." This is the *law of retribution (jus talionis)*—it being understood, of course, that this is applied by a court as distinguished from private judgment—can definitely assign both the quality and the quantity of a just penalty. All other standards are wavering and uncertain; and on account of other considerations involved in them, they contain no principle conformable to the sentence of pure and strict justice.

But what does it mean to say, If you steal from someone, you steal from yourself? Whoever steals makes the property of everyone else insecure and therefore deprives himself (by the principle of retribution) of security in any possible property. He has nothing and can also acquire nothing; but he still wants to live, and this is now possible if others provide for him. But since the state will not provide for him free of charge, he must let it have his powers for any kind of work it pleases (in convict or prison labor) and is reduced to the status of a slave for a certain time, or permanently if the state sees fit. If, however, he has committed murder he must *die*. Here there is no substitute that will satisfy justice. There is no similarity between life, however wretched it may be, and death, hence no likeness between the crime and the retribution unless death is judicially carried out upon the wrongdoer, although it must still be freed from any mistreatment that could make the humanity in the person suffering it into something abominable. Even if a civil society resolved to dissolve itself with the consent of all its members—as might be supposed in the case of a people inhabiting an island resolving to separate and scatter themselves throughout the whole world—the last murderer lying in prison ought to be executed before the resolution was carried out. This ought to be done in order that every one may realize the desert of his deeds, and that bloodguiltiness may not remain upon the people; for otherwise they will all be regarded as participators in the murder as a public violation of justice.[6]

This is a classic expression of the retributivist position, for it bases punishment solely on the issue of whether or not the subject in question has committed a crime and punishes him accordingly. All other considerations—eudaimonistic or utilitarian—are to be rejected as irrelevant to punishment. For example, Kant considers the possibility that a capital criminal might allow himself to be a subject in a medical experiment as a substitute for capital punishment and to benefit society. He rejects the suggestion. "A court would reject with contempt such a proposal from a medical college, for justice ceases to be justice if it can be bought for any price whatsoever." I have heard the phrase "that bloodguiltiness may not remain upon the people" interpreted as implying utilitarian consideration, signifying that the people will be cursed in the future. Perhaps a more charitable interpretation is that failure to punish constitutes an endorsement of the criminal act and thus a kind of criminal complicity after the act.[7]

Kant and the classic retributivist position in general have three theses about the justification of punishment:

1. Guilt is a necessary condition for judicial punishment. That is, *only* the guilty may be punished.

2. Guilt is a sufficient condition for judicial punishment. That is, *all* the guilty must be punished. If you have committed a crime, morality demands that you suffer an evil for it.

3. The correct amount of punishment imposed upon the morally (or legally) guilty offender is the amount equal to the moral seriousness of the offense.

Punishment restores the scales of justice and the social equilibrium of benefits and burdens, and it is backward looking. We might put the argument this way:

1. In breaking a primary rule of society, a person obtains an unfair advantage over others.

2. Unfair advantages ought to be redressed by society if possible.

3. Punishment is a form of redressing the unfair advantage.

4. Therefore, we ought to punish the offender for breaking the primary rule. Punishment restores the social equilibrium of burdens and benefits by taking from the agent what he or she unfairly got and now owes, thus exacting his or her debt.

Mitigating circumstances may be taken into consideration to lessen the severity of the punishment, but the aim is to bring about moral homeostasis, a social order in which the good are rewarded and the bad are punished in proportion to their deeds.

Although the retributivist theory has broad intuitive appeal, it is not without problems. One problem is to make sense out of the notion of balancing the scales of justice. The metaphor suggests a cosmic scale that is put out of balance by a crime, but such a scale might not exist, or if one does, it may not be our duty to maintain it through punishment. That may be God's role. Furthermore, retributivism seems unduly retrospective. If we can restore the repentant criminal to moral integrity through rehabilitative processes, insisting on a pound of flesh seems barbaric. While retributivists usually moderate their stance in the light of these objection, the question is whether a sufficiently qualified retributivism is really a retributivism at all rather than a version of utilitarianism.

Utilitarian Theories Utilitarian theories are theories of deterrence, reform, and prevention. The emphasis is not on the gravity of the evil done, but on deterring and preventing future evil. The motto of utilitarians might be "Don't cry over spilt milk!" Unlike retributivist theories, which are backward looking and based on *desert*, Utilitarian theories are *forward* looking, based on social improvement. Jeremy Bentham (1748–1832) and John Stuart Mill (1806–1873) are classic utilitarians. Their position can be analyzed into three theses:

1. Social utility (including reform, prevention, and deterrence) is a necessary condition for judicial punishment.

2. Social utility is a sufficient condition for judicial punishment.

3. The proper amount of punishment to be imposed upon the offender is the amount that will do the most good (or least harm) to all those who will be affected by it. Stanley Benn puts it well: "The margin of increment of harm inflicted on the offender should be preferable to the harm avoided by fixing that penalty rather than one slightly lower."[8]

Punishment is a technique of social control, justified so long as it prevents more evil than it produces. If there is a system of social control that will give a greater balance (for example, Rehabilitation), the utilitarian will opt for that. The utilitarian doesn't accept Draconian laws that would deter because the punishment would be worse than the crime, causing greater suffering than the original offense. Only three grounds are permissible for punishment: (1) to prevent a repetition (2) to deter others—the threat of punishment deters potential offenders and (3) to rehabilitate the criminal (this need not be seen as punishment, but it may involve that).

The threat of punishment is everything. Every act of punishment is to that extent an admission of the failure of the threat. If the threat were successful, no punishment would be needed, and the question of justification would not arise.

One problem with the utilitarian theory is simply that it goes against our notion of desert. It says that social utility is a necessary condition for punishment. But I would be in favor of punishing at least the most egregious offenders even if I knew they would never commit another crime. Suppose we discovered Adolf Hitler living quietly in a small Argentine town and were sure that no good (in terms of deterrence or prevention) would come of punishing him. Shouldn't we still bring him to trial and punish him appropriately?

A further problem is that utilitarianism seems to allow punishment for prospective crimes. If the best evidence we have leads us to believe that a person or a group of people will commit a crime, we are justified in applying punitive measures if our actions satisfy a cost-benefit analysis.

The main weakness of utilitarianism is that it seems to allow the punishment of the innocent if that will deter others from crime. We want only criminals punished, but utilitarians focus on results, not justice. If we can frame an innocent bum for a rape and murder to prevent a riot, the utilitarian would be tempted to do so. This violates the essence of justice.

Rehabilitative Theories   Crime is a disease, and a criminal is a sick person who needs to be cured, not punished. Rehabilitationists such as B. F. Skinner, Karl Menninger, and Benjamin Karpman point to the failure and cruelties of our penal system and advocate an alternative of therapy and reconditioning. "Therapy not torture" might be said to be their motto. Criminals are not really in control of their behavior but are suffering personality disorders. Crime is by and large a result of adverse early environment, so what must be done is to recondition the criminal through positive reinforcement. Punishment is a prescientific response to antisocial behavior. At best, punishment temporarily suppresses adverse behavior, but if untreated, Skinner argues, it will resurface again as though the punishment never occurred. It is useless as a deterrent. Rehabilitationists charge that retributivists are guilty of holding an antiquated notion of human beings as possessing free wills and being responsible for their behavior. We, including all of our behavior, are all products of our heredity and, especially, our environment.

Menninger sees rehabilitation as a replacement for the concept of justice in criminal procedure.

> The very word *justice* irritates scientists. No surgeon expects to be asked if an operation for cancer is just or not. No doctor will be reproached on the grounds that the dose of penicillin he has prescribed is less or more than *justice* would stipulate. . . . It does not advance a solution to use the word *justice*. It is a subjective emotional word. . . . the concept is so vague, so distorted in its application, so hypocritical, and usually so irrelevant that it offers no help in the solution of the crime problem which it exists to combat but results in its exact opposite—injustice, injustice to everybody.[9]

Of course we need to confine criminals for their own good and society's, but a process of positive reinforcement must be the means of

dealing with criminals and their "crimes." Benjamin Karpman, one of the proponents of this theory, puts it this way,

> Basically, criminality is but a symptom of insanity, using the term in its widest generic sense to express unacceptable social behavior based on unconscious motivation flowing from a disturbed instinctive and emotional life, whether this appears in frank psychoses, or in less obvious form in neuroses and unrecognized psychoses. . . . If criminals are products of early environmental influences in the same sense that psychotics and neurotics are, then it should be possible to reach them psychotherapeutically.[10]

Let me begin my criticism of Rehabilitation by relating a retelling of the Good Samaritan story. You recall that a Jew went down from Jerusalem to Jericho and fell among thieves who beat him, robbed him, and left him dying. A priest and a Levite passed by, but an outcast Samaritan came to his rescue, bringing him to a hotel for treatment and paying his bills.

The contemporary version of the story goes like this. A man is brutally robbed and left on the side of the road by his assailants. A priest comes by but regrets having to leave the man in his condition, since the priest will be late for the church service that he must lead. Likewise a lawyer passes by, rushing to meet a client. Finally, a psychiatrist sees our subject, rushes over to him, places the man's head in his lap, and in a distraught voice cries out, "Oh, this is awful! How deplorable! Tell me, Sir, who did this to you? He needs help."

Not all psychiatrists fit this description of mislocating the victim, but the story cannot be dismissed as merely a joke in poor taste. It fits an attitude that substitutes the concept of sickness for moral failure. Let me briefly note some of the problems with the whole theory of rehabilitation as a substitute for punishment. First, this doctrine undermines the very notion of human autonomy and responsibility. Individuals who are not mentally ill are free agents whose actions should be taken seriously as flowing from free decisions.[11] If a person kills in cold blood, he or she must bear the responsibility for that murder. Rehabilitative theories reduce moral problems to medical problems.

Furthermore, rehabilitation doesn't seem to work. Rehabilitation is a form of socialization through sophisticated medical treatment. Although humans are malleable, there are limits to what socialization and medical technology can do. Socialization can be relatively effective in infancy and early childhood, less so in late childhood, and even less effective in adulthood. Perhaps at some future time when brain manipulation becomes possible, we will make greater strides toward behavior modification. Perhaps we will be able to plant electrodes in a criminal's brain and so affect his cerebral cortex that he "repents" of his crime and is restored to society. The question then will be whether we have a right to tamper with someone's psyche in this manner. Furthermore, would a neurologically induced repentance for a crime really be repentance, or would it be an overriding of the criminal's autonomy and personality? And wouldn't that tampering itself be a form of punishment?

CONCLUSION

Let me bring this part of our work to a close by suggesting that there are elements of truth in all three theories of punishment. Rehabilitationism, insofar as it seeks to restore criminals to society as morally whole beings, has merit as an aspect of the penal process, but it cannot stand alone. The retributivist theory is surely correct to make guilt a necessary condition for punishment and to seek to make the punishment fit the crime. Its emphasis on desert is vital to our theory of rewards and punishment, and with this it respects humans as rational, responsible agents who should be treated in a manner fitting to their deserts. However, it may be too rigid in its *retrospective* gaze and in need of mercy and *prospective* vision. Utilitarianism seems correct in emphasizing this prospective feature of treatment with the goal of promoting human flourishing. But it is in danger of manipulating people for the social good—even of punishing the innocent or punishing the guilty more than they deserve (for social purposes). One way of combining retributivism and utilitarianism has been suggested by John Rawls in a classic paper, "Two Concepts of Rules." Rawls attempts to do justice to both the retributivist and the utilitarian theories of punishment.[12] He argues that there is a difference between justifying an institution and justifying a given instance in which the institution is applied. The question "Why do we have law or system?" is of a different nature from the question "Why are we applying the law in the present situation in this mode?" Applied to punishment: (1) "Why do we have a system of punishment?" and (2) "Why are we harming John for his misdeed?" are two different sorts of questions. When we justify the institution of punishment, we resort to utilitarian or consequentialist considerations: A society in which the wicked prosper offers inadequate inducement to virtue. The society will get on better if some rules are made and enforced than will a society in which either no rules exist or the rules are not enforced. However, when we seek to justify an individual application of punishment, we resort to retributivist considerations, for example, when someone commits a breach against the law and merits a fitting punishment.

Part Two: The Death Penalty

> Even if a civil society resolved to dissolve itself with the consent of all its members—as might be supposed in the case of a people inhabiting an island resolving to separate and scatter themselves throughout the whole world—the last murderer lying in prison ought to be executed before the resolution was carried out. This ought to be done in order that every one may realize the desert of his deeds, and that bloodguiltiness may not remain upon the people; for otherwise they will all be regarded as participators in the murder as a public violation of justice. Kant[13]

We now turn to the question of the death penalty and apply our discussion of punishment to capital punishment. First we discuss the Retributivist argument, then the Utilitarian, and finally the Golden Rule argument for the death penalty.

THE RETRIBUTIVIST ARGUMENT FOR THE DEATH PENALTY

Let me say a word about the notion of *desert.* Part of justice, going back to Plato, Aristotle, Kant, the Biblical tradition, and virtually every major religion, holds that people ought to get what they deserve. Those who work hard for worthy goals deserve reward; those who do not make the effort deserve nothing; and those who purposefully do evil deserve punishment. The virtuous deserve to flourish to the degree of their virtue, and the vicious deserve to suffer to the degree of their vice. "Whatsoever a man soweth, that shall he reap," is an ancient adage perhaps as old as its metaphysical counterpart of eternal judgment (Jewish/Christian tradition) or karma (Hindu/Buddhist tradition)—that what one does in this life will be part of one's essential constitution in the next life. This notion presumes the notion of responsibility, that people are accountable for their actions and should be rewarded and punished accordingly. Even Karl Marx objected to applying the principle "From each according to his ability, to each according to his need," to people who did not work, who did not deserve to be helped.[14] Only in contemporary liberalism, such as Rawls's theory of justice as fairness, has the notion of natural desert been seriously undermined. But Rawls is wrong here. Although we may not deserve our initial endowments or capacities, we do deserve what we make with them. Our effort and contribution are worthy of moral assessment, and as agents we can be held accountable for our effort and contributions. That is, without the concept of desert, responsibility has no validity, and without the notion of responsibility, neither morality nor law has a footing.

Suppose, as most of us do, that each person has a right to life. That right, however, is not absolute, but conditional (otherwise we could not kill even in self-defense). Like our right to property and liberty, it can be overridden for weighty moral reasons. When an offender threatens or attempts to kill an innocent person, the offender deserves a punishment appropriate to the severity of the crime. When an offender with malice aforethought takes the life of an innocent person, he or she forfeits his or her own life. But the main idea in the retributivist theory is that not only is the death penalty permissible for the murderer, it is also deserved. The guilty deserve punishment, and that punishment should be proportional to the severity of their crime. A complete retributivist like Kant (see the quotation at the beginning of this part) holds that all and only those who are guilty should be so punished. The moderate retributivist holds that only the guilty should be so punished—but not necessarily all of the guilty. Mitigating circumstances, the external costs of punishment, the possibility of reform, and so forth may prescribe lesser degrees of punishment than are deserved. Hell itself may be a just desert for Hitler, but morality doesn't require that we torture him. The moderate retributivist holds that giving people what they deserve (positive and negative) is a *prima facie* duty, not an absolute, nonoverridable one.

Some have objected that the death penalty is itself murder. To quote eighteenth-century abolitionist Cesare di Beccaria, "Putting the criminal to death only compounds evil. If killing is an evil, then the State actually doubles the evil by executing the murderer. The State violates the criminal's right to life. It carries out *legalized murder.* The death penalty cannot be useful because of the example of barbarity it gives to men. . . . it seems to me absurd that the laws which punish homicide should themselves commit it." But there is a difference. The murderer volunteered for his crime. The victim didn't volunteer for his fate. The murderer had reason to believe that he would be justly and severely punished for his crime, so he has no reason to complain when the state executes him. The murderer violated the victim's right to life, thereby forfeiting his own *prima facie* right to life. The Fifth and Fourteenth Amendments of our Bill of Rights state that no one should be deprived of life, liberty, or property without due process of the law, implying that so long as due process of the law has been observed, condemning a murderer to death is both legally and morally justified.

Society may rank punishments corresponding roughly to the gravity of the crimes. That is, it draws up two lists. The first list consists of a list of crimes, from the most to the least serious. The second is a list of punishments that it considers acceptable, from the most severe to the least severe. So long as there is a rough correspondence between the two lists, a society is permitted to consult its own sense of justice in linking the various punishments with each crime in question. The death penalty, it seems, is at the head of the list of severe punishments, linked retributively with the worst crimes. Whether torture is also permitted for a torturer, mutilation for a rapist, and so forth, may be debated. Strictly speaking I have no argument against the appropriate use of torture, though I think it is not necessary. It seems to me that death is a sufficient punishment for the most heinous crimes, but it's not part of my thesis to sort out these matters. Where to put the limit of harm to be imposed on the murderer is partly a cultural matter, as the history of legal punishment indicates.[15] Our notion of what is or is not "humane," connected with repulsion against torture and corporal punishment in general, is largely a cultural matter. It has to do with how we have been socialized. Torture shocks our sensibilities, but not those of our ancestors, and not necessarily our moral principles. Although I am a moral objectivist, holding that moral truth exists, part of morality is relative to culture, to the sensibilities of the majority of its members.

One objection to the retributivist argument is that although a criminal may deserve the death penalty, the justification of the State's execution of the criminal is another matter. It needs a separate justification. The correct response is that justice consists of giving people what they deserve. As Locke noted, in the state of nature we would each have the right and duty to punish the offender, but in organized society, we surrender that right and duty to the State. We may override justice because of mitigating circumstances, but insofar as the State has duty to dispense justice, it is justified in executing those who commit murder.

The Utilitarian Argument

The utilitarian argument for capital punishment is that it deters would-be offenders from committing first-degree murder. If the death penalty deters, we have an auxiliary argument for its use. This argument may supplement (but not replace) the retributivist argument. Isaac Ehrlich's study, to my knowledge the most thorough study to date, takes into account the complex sociological data and concludes that over the period 1933–1969, "an additional execution per year. . . . may have resulted on the average in seven or eight fewer murders."[16] Ehrlich's findings have been challenged by many opponents with the result that the issue is left in doubt. It seems an enormous undertaking to prove either that the death penalty deters or that it does not deter. The statistical evidence is inconclusive—which is different from saying that it is "zero," as abolitionists sometimes claim.

Commonsense reasons exist for believing that the death penalty deters some would-be murderers from murdering. Richard Herrnstein and James Q. Wilson have argued in *Crime and Human Nature* that a great deal of crime is committed in a cost-benefit scheme, wherein the criminal engages in some form of risk assessment as to his or her chances of getting caught and punished in some manner. If a would-be criminal estimates the punishment to be mild, the crime will become inversely attractive, and vice versa. If a potential murderer judges that he may be punished by imprisonment or death, he will be more deterred than if he judges that he will be punished only by imprisonment. Doesn't the fact that those condemned to death do everything in their power to postpone it, and to get their sentences reduced to long-term prison sentences, show that the death penalty is feared as an evil to be avoided? The potential criminal need not go through deliberate cost-benefit analysis. The association of murder with the death penalty may have embedded in the subconscious mind of potential criminals a powerful deterrence. Perhaps the abolition of the death penalty from the 1960s until the late 1970s, and the fact that it is only recently being carried out with any regularity, have eroded the association, accounting for the increased murder rate from 1980 until 1993. The fact that the death penalty is beginning to be carried out may partially account for the decrease of homicides in recent years.

Former Prosecuting Attorney for the State of Florida, Richard Gernstein, has set forth the commonsense case for deterrence. First of all, the death penalty certainly deters the murderer from commiting any further murders, including those he or she might commit within the prison in which he is confined. Second, statistics cannot tell us how many potential criminals have refrained from taking another's life through fear of the death penalty. As Hyman Barshay puts it:

> The death penalty is a warning, just like a lighthouse throwing its beams out to sea. We hear about shipwrecks, but we do not hear about the ships the lighthouse guides safely on their way. We do not have proof of the number of ships it saves, but we do not tear the lighthouse down.

Some of the commonsense evidence is anecdotal, as reported by British member of parliament Arthur Lewis, who was converted from being an abolitionist to a retentionist:

One reason that has stuck in my mind, and which has proved to me beyond question, is that there was once a professional burglar in my constituency who consistently boasted of the fact that he had spent about one-third of his life in prison. . . . he said to me, "I am a professional burglar. Before we go out on a job we plan it down to every detail. Before we go into the boozer to have a drink we say, 'Don't forget, no shooters'—shooters being guns." He adds, "We did our job and didn't have shooters because at that time there was capital punishment. Our wives, girlfriends and our mums said, 'Whatever you do, do not carry a shooter because if you are caught you might be topped.' If you do away with capital punishment they will all be carrying shooters."

It's difficult to know how widespread this kind of reasoning is. My own experience, growing up in a neighborhood where some of my acquaintances were criminals, corroborates this testimony. These criminals admitted being constrained in their behavior by the possibility of the death penalty. No doubt some crimes are committed in the heat of passion or by the temporarily insane, but not all crime fits that mold. Perhaps rational risk assessment, which involves the cost-benefit analysis of crime, is mainly confined to certain classes of potential and professional criminals, including burglars and kidnappers. It probably applies to people who are tempted to kill their enemies. We simply don't know how much capital punishment deters, but this sort of commonsense, anecdotal evidence cannot be dismissed as worthless. Common sense tells us that people will be deterred by greater punishments such as death than by lesser ones such as imprisonment.

I have been arguing that we do have some statistical and commonsense evidence that the death penalty deters would-be killers. Even if you are skeptical about that evidence, another argument, based on the *possibility* that it deters, is available to us. This is the argument set forth by Ernest van den Haag, which he calls the "Best Bet argument."[17] Van den Haag argues that even though we don't know for certain whether the death penalty deters or prevents other murders, we should bet that it does. Indeed, due to our ignorance, any social policy we take is a gamble. Not to choose capital punishment for first-degree murder is as much a bet that capital punishment doesn't deter as choosing the policy is a bet that it does. There is a significant difference in the betting, however: to bet *against* capital punishment is to bet against the innocent and for the murderer; while to bet *for* it is to bet against the murderer and for the innocent.[18]

The point is this: we are accountable for what we let happen as well as for what we actually do. If I fail to bring up my children properly and they are a menace to society, I am to some extent responsible for their bad behavior. I could have caused it to be somewhat better. If I have good evidence that a bomb will blow up the building in which you are working and I fail to notify you (assuming that I can), I am partly responsible for your death, if and when the bomb explodes. To refrain purposefully from a lesser evil that we know will allow a greater evil to occur, is to be at least partially responsible for the greater evil.

This responsibility for our omissions underlies van den Haag's argument, to which we now return. Suppose that we choose a policy of capital punishment for capital crimes. In this case we are betting that the death of some murderers will be more than compensated for by the lives of some innocents who will not be murdered (by either these murderers or others). If we're right, we have saved the lives of the innocent. If we're wrong, unfortunately, we've sacrificed the lives of some murderers. Suppose we choose not to have a social policy of capital punishment. If capital punishment doesn't work as a deterrent, we've come out ahead, but if it does, we've missed an opportunity to save innocent lives. If we value the saving of innocent lives more highly than the loss of the guilty, betting on a policy of capital punishment turns out to be rational. The reasoning goes like this: Let "CP" stand for Capital Punishment:

The Wager

	CP works	CP doesn't work
We bet on CP	a. We win: some murderers die and some innocents are saved.	b. We lose: some murderers die for no purpose.
We bet against CP	c. We lose: murderers live and some innocents die needlessly.	d. We win: murderers live and the lives of others are unaffected.

Suppose that we estimate the utility value of a murderer's life a 5 while the value of an innocent's life is 10. Although we cannot give lives exact numerical values, we can make rough comparative estimates: Mother Teresa's life is greater than Adolf Hitler's, and all things being equal, the life of an innocent person is at least twice the value of a murderer's. (My own sense is that the murderer has forfeited most, if not all, of his worth, but if I had to put a figure on it, that figure would be 1,000 to 1). Given van den Haag's figures, the sums work out this way:

A murderer saved	+5
A murderer executed	-5
An innocent saved	+10
An innocent murdered	-10

Suppose that for each execution only two innocent lives are spared. Then the outcomes read as follows:

a. -5 + 20 = +15

b. -5

c. +5 -20 = -15

d. +5

If all of the possibilities are roughly equal, we can sum their outcomes as follows:

If we bet on capital punishment, (a) and (b) obtain = +10.

If we bet against capital punishment, (c) and (d) obtain = -10.

So to execute convicted murderers turns out to be a good bet. To abolish the death penalty for convicted murderers would be a bad bet. We unnecessarily put the innocent at risk.

Even if we value the utility of an innocent life only slightly more than that of a murderer, it is still rational to execute convicted murderers. As van den Haag writes, "Though we have no proof of the positive deterrence of the penalty, we also have no proof of zero or negative effectiveness. I believe we have no right to risk additional future victims of murder for the sake of sparing convicted murderers; on the contrary, our moral obligation is to risk the possible ineffectiveness of executions."[19]

THE GOLDEN RULE ARGUMENT

One more argument should be set forth, and that is the Golden Rule argument for the death penalty. The Golden Rule states that we should do unto others as we would have them do unto us if we were in their shoes. Reflect on the evil deeds perpetrated by Nazi war criminals, or by those who blew up the Murrah Federal Building in Oklahoma City on April 19, 1995, killing 168 people, or on any number of heinous murders well known to us. If you had yielded to temptation and blown up the Federal Building, or like Steven Judy had raped and murdered a helpless woman and then drowned her three small children, or if you had kidnapped a young girl, placed her in your trunk and then killed her, what punishment do you think would be fitting for *you*? What would you deserve? Would you want to live? Would not the moral guilt that you would doubtless feel demand the death penalty? And would you not judge that such moral guilt was appropriate and that anyone who did not feel it was morally defective? Would you not agree that you had forfeited your right to life, that you had brought upon yourself the hangman's noose? Would you not agree that you deserved nothing less than death? Should we not apply these sentiments to murderers?

OBJECTIONS TO CAPITAL PUNISHMENT

Let us examine three major objections to capital punishment, as well as the retentionist's responses to those objections.

1. Objection: Capital punishment is a morally unacceptable thirst for revenge. As former British Prime Minister Edward Heath put it,

> The real point which is emphasized to me by many constituents is that even if the death penalty is not a deterrent, murderers deserve to die. This is the question of revenge. Again, this will be a matter of moral judgment for each of us. I do not believe in revenge. If I were to become the victim of terrorists, I would not wish them to be hanged or killed in any other way for revenge. All that would do is deepen the bitterness which already tragically exists in the conflicts we experience in society, particularly in Northern Ireland.[20]

Response: Retributivism is not the same thing as revenge, although the two attitudes are often intermixed in practice. Revenge is a personal response to a perpetrator for an injury. Retribution is an impartial and impersonal response to an offender for an offense done against someone. You cannot desire revenge for the harm of someone to whom you are indifferent. Revenge always involves personal concern for the victim. Retribution is not personal but based on objective factors: the criminal has deliberately harmed an innocent party and so deserves to be punished, whether I wish it or not. I would agree that I, my son, or my daughter deserves to be punished for our crimes, but I don't wish any vengeance on myself, my son, or my daughter.

Furthermore, while revenge often leads us to exact more suffering from the offender than the offense warrants, retribution stipulates that the offender be punished in proportion to the gravity of the offense. In this sense, the *lex talionis* that we find in the Old Testament is actually a progressive rule, where retribution replaces revenge as the mode of punishment. It says that there are limits to what one may do to an offender. Revenge demands a life for an eye or a tooth, but Moses provides a rule that exacts a penalty equal to the harm done by the offender.

2. Objection: Miscarriages of justice occur. Capital punishment is to be rejected because of human fallibility in convicting innocent parties and sentencing them to death. In a survey done in 1985, Hugo Adam Bedau and Michael Radelet found that of the 7,000 persons executed in the United States between 1900 and 1985, 25 were innocent of capital crimes.[21] Although some compensation is available to those unjustly imprisoned, the death sentence is irrevocable. We can't compensate the dead. As John Maxton, a member of the British Parliament, puts it, "If we allow one innocent person to be executed, morally we are committing the same, or, in some ways, a worse crime than the person who committed the murder."[22]

Response: Mr. Maxton is incorrect in saying that mistaken judicial execution is morally the same as or worse than murder. A deliberate intention to kill the innocent occurs in a murder, whereas no such intention occurs in wrongful capital punishment.

Sometimes the objection is framed this way: It is better to let ten criminals go free than to execute one innocent person. If this dictum is a call for safeguards, it is well taken, but somewhere there seems to be a limit on the society's tolerance of capital offenses. Would these abolitionists argue that it is better that 50 or 100 or 1,000 murderers go free than that one innocent person be executed? Society has a right to protect itself from capital offenses even if this means taking a finite chance of executing an innocent person. If the basic activity or process is justified, it is regrettable but morally acceptable that some mistakes are made. Fire trucks occasionally kill innocent pedestrians while racing to fires, but we accept these losses as justified by the greater good of the activity of using fire trucks. We judge the use of automobiles to be acceptable even though such use causes an average of 50,000 traffic fatalities each year. We accept the morality of a defensive war even though it will result in our troops accidentally or mistakenly killing innocent people.

The fact that we can err in applying the death penalty should give us pause and cause us to build an appeals process into the judicial system. Such a process is already in the American and British legal systems. Occasional errors may be made, but as regrettable as this is, it is not a sufficient reason for us to refuse to use the death penalty if, on balance, it serves a just and useful function.

Furthermore, abolitionists are simply misguided in thinking that prison sentences are a satisfactory alternative. It's not clear that we can always or typically compensate innocent parties who waste away in prison. Jacques Barzun has argued that a prison sentence can be worse than death and carries all the problems that the death penalty does regarding the impossibility of compensation:

> In the preface of his useful volume of cases, *Hanged in Error,* Mr. Leslie Hale refers to the tardy recognition of a minor miscarriage of justice—one year in jail: "The prisoner emerged to find that his wife had died and that his children and his aged parents had been removed to the workhouse. By the time a small payment had been assessed as 'compensation' the victim was incurably insane." So far we are as indignant with the law as Mr. Hale. But what comes next? He cites the famous Evans case, in which it is very probable that the wrong man was hanged, and he exclaims: "While such mistakes are possible, should society impose an irrevocable sentence?" Does Mr. Hale really ask us to believe that the sentence passed on the first man, whose wife died and who went insane, was in any sense *revocable?* Would not any man rather be Evans dead than that other wretch "emerging" with his small compensation and his reason for living gone?[23]

The abolitionist is incorrect in arguing that death is different than long-term prison sentences because it is irrevocable. Imprisonment also takes good things away from us that may never be returned. We cannot restore to an inmate the freedom or opportunities he or she lost. Suppose an innocent twenty-five-year-old man is given a life sentence for murder. Thirty years later the mistake is discovered and he is set free. Suppose he equates three years of freedom to every one year of life. That is, he would rather live ten years as a free man than thirty as a prisoner. Given this man's values, the criminal justice system has taken the equivalent of ten years of life from him. If he lives until he is sixty-five, he has, by his estimate, lost ten years, so he may be said to have lived only fifty-five years.[24]

The numbers in this example are arbitrary, but the basic point is sound. Most of us would prefer a short life of high quality to a longer one of low quality. Death prevents all subsequent quality, but imprisonment also irrevocably harms one in diminishing the quality of life of the prisoner.

3. *Objection:* The death penalty is unjust because it discriminates against the poor and minorities, particularly African Americans. Former Supreme Court Justice William Douglas wrote that "a law which reaches that [discriminatory] result in practice has no more sanctity than a law which in terms provides the same."[25] Nathanson argues that "in many cases, whether one is treated justly or not depends not only on what one deserves but on how other people are treated."[26] He offers the example of unequal justice in a plagiarism case. "I tell the students in my class that anyone who plagiarizes will fail the course. Three students plagiarize papers, but I give only one a failing grade. The other two, in describing their motivation, win my sympathy, and I give them passing grades." Arguing that this is patently unjust, he likens this case to the imposition of the death penalty and concludes that it too is unjust.

Response: First of all, it is not true that a law applied in a discriminatory manner is unjust. Un-

equal justice is no less justice, however uneven its application. The discriminatory application, not the law itself, is unjust. A just law is still just, even if it is not applied consistently. For example, a friend of mine once got two speeding tickets during a 100-mile trip (having borrowed my car). He complained to the police officer who gave him his second ticket that many drivers were driving faster than he was at the time. They had escaped detection, he argued, so it wasn't fair for him to get two tickets on one trip. The officer acknowledged the imperfections of the system but, justifiably, had no qualms about giving him the second ticket. Unequal justice is still justice, however regrettable. So Justice Douglas is wrong in asserting that discriminatory results invalidate the law itself. The discriminatory practice should be reformed, and in many cases it can be. But imperfect practices in themselves do not entail that the laws engendering these practices are themselves unjust.

With regard to Nathanson's analogy in the plagiarism case, two things should be said against it. First, if the teacher is convinced that the motivational factors are mitigating factors, then he or she may be justified in passing two of the plagiarizing students. Suppose that one student did no work whatsoever, showed no interest (Nathanson's motivation factor) in learning, and exhibited no remorse in cheating, whereas the other two spent long hours seriously studying the material and, upon apprehension, showed genuine remorse for their misdeeds. To be sure, they yielded to temptation at certain—though limited—sections of their long papers, but the vast majority of their papers represented their own diligent work. Suppose also that all three had C averages at this point. The teacher gives the unremorseful, gross plagiarizer an F but relents and gives the other two Ds. Her actions parallel the judge's use of mitigating circumstances and cannot be construed as arbitrary, let alone unjust.

The second problem with Nathanson's analogy is that it would have disastrous consequences for law and benevolent practices alike. If we concluded that we should abolish a rule or practice unless we always treated everyone by exactly the same rules, we would have to abolish, for example, traffic laws and laws against imprisonment for rape, theft, and even murder. Carried to its logical limits, we would also have to refrain from saving drowning victims if a number of people were drowning but only a few of them could be saved. Imperfect justice is the best that we humans can attain. We should reform our practices as much as possible to eradicate unjust discrimination wherever we can, but if we are not allowed to have a law without perfect application, we will be forced to have no laws at all.

Nathanson acknowledges this response but argues that the case of death is different. "Because of its finality and extreme severity of the death penalty, we need to be more scrupulous in applying it as punishment than is necessary with any other punishment."[27] The retentionist agrees that the death penalty is a severe punishment and that we need to be scrupulous in applying it. The difference between the abolitionist and the retentionist seems to lie in whether we are wise and committed enough as a nation to reform our institutions so that they approximate fairness. Apparently Nathanson is pessimistic here, whereas I have faith in our ability to learn from our mistakes and reform our systems. If we can't reform our legal system, what hope is there for us?

More specifically, the charge that a higher percentage of blacks than whites are executed was once true but is no longer so. Many states have made significant changes in sentencing procedures, with the result that currently whites convicted of first-degree murder are sentenced to death at a higher rate than blacks.[28]

One must be careful in reading too much into these statistics. Although great disparities in statistics should cause us to examine our judicial procedures, they do not in themselves prove injustice. For example, more males than females are convicted of violent crimes (almost 90 percent of those convicted of violent crimes are males—a virtually universal statistic), but this is not strong evidence that the law is unfair, for there are psychological explanations for the disparity in convictions. Males are on average and by nature more aggressive (usually tied to testosterone) than females. Likewise, there may be good explanations for why people of one ethnic group commit more crimes than do those of other groups, explanations that do not impugn the processes of the judicial system.[29]

4. Objection: The death penalty is a "cruel and unusual punishment." It constitutes a denial of the wrongdoer's essential dignity as a human being. No matter how bad a person becomes, no matter how terrible one's deed, we must never cease to regard a person as an end in himself or herself, as someone with inherent dignity. Capital punishment violates that dignity. As such, it violates the Constitution of the United States of America, which forbids "cruel and unusual" punishments. Here is how Justice Thurgood Marshall stated it in *Gregg v. Georgia:*

> To be sustained under the Eighth Amendment, the death penalty must [comport] with the basic concept of human dignity at the core of the Amendment; the objective in imposing it must be [consistent] with our respect for the dignity of [other] men. Under these standards, the taking of life "because the wrongdoer deserves it" surely must fail, for such a punishment has as its very basis the total denial of the wrongdoer's dignity and worth. The death penalty, unnecessary to promote the goal of deterrence or to further any legitimate notion of retribution, is an excessive penalty forbidden by the Eighth and Fourteenth Amendments. [30]

Similarly, in *Furman v. Georgia* (1972) Justice William Brennan condemned capital punishment because it treats "members of the human race as nonhumans, as objects to be toyed with and discarded," adding that it is "inconsistent with the fundamental premise of the Clause that even the vilest criminal remains a human being possessed of common human dignity."[31]

Response: First of all, Justice Marshall differs with the framers of the Constitution about the meaning of "cruel and unusual" in declaring that the death penalty violates the Eighth Amendment's prohibition against "cruel and unusual" punishments—unless one would accuse the framers of the Constitution of contradicting themselves. The Fifth and Fourteenth Amendments clearly authorize the death penalty.[32] The phrase "cruel and unusual" in the Eighth Amendment seems to mean cruel and *uncustomary or new* punishments, for, as van den Haag notes, "the framers did not want judges to invent *new* cruel punishments, but did not abolish customary ones."[33] However, even if the framers did intend to prohibit the death penalty, I would argue that it is morally justified. The law is not always identical to what is morally correct.

Rather than being a violation of a wrongdoer's dignity, capital punishment may constitute a recognition of human dignity. As noted in the discussion of Kant's view of retribution, the use of capital punishment respects the worth of victims in calling for an equal punishment to be exacted from offenders, and it respects the dignity of the offenders in treating them as free agents who must be respected for their decisions and who must bear the cost of their acts as responsible agents.

Let's look at these two points a bit more closely. The first—that capital punishment respects the worth of the victim—is bluntly articulated by newspaper columnist Mike Royko:

> When I think of the thousands of inhabitants of Death Rows in the hundreds of prisons in this country, I don't react the way the kindly souls do—with revulsion that the state would take these lives. My reaction is: What's taking us so long? Let's get that electrical current flowing. Drop the pellets now!
>
> Whenever I argue this with friends who have opposite views, they say that I don't have enough regard for that most marvelous of miracles—human life.

> Just the opposite: It's because I have so much regard for human life that I favor capital punishment. Murder is the most terrible crime there is. Anything less than the death penalty is an insult to the victim and society. It says, in effect, that we don't value the victim's life enough to punish the killer fully.[34]

It is precisely because the victim's life is sacred that the death penalty is sometimes the only fitting punishment for first-degree murder. I am accepting here the idea that there is something "sacred" or "dignified" about human life, although earlier I gave reasons that should cause secularists to doubt this.

Second, it's precisely because murderers are autonomous, free agents that we regard their acts of murder as their own and hold them responsible. Not to hold a murderer responsible for his crime is to treat him as less than autonomous. Just as we praise and reward people in proportion to the merit of their good deeds, so we blame and punish them in proportion to the evil of their bad deeds. If there is evidence that the offender did not act freely, we would mitigate his sentence, but if he acted of his own free will, he bears the responsibility for those actions and deserves to be punished accordingly.

Of course, there are counterresponses to all of the retentionist's responses. Consider the utilitarian matter of cost. The appeals process, which is necessary to our system of justice, is so prolonged and expensive that it might not be worth the costs simply to satisfy our sense of retribution. Furthermore, most moderate retributivists do not argue that there is an absolute duty to execute first-degree murderers. Even the principle that the guilty should suffer in proportion to the harm they caused is not absolute; it can be overridden by mercy. But such mercy must be judicious, serving the public good.

In the same vein many argue that life imprisonment without parole will accomplish just as much as the death penalty. The retentionist would respond that death is a more fitting punishment for one who kills in cold blood, and utilitarians (deterrentists) would be concerned about the possibility of escape, murders committed by the murderer while incarcerated, and the enormous costs of keeping a prisoner incarcerated for life. Imprisonment without parole, advocated by many abolitionists as an alternative to the death penalty, should be given serious consideration in special cases, such as when there is evidence that the murderer has suitably repented. Even in these cases, however, the desert argument and the Best Bet argument lean toward the death penalty.

No doubt we should work toward the day when capital punishment is no longer necessary: when the murder rate becomes a tiny fraction of what it is today, when a civilized society can safely incarcerate the few violent criminals in its midst, and when moral reform of the criminal is a reality. Perhaps this is why several European nations have abolished capital punishment (e.g., the murder rate in one year in Detroit alone was 732 times that of the nation of Austria). I for one regret the use of the death penalty. I would vote for its abolition in an instant if only one condition were met: that those contemplating murder would set an example for me. Otherwise, it is better that the murderer perish than that innocent victims be cut down by the murderer's knife or bullet.

Endnotes

1. "Jail for Crime that Shocked Even the Jaded," *The New York Times,* 16 August 1990.
2. National Center of Health Statistics. Available from the National Center for Disease Control. The National Center for Injury Prevention and Control reports that in 1994, 8,116 young people 15–24 years old were victims of homicide. This amounts to an average of 22 youth victims per day in the United States. This homicide rate is 10 times higher than in Canada, 15 times higher than in Australia, and 28 times higher than in France or in Germany. In 1994, 102,220 rapes and 618,950 robberies were reported.
3. The United States 1994 Uniform Crime Report states that 1,864,168 violent crimes occurred in 1994; 25,052 offenders were listed. "Of those [whose] sex and age were reported 91 percent of the offenders were males, and 84 percent were persons 18 years of age or older. . . . Of offenders for whom race was known, 56 percent were black, 42 percent white, and the remainder were persons of other races." (p. 14)
4. In the following analysis, I am indebted to Anthony Flew, "Justification of Punishment," *Philosophy* (1954); Joel Feinberg, "Punishment," *Philosophy of Law,* 2d ed., eds. Joel Feinberg and Hyman Gross (Belmont, CA: Wadsworth, 1980); and Herbert Morris, "Persons and Punishment" *The Monist* 52 (October 1968). See also Tziporah Kasachkoff, "The Criteria of Punishment: Some Neglected Considerations" *Canadian Journal of Philosophy,* vol. 2, 3, (March 1973).
5. H. L. A. Hart, *Punishment and Responsibility* (Oxford: Oxford University Press, 1968) 234.

6. Immanuel Kant, *The Metaphysics of Morals* (1779), trans. E. Hastie (Edinburgh, 1887), 155–156.
7. I am grateful to Jeffrey Reiman for pointing this out to me.
8. Stanley Benn, "Punishment," *Encyclopedia of Philosophy,* ed. Paul Edwards (New York: Macmillan, 1967), vol. 7: 29–35.
9. Karl Menninger, *The Crime of Punishment* (New York: Viking Press, 1968), 17, 10–11. The passage is remarkable for its apparent denial and assertion of the objective reality of justice.
10. Benjamin Karpman, "Criminal Psychodynamics," *Journal of Criminal Law and Criminology* 47 (1956), 9. See also B. F. Skinner, *Science and Human Behavior* (New York: Macmillan, 1953), 182–193.
11. I am assuming that the case for free will and responsibility is cogent. For a good discussion see the readings by Harry Frankfurt, Gary Watson, and Peter van Inwagen in *Moral Responsibility,* ed. John Martin Fischer (Ithaca: Cornell University Press, 1986).
12. John Rawls, "Two Concepts of Justice," *Philosophical Review* (1955).
13. Immanuel Kant, *The Metaphysics of Morals,* trans. John Ladd (Indianapolis: Bobbs-Merrill, 1965), 103.
14. Karl Marx, "Critique of the Gotha Program," *Karl Marx: Selected Writings,* ed. B. McLellan (Oxford: Oxford University Press, 1977). For a fuller discussion of desert, see my article "Equality and Desert," *What Do We Deserve* eds. L. Pojman and O. McLeod (Oxford: Oxford University Press, 1998).
15. Michael Davis has an excellent discussion of "humane punishment" in "Death, Deterrence, and the Method of Common Sense," *Social Theory and Practice* (summer 1981).

16. Isaac Ehrlich, "The Deterrent Effect of Capital Punishment: a Question of Life and Death," *American Economic Review* 65 (June 1975): 397-417.

17. Ernst van den Haag, "On Deterrence and the Death Penalty," *Ethics,* 78 (July 1968).

18. The Best Bet argument rejects the passive–active distinction involved in killing and letting die. Many people think that it is far worse to kill someone than to let him die, even with the same motivation. More generally, they hold that it is worse to *do* something bad than to *allow* something bad to happen. I think people feel this way because they are tacitly supposing different motivational stances. Judith Jarvis Thomson gives the following counterexample to this doctrine: John is a trolley driver who suddenly realizes that his brakes have failed. He is heading for a group of workers on the track before him and will certainly kill them if something isn't done immediately. Fortunately, there is a side track to the right onto which John can turn the trolley. Unfortunately, there is one worker on that track who will be killed if John steers the trolley onto the side track.

If the passive–active distinction holds, John should do nothing but simply allow the trolley to take its toll of the five men on the track before him, but that seems terrible. Surely by turning quickly and causing the trolley to move onto the side track, John will be saving a total of four lives. It seems morally preferable for John to turn the trolley onto the side track and actively cause the death of one man rather than passively allow the death of five. John is caught in a situation in which he cannot help doing or allowing harm, but he can act so that the lesser of the evils obtains.

19. van den Haag, op. cit.

20. British Parliamentary Debates, 1982, quoted in Sorrell, *Moral Theory,* 43.

21. Hugo Adam Bedau and Michael Radelet, *Miscarriages of Justice in Potential Capital Cases* (1st draft Oct. 1985, on file at Harvard Law School Library), quoted in E. van den Haag, "The Ultimate Punishment: A Defense," *Harvard Law Review,* 99, no. 7 (May 1986): 1664.

22. Ibid., 47.

23. Jacques Barzun, "In Favor of Capital Punishment," *The American Scholar,* 31, no. 2, (spring 1962).

24. I have been influenced by similar arguments by Michael Levin (unpublished manuscript) and Michael Davis, "Is the Death Penalty Irrevocable?" *Social Theory and Practice* 10:2 (summer 1984).

25. Justice William Douglas in *Furman v. Georgia* 408 U.S. 238 (1972).

26. Stephen Nathanson, *An Eye for an Eye?*, (Totowa, NJ: Roman & Littlefield, 1987) 62.

27. Ibid., 67.

28. The Department of Justice's *Bureau of Justice Statistics Bulletin* for 1994 reports that between 1977 and 1994, 2,336 (51%) of those arrested for murder were white, 1838 (40%) were black, 316 (7%) were Hispanic. Of the 257 who were executed, 140 (54%) were white, 98 (38%) were black, 17 (7%) were Hispanic, and 2 (1%) were of other races. In 1994, 31 prisoners, 20 white men and 11 black men, were executed, although whites made up only 7,532 (41%) and blacks 9,906 (56%) of those arrested for murder. Of those sentenced to death in 1994, 158 were white men, 133 were black men, 25 were Hispanic men, 2 were Native American men, 2 were white women, and 3 were black women. Of those sentenced, relatively more blacks (72%) than whites (65%) or Hispanics (60%), had prior felony records. Overall, the criminal justice system does not seem to favor white criminals over black, though it does seem to favor rich defendants over poor ones.

29. For instance, according to FBI figures for 1992, the U.S. murder rate was 9.3, far higher than that of France (4.5), Germany (3.9) or Austria (3.9). Of the 23,760 murders committed in the United States that year, 55% of the offenders whose race was known were black and 43% white. Since blacks compose 12.1% of the U.S. population, the murder rate for blacks in 1992 was 45 per 100,000, while that for whites was 4.78—a figure much closer to that for European whites.

30. Justice Thurgood Marshall, *Gregg v. Georgia,* (1976).

31. Justice William Brennan, *Furman v. Georgia,* (1972).

32. The Fifth Amendment permits depriving people of "life, liberty or property" if the deprivation occurs with "due process of law," and the Fourteenth Amendment applies this provision to the states: "no State shall . . . deprive any person of life, liberty, or property, without due process of law."

33. Ernest van den Haag, "Why Capital Punishment?" *Albany Law Review* 54 (1990).

34. Mike Royko, *Chicago Sun-Times,* September 1983.

Chapter 13

Animal Rights

Sentience as Significant

Brute beasts, not having understanding and therefore not being persons, cannot have any rights. . . . The conclusion is clear. We have no duties to them,—not of justice, . . . not of religion . . .

JOSEPH RICKABY, S.J., *Moral Philosophy of Ethics and Natural Law,* 1889

In their behavior towards creatures, all men are Nazis.

ISAAC BASHEVIS SINGER, *Enemies: A Love Story*

Introduction: All is Not Well in the Animal Kingdom

Every minute of every day, an average of 100 animals are killed in laboratories in the United States. Fifty million experimental animals are put to death each year.[1] Some die in the testing of industrial and cosmetic products, some are disposed of because they are female, some are killed after being force-fed or after being tested for pharmaceutical drugs. Insecticides, pesticides, antifreeze chemicals, brake fluids, bleaches, Christmas tree sprays, silver cleaners, oven cleaners, deodorants, skin fresheners, baby preparations, bubble baths, bath salts, freckle creams, eye makeup, crayons, fire extinguishers, inks, suntan oils, nail polish, mascara, hair sprays, zipper lubricants, paints—all are tested on animals before humans are allowed to use them. Although not required in all cases, many companies have traditionally performed animal tests to gain approval of their products by the government. Legal requirement that animals be anesthetized can be circumvented in many experiments, and in others the nature of the tests precludes the use of anesthesia. In the Draize eye test, concentrated solutions of commercial products are instilled into rabbits' eyes and the damage is then recorded according to the size of the area injured. Monkeys have also been used for these experiments. After the tests, the animals are destroyed.[2]

Civet cats are confined in small cages in dark rooms where the temperature is 110°F, until they die. The musk, which is scraped from their genitals once a day for as long as they can survive, makes the scent of perfume last a bit longer after each application. In recent years progress has been made in that several cosmetic companies are abandoning the use of animals for testing in cosmetic products.

In military primate equilibrium studies monkeys are set in simulated flying platforms and tested for their ability to keep their balance under duress. They are subjected to high doses of radiation and chemical warfare agents to see how these would affect their ability to fly. When they become nauseated and begin to vomit from the doses of radiation, they are forced to keep their platform horizontal through the inducement of electric shocks.

In July 1973 Representative Les Aspin of Wisconsin discovered that the United States Air Force was planning to purchase 200 beagle puppies, with vocal cords tied to prevent normal barking, to be used for testing poisonous gases. At the same time the Army was preparing to use 400 beagles for similar tests. More recently, Army laboratories fed 60 beagles doses of TNT to determine the effects of the explosive on animals.[3]

At several universities dogs, monkeys, and rats have been confined to small rooms, where they are unable to escape from electric shocks emanating from the steel grid floors, to determine how they react to unavoidable pain. In toxicity tests, animals are placed in sealed chambers and forced to inhale sprays, gases and vapors. In dermal toxicity tests, rabbits have their fur removed so that a test substance can be placed on their skin. The skin may bleed, blister, and peel. In immersion studies, animals are placed in vats of diluted substances, sometimes causing them to drown before the results can be obtained.

Rhesus monkeys have been given massive doses of cocaine until they began to mutilate themselves and eventually die of cocaine abuse. In 1984 at a major university, experiments were performed on baboons to determine brain damage from head injuries. The subjects were strapped down in boxlike vices and had specially designed helmets glued to their skulls. Then a pneumatic device delivered calibrated blows to the helmet, causing brain injuries to the baboons. Videotapes showed that while the head injuries were being inflicted, the researchers stood by joking about their subjects.[4]

Neither is all well down at McDonald's farm. Factory farming, with its high-tech machinery, has replaced the bucolic pleasantries of free-range agriculture. Farmer McDonald doesn't visit his hens in barns to pick an egg from a comfortable nest. Now as soon as the chicks are hatched, they are placed in small cages. Between five and eight (up to nine) chickens are pressed close together in cages about 18 inches by 10 inches over thin wired floors that hurt their feet. They cannot move around. They are painfully debeaked so that they cannot attack each other in these unnatural quarters. In other chicken factories, the chickens are hung by their feet from a conveyer belt that escorts them through an automatic throat-slicing machine. Three billion chickens are killed in the United States each year. Likewise, pigs and veal calves are kept in pens so small that they cannot move or turn around and develop muscles. They are separated from their mother so they cannot be suckled and are fed a diet low in iron so that we can eat very tender meat.[5] James Rachels describes the process this way:

> Veal calves spend their lives in pens too small to allow them to turn around or even to lie down comfortably—exercise toughens the muscles, which reduces the "quality" of the meat, and besides, allowing the animals adequate living space would be prohibitively expensive. In these pens the calves cannot perform such basic actions as grooming themselves, which they naturally desire to do, because there is no room for them to twist their heads around. It is clear that the calves miss their mothers, and like human infants they want something to suck: they can be seen trying vainly to suck the sides of their stalls. In order to keep their meat pale and tasty, they are fed a liquid diet deficient in both iron and roughage. Naturally they develop cravings for these things, because they need them. The calf's craving for iron is so strong that, if it is allowed to turn around, it will lick at its own urine, although calves normally find this repugnant. The tiny stall, which prevents the animal from turning, solves this "problem." The craving for roughage is especially strong for bedding, since the animal would be driven to eat it, and that would spoil the meat. For these animals the slaughterhouse

is not an unpleasant end to an otherwise contented life. As terrifying as the process of slaughter is, for them it may actually be regarded as a merciful release.[6]

Are animal experiments justified? If so, should there be constraints on them to minimize suffering? Is it morally permissible to eat animals? Why or why not? In sum, do animals have rights? These are the questions discussed in this chapter. We will first examine five major theories regarding our obligations to animals and then examine specific issues, such as vegetarianism, animal experimentation, and hunting for sport.

Five Theories of Obligation to Animals

Five theories on the moral status of animals appear in the history of Western philosophy and religion, from assigning animals no status on the one extreme to assigning them equal status with humans on the other extreme.

1. THE NO STATUS THEORY

The *No Status theory* was set forth by French philosopher René Descartes (1596–1650), who held that animals have no rights or moral status because they have no souls. According to Descartes, since the soul is necessary for consciousness, animals cannot feel pain or pleasure. They are mere machines. "From this aspect the body is regarded as a machine which, having been made by the hands of God, is incomparably better arranged, and possesses in itself movements which are much more admirable than any of those which can be invented by man."[7]

Animals are automata who move and bark and utter sounds like well-wound clocks. Because they lack a soul, which is the locus of consciousness and value, they have no moral status whatsoever. It is no more morally wrong to pull the ears off a dog or eat a cow than it is to kick a stone or eat a carrot.

In Descartes's time animals were subjected to excruciating tortures in physiological experiments. Dogs were restrained by nailing their paws to boards so that they could be more easily observed while being cut open. Sometimes their vocal chords were cut so that their shrieks would not disturb the anatomists. In the next century Nicholas Fontaine observed the following:

> [The anatomists] administered beatings to dogs with perfect indifference, and made fun of those who pitied the creatures as if they felt pain. They said the animals were clocks; that the cries they emitted when struck were only the noise of a little spring that had been touched, but that the whole body was without feeling. They nailed poor animals up on boards by their four paws to vivisect them and see the circulation of the blood which was a great subject of conversation.[8]

We now know that these philosophers were wrong about the mental life of animals. Animals do feel pain and pleasure. They have consciousness and engage in purposeful behavior. Dogs and cats manifest intelligence, gorillas and chimpanzees exhibit complex abstracting and reasoning abilities and have the capacity to communicate through language. The differences between humans and other animals are more a matter of degree than of kind.

Nineteenth-century British philosopher William Whewell seems to have held a slightly different version of the No Status view: "The pleasures of animals are elements of a very different order from the pleasures of man. We are bound to endeavor to augment the pleasures of men, not only because they are pleasures, but because they are human pleasures. We are bound to men by the universal tie of humanity, of human brotherhood. We have no such tie to animals."[9]

This modified Cartesian view is reflected in Nobel Prize–winning microbiologist David Baltimore's claim that no moral issue is involved in animal research and in the writings of psychologists G. Gallup and S. D. Suarez, who write that "the evolution of moral and ethical behavior in man may be such that it is not applicable to other species." Similarly, veterinarian F. S. Jacobs writes that "domestic animals exist in this world because they fulfill man's needs. . . . Therefore it is meaningless to speak of their rights to existence, because they would not exist if man did not exist."[10]

According to the *No Status theory,* animals have no rights, and we have no positive obligations to them. They are merely resources for us to dispose of as we will.

2. THE INDIRECT OBLIGATION THEORY

The dominant position in Western philosophy and religion has been the view that although animals have no rights in their own right, we ought to treat them kindly. We have duties to them because we have obligations to rational beings, God, and other people who own them. Furthermore, if we treat animals cruelly, we may adopt bad habits and so treat humans cruelly.

The creation story of Genesis supports a stewardship model of creation. All of nature has been given to human beings for their use, but humanity must use it properly for God's sake. "And God blessed [man and woman] and God said to them, 'Be fruitful and multiply, and fill the earth and subdue it; and have dominion over the fish of the sea and over the birds of the air and over every living thing that moves upon the earth.' And God said, 'Behold, I have given you every plant yielding seed which is upon the face of all the earth, and every tree with seed in its fruit; you shall have them for food.' "[11]

Philosophers Thomas Aquinas (1225–1274) and Immanuel Kant (1724–1804) hold that cruelty to animals is wrong because it forms bad character and it leads to cruelty to human beings. Aquinas holds a hierarchical view that permits humans to use animals for human purposes:

> There is no sin in using a thing for the purpose for which it is. Now the order of things is such that the imperfect are for the perfect . . . thing, like plants which merely have life, are all alike for animals, and all animals are for man. Where-

fore it is not unlawful if men use plants for the good of animals, and animals for the good of man, as the Philosopher [Aristotle] states.

Now the most necessary use would seem to consist in the fact that animals use plants, and men use animals, for food, and this cannot be done unless these be deprived of life, wherefore it is lawful both to take life from plants for the use of animals and animals for the use of men. In fact this is in keeping with the commandment of God himself. (Genesis 1:29, 30 and Genesis 9:3)

Aquinas continues: "If any passages of Holy Writ seem to forbid us to be cruel to dumb animals, for instance to kill a bird with its young: this is either to remove man's thoughts from being cruel to other men, and lest through being cruel to animals one becomes cruel to human beings: or because injury to an animal leads to the temporal hurt of man, either of the doer of the deed, or of another."[12]

Kant repeats Aquinas's view. We have "no direct duties" to animals, for they "are not self-conscious and are there merely as a means to an end."

> The end is man. . . . Our duties towards animals are merely indirect duties towards humanity. Animal nature has analogies to human nature, and by doing our duties to animals in respect to manifestations of human nature, we indirectly do our duty to humanity. . . . If a man shoots his dog because the animal is no longer capable of service, he does not fail in his duty to the dog, for the dog cannot judge, but his act is inhuman and damages in itself that humanity which it is his duty to show towards mankind. If he is not to stifle his human feelings, he must practice kindness towards animals, for he who is cruel to animals becomes hard also in his dealing with men.[13]

The weakness of the Indirect Obligation view is that it makes rational self-consciousness the sole criterion for being morally considerable. Although such self-consciousness may be the criterion for having full-blooded rights and for being a morally responsible agent, it is not the only thing of moral importance. Causing pain and suffering are bad in themselves, and we have duties not to do such things but rather to ameliorate and eliminate pain and suffering.

3. THE EQUAL STATUS VIEW

K. McCabe, the codirector of the animal rights group People for the Ethical Treatment of Animals (PETA) has said, "There is no rational basis for separating out the human animal. A rat is a pig is a dog is a boy. They're all mammals. . . . In time, we'll look on those who work in [animal laboratories] with the horror now reserved for the men and women who experimented on Jews in Auschwitz. . . . That, too, the Nazis said, was 'for the greater benefit of the master race.' "[14]

We call the view that equates human beings with animals the Equal Status thesis. Its foremost proponent is philosopher Tom Regan, who holds three goals for the treatment of animals: (1) The total abolition of the use of animals in science; (2) the total dissolution of commercial animal agriculture; and (3) the total elimination of commercial and sport hunting and trapping. Even though Regan concedes that some individual uses of animals for biomedical experimentation might be justified and free-range grazing farming is better than factory farming, all of these uses constitute infringements on animal rights, and the exceptional cases are so isolated as to serve only to confuse the issue.

What is wrong is not the pain caused, the suffering, or the deprivation, although these compound the wrong. What's fundamentally wrong is "the system that allows us to view animals as *our resources,* here for us—to be eaten, or surgically manipulated, or put in our cross hairs for sport or money."[15]

Why is it wrong to treat animals as our resources? Because they have *inherent value* and are ends in themselves, just like us. They are of *equal worth* to human beings.

To say we have such value is to say that we are something more than, something different from, mere receptacles. Moreover, to insure that we do not pave the way for such injustices as slavery or sexual discrimination, we must believe that all who have inherent value have it equally, regardless of their sex, race, religion, birthplace, and so on. Similarly to be discarded as irrelevant are one's talents or skills, intelligence and wealth, personality or pathology, whether one is loved or admired—or despised and loathed. The genius and the retarded child, the prince and the pauper, the brain surgeon and the fruit vendor, Mother Theresa and the most unscrupulous used car salesman—all have inherent value, all possess it equally, and all have an equal right to be treated with respect, to be treated in ways that do not reduce them to the status of things, as if they exist as resources for others.[16]

What is the basis of the equal inherent value? Just this: "We are each of us the experiencing subject of a life, each of us a conscious creature having an individual welfare that has importance to us whatever our usefulness to others. We want and prefer things; believe and feel things; recall and expect things."

Regan's Deontological Egalitarianism (Rights and Respect) argument can be stated thus:

1. All humans (or all subject-of-life humans) have equal positive value.

2. There is no morally relevant difference between humans and (some) animals (for example, mammals).

3. Therefore all (some) animals have equal positive worth with humans.

4. Moral rights derive from the possession of value.

5. Since humans have rights (to life, not to be harmed, etc.) animals have the same rights.

Several problems arise in Regan's theory of equal inherent value. First, he hasn't explained why being an experiencing subject entails pos-

sessing inherent value. The reply given by his defenders is "The subject experiences the value— hence the subject has inherent value." This seems confused. One can't validly argue from valuing something, V, to being V without additional premises. The subject may be unhealthy but still value health, or I may value reason without being rational. Further, how do we know that being "subject-to-a-life" grants one such inalienable positive value? Is it supposed to be intuitively self-evident? If so, then it would also seem self-evident to some that merely being conscious entails less value than being *self-conscious,* especially *rationally* self-conscious. Someone in a daze or dream may be minimally conscious, but that is a state less valuable than being fully self-conscious, with plans and projects. It is desirable to have more reason or intelligence rather than less. Intelligence, knowledge, and freedom are inherent values, but animals have less of them than humans. It's true that humans have varying degrees of them, but as a species (on average) we have more of what makes for worth than do other species, so there must be degrees of value, interspecies and intraspecies. If so, we must feel dissatisfied with Regan's assessment. He simply has not given any evidence for the thesis that all animals have equal worth and are to be treated with equal respect.

Regan rejects the notion of differing degrees of inherent value based on differing degrees of self-awareness or some other mental capability, affirming that this leads to the view that mentally superior people have stronger moral rights than mentally inferior people.

There are at least two ways to respond to Regan here. First, following deontologists such as Kant and Rawls, some may appeal to the threshold view of self-consciousness and argue that all and only those who are capable of rational deliberation and life plans are to be accorded a serious right to life. There may be differences between humans with regard to the ability to reason, but almost all (except infants, the mentally ill, the senile, and the seriously retarded and brain damaged) have sufficient ability to be counted within the circle of full moral citizenry. Some higher animals, such as dolphins, gorillas, and chimpanzees, may also belong to this group. The threshold argument seems arbitrary, ad hoc, and hence unsound. It invites the question, Why draw a line where none exists in reality? If self-consciousness and rationality are decisive qualities for moral appraisal, then isn't more better than less, meaning that individuals with more of the qualities should be respected more highly than those with less?[17]

The second way to respond to Regan's anti-hierarchical notion of value is to take a contractarian approach to ethics, arguing that there are no inherent values and that animals are not normally part of the social contract. Since rights derive from contract, animals do not have any rights.[18] Of course, contractarians may still recommend kindness to creatures outside the contract, but where human interests are compelling, animals may be sacrificed to those interests in ways that humans may not.

What seems to underly Regan's egalitarianism is the Sanctity of Life principle, or rather the Sanctity of a *Subject-of-a-Life* principle, since he views being "subject-of-a-life" (i.e., having beliefs and desires) as intrinsically valuable. But just as the Sanctity of Life principle fails to distinguish between quality of life (the life of a bacteria is equal to that of Mother Teresa), the Subject-of-a-Life criterion does the same within a narrower scope. Whereas the former presupposes an outmoded vitalism, the latter presupposes a deeper metaphysic (than Regan offers) in support of his absolutist goals: the total abolition of the use of animals in scientific experimentation; the total dissolution of commercial animal agriculture; and the total elimination of commercial and sport hunting and trapping. Until Regan gives us reason to accept his Sanctity of a Subject-of-a-Life principle, his arguments will fail to support any of these aims.

One further problem with Regan's approach should be mentioned. This approach fails to explain why we shouldn't intervene in the animals world, eliminating animal cruelty. Shouldn't radical zoophiles go into the wild and protect helpless rabbits, deer, and birds from marauding predators, members of the cat family (lions, tigers, leopards), wolves, and other carnivores? Perhaps carnivores could be confined to separate quarters and fed the carcasses of other animals, including human beings. How can these animal egalitarians rest until all of nature is turned into the Peaceable Kingdom, where the lion is made to lie down with the lamb? The suffering that wolves cause rabbits or leopards and tigers cause antelope and deer is far more devastating than that inflicted by the clean shot of an expert hunter's rifle.

Both Regan and Paul Taylor have difficulty with the violent behavior of wild animals. It doesn't fit their vision of a Peaceable Kingdom, but they can't say that we have duties to eliminate all predatory behavior, let alone all carnivores, to make the world safe for pacifist herbivores and plants, for carnivores can't help their need for meat. Their "respect for nature" doesn't allow humans to intervene as environmental imperialists. So what are we to say about the rights of sheep and rabbits not to be torn asunder and harmed by wolves and other predatory animals? Here is Regan's reply: Even though the sheep and rabbits have a right to life and a right not to be harmed, the wolf has no duty to respect those rights, since *ought* implies *can*. The wolf is only doing what is natural and cannot do otherwise. If we intervene, we are violating the wolf's right to dinner. Here is Regan's argument:

[I have] defended [the thesis] that moral patients have *no* duties and thus do not have the particular duty to respect the rights of others. *Only moral agents can have duties,* and this because only these individuals have the cognitive and other abilities necessary for being held morally accountable for what they do or fail to do. Wolves are not moral agents. They cannot bring impartial reason to bear on their decision making—cannot, that is, apply the formal principle of justice or any of its normative interpretations. That being so, wolves in particular and moral patients generally cannot *themselves* meaningfully be said to have duties to anyone, nor, therefore, the particular duty to respect the rights possessed by other animals. In claiming that we have a prima facie duty to assist those animals *whose rights are violated,* therefore, we are not claiming that we have a duty to assist the sheep against the attack of the wolf, since the wolf neither can nor does violate anyone's rights. The absurd results leveled against the attribution of rights to animals simply do not materialize.[19]

I think that Regan is wrong here. If the sheep has a positive right to live in peace, then we have a duty to try to help him. If a boulder came hurtling down and was about to crush the sheep, wouldn't we be remiss in our duty if we didn't take reasonable steps to get the sheep out of harm's way? Likewise, even if the wolves' actions are natural, we have a duty to the sheep to save it from the world.

Furthermore, can't Regan's argument be used to prohibit us from saving humans from wild animals? From bacteria? From insane humans who are only following their nature in raping and killing? Consider the policeman coming to the distraught parents of a child who has been brutally raped and killed by a homicidal maniac. "Well, I would have intervened when I saw Mr. Smith brutalizing your daughter, Mrs. Brown, but then I realized that he was only following his nature as a violent animal, so I was obliged to leave him alone." Or to paraphrase Regan, "You see, Mrs. Brown, in claiming that we have a *prima facie* duty to assist children *whose rights are violated,* we are not claiming that we have a duty to assist them against the attack of a madman, since the madman neither can nor does violate anyone's rights."

One should note that Regan is inconsistent, for (only eleven pages after saying that we may not intervene in favor of the sheep) he argues that we may kill a rabid dog when it attacks a human. How is this different from a rabid wolf's or dog's attacking a sheep?

In the end Regan hasn't justified either his position or the implications of that position. He holds a deep intuition that all people are of equal worth and appeals to a philosophical consensus on that assumption, which provides a basis for his entire moral theory. From there he argues that since there is no relevant difference between humans and other mammals (over the age of one), we should treat all such mammals equally, as possessing equal worth. But if there is no reason to believe that all people, let alone all other mammals over the age of one, possess equal positive value, what is left of Regan's moral system? Are we left with any morality at all? Does his system lead to moral nihilism? I must leave you to decide the issue.

4. THE EQUAL CONSIDERATION THEORY

The Equal Consideration theory was first set forth by Jeremy Bentham (1748–1832), the father of classical utilitarianism, and developed by Peter Singer in his epoch-making book, *Animal Liberation* (1975). It holds that animals are just like us in basic morally relevant ways and so merit our moral regard. As a hedonistic utilitarian, Bentham believed that the essence of morality was to maximize pleasure or happiness and minimize pain and suffering. Furthermore, each sentient being was to count for one and no one was to count as more than one in the utilitarian calculus. In a classic passage written in 1789, Bentham compares the irrationality of our views toward animals with the irrationality of our views toward other races.

> The day *may come,* when the rest of the animal creation may acquire those rights which never could have been withholden from them but by the hand of tyranny. The French have already discovered that the blackness of the skin is no reason why a human being should be abandoned without redress to the caprice of a tormentor. It may come one day to be recognized,

that the number of the legs [or] the [color] of the skin are reasons equally insufficient for abandoning a sensitive being to the same fate. What else is it that should trace the insuperable line? Is it the faculty of reason, or, perhaps, the faculty of discourse? But a full-grown horse or dog is beyond comparison a more rational, as well as a more conversable animal, than an infant of a day, or a week, or even a month, old. But suppose the case were otherwise, what would it avail? the question is not, Can they *reason?* nor Can they *talk?* but, Can they *suffer?*[20]

Animals are *sentient beings,* capable of happiness and suffering, and since sentience is the sole criterion for moral consideration, they are morally considerable in the same way that human beings are.

Bentham's theory was criticized in his own day as crudely *hedonistic,* for reducing all morality to considerations of pleasure and pain. If this were so, then it might be morally right for five sadists who receive a total of 100 *hedons* in the process, to torture a child who only suffers 50 *dolors* (antihedons). Or if a burglar will get more pleasure from my artwork than I do, he has a right to steal it (if in doing so he doesn't produce additional harm).

Sometimes utilitarians like Bentham write as though the single concern of morality were to eliminate suffering in the world. If this were morality's only concern, we would have an obligation to eliminate all sentient life as painlessly as possible, since the only way to eliminate suffering (even gratuitous suffering) is to kill every living organism.

At other times Bentham seems to say that promoting positive pleasure (and in the process, eliminating pain) is the essence of morality. For this reason his version of utilitarianism was labeled "the pig philosophy" by his contemporary critics. Better a pig satisfied than Socrates dissatisfied! In an experiment done on rats, electrodes are wired to the limbic areas of their cerebral cortex, and the rats are shown a button

that, when pressed, stimulates a reward or pleasure center in the brain. I'm told that the rats in the experiment become addicted to the stimulation, so they lose interest in food and sex and spend most of their time pressing the stimulation button until they die. If the maximization of pleasure is what morality is all about, we ought to plug everyone, animals and humans, up to these pleasure machines.

Peter Singer, aware of the dangers of classical utilitarianism, has modified Bentham to present a more plausible version of utilitarianism. The one thing Singer does accept from Bentham is the idea that all sentient beings are linked by their capacity to suffer. From this Singer develops his notion of Animal Liberation, a global theory of duties to animals. He has four essential points:

(1) The Principle of Equality: every sentient being deserves to have his or her needs and interests given equal consideration. Following Bentham, each sentient being is to count for one and only for one. Status and privilege should play no part in doling out benefits. Rather we should distribute goods on the basis of need and interest.

> Equality is a moral idea, not an assertion of fact. There is no logically compelling reason for assuming that a factual difference in ability between two people justifies any difference in the amount of consideration we give their needs and interests. *The principle of equality of human beings is not a description of an alleged actual equality among humans: it is a prescription of how we should treat them.*[21]

(2) The Principle of Utility: the right act is the one that maximizes utility or happiness (or minimizes suffering or unhappiness). Singer holds a version of *Preference Utility:* we ought to satisfy the actual preferences of sentient beings.

(3) The Rejection of *Speciesism,* which constitutes a violation of the Principle of Equality. Singer compares speciesism, the arbitrary favoring of one's species, with racism. "The racist . . .

[gives] greater weight to the interests of members of his own race, when there is a clash between their interests and the interests of another race. Similarly the speciest allows the interests of his own species to override the greater interests of members of other species."[22]

(4) The Relevance of Self-Consciousness. There is a difference between our equal ability to suffer and our equal worth as rational, self-conscious agents. Singer values rational self-consciousness over mere sentience, but he agrees that sentience, or the ability to suffer, gives us a baseline equality for some considerations.

Singer makes a distinction between activities that cause suffering and those that cause death. It may be worse to cause animals to suffer than to kill them, since the latter may be done with minimum pain and the animal generally does not have an understanding of life and death. With humans the situation is the other way around. Since humans generally prefer life with pain (up to a limit) to death, it is worse to kill humans than to cause them suffering.

Not all animals are of equal worth. As Singer says,

> A rejection of speciesism does not imply that all lives are of equal worth. While self-awareness, intelligence, the capacity for meaningful relations with others, and so on are not relevant to the question of inflicting pain— since pain is pain, whatever other capacities, beyond the capacity to feel pain, the being may have—these capacities may be relevant to the question of taking life. It is not arbitrary to hold that the life of a self-aware being, capable of abstract thought, of planning for the future, of complex acts of communication, and so on, is more valuable than the life of a being without these capacities. To see the difference between the issues of inflicting pain and taking life, consider how we would choose within our own species. If we had to choose to save the life of a normal human or a mentally defective human, we would probably choose to save the life of the normal human; but if we had to

choose between preventing pain in the normal human or the mental defective—imagine that both have received painful but superficial injuries, and we only have enough painkiller for one of them—it is not nearly so clear how we ought to choose. The same is true when we consider other species. The evil of pain is, in itself, unaffected by the other characteristics of the being that feels the pain; the value of life is affected by these other characteristics.[23]

So it is irrelevant whether animals and humans are of equal worth *when it comes to suffering*. In suffering we are to be given equal consideration. Since sentience lies at the core of our moral thinking, and language and intelligence lie nearer the periphery, a large part of our morality will have to do with liberating people and animals from suffering.

Regarding animal experimentation, Singer points out that our current practices are speciesist. He admits that some animal experimentation is justified on utilitarian grounds but points out that this argument also justified experimentation on small and retarded children. When the advocate of animal experimentation asks, "Would you be prepared to let thousands of humans die if they could be saved by experimenting on a single animal?" Singer responds, "Would the experimenter be prepared to perform his experiment on an orphaned human infant, if that were the only way to save many lives?" If the experimenter is not prepared to use an orphaned human infant, his readiness to use nonhumans is simple discrimination, since adult apes, cats, mice, and other mammals are more aware of what is happening to them, more self-directed, and, so far as we can tell, at least as sensitive to pain as any human infant."[24]

Although Singer's views on the prejudice of speciesism compel us to rethink the moral status of animals, these views still have problems. They have some of the weaknesses attributed to Bentham—weaknesses inherent to utilitarianism. If jealous John will suffer 100 *dolores* is he is denied my $100, but I will suffer only 80 *dolores* if he steals my $100, John has a moral right to steal my money.

There is a deeper problem with Singer's Preference Act Utilitarianism that resides in the very notion of *preference* itself. For Singer, the morally right act is the one that yields the highest preference satisfaction. No doubt an animal's desire not to suffer outweighs my desire for the taste of meat, but this does not take us to the conclusion that preferences should be considered equally or that preference maximization is the only relevant criterion to be considered.

Even if a dog or mouse is suffering more pain than a child, it is, nevertheless, deeply counterintuitive to say that we have a duty to give the single pain reliever to the dog or mouse. If the child is my child, then I think I have a strong duty to give it to him or her—even if the dog is my dog. The utilitarian might respond that this may be true because the child will live longer than the dog or mouse and have painful memories of the pain for a longer time. Well, imagine that it is an elderly man who is not likely to live longer than the puppy. I still sense that it would be right (or at least not wrong) to give the pill to the elderly man.

In fact, it seems to me that I should prefer my grandfather's vital interests more than those of all the dogs and mice in the world. If my grandfather were in danger of losing a leg and forty dogs were each in danger of losing a leg, and I could either save my grandfather's leg or the legs of all forty dogs, I wouldn't hesitate to operate on my grandfather. No matter how many dogs' legs I could save, I'd feel it my duty to save my grandfather's.

Singer, of course, might argue that this only proves that I am still an immoral speciesist. Isolated intuitions prove nothing. And so they don't. Let's proceed further.

Suppose that ten people will inherit my grandmother's vast wealth. Each has a strong preference that my grandmother die so they can pay their bills. The total of their preference units is 1,000. Suppose my grandmother's desire to continue to live is only 900 units. Wouldn't I—supposing that as a utilitarian I can pull it off without too much guilt—have a duty to kill my grandmother as painlessly as possible?

"No," the Preference Utilitarian exclaims. "For you have forgotten the unintended side effects of creating fear in the minds of others that this might be done to them and so magnifying the negative preference points."

Well, then, all I have to do is be pretty sure that the poison I administer to my grandmother's tea, which induces a heart attack, is the kind that leaves no trace.

In fact, can't the Preference Utilitarian do anything he or she wants, including killing people, taking their property, and breaking promises to them, just so long as his or her preference (or the aggregate preferences of his group) outweigh the preference of the victim? If you suddenly become despondent and no longer value life, why can't I utilitarianly kill you if it satisfies a preference to do so? If I can get you to care less than you do about your Mercedes Benz, and can ensure that only minimal bad side effects will follow, can I not steal your car with complete utilitarian approval?

You might reply that this would be exploitation. Well, why is exploitation wrong? If I desire to exploit you more than you dislike being exploited, doesn't my preference win out over yours?

Likewise, couldn't we justify slavery just by brainwashing the slaves to prefer slavery to freedom or at least not to value freedom more than we value having slaves?

In the end Singer doesn't gain much advantage, if any, over Bentham's crude hedonic calculus. It's simply that instead of people being *pleasure/pain* receptacles, they now become *preference* receptacles.

One final criticism that deeply affects Singer's argument turns on the fact that his Principle of

Equality, the principle of equal consideration, is not really about equality at all. Equal consideration according to what? It is the *what* that is doing all the work. It is the *what* of being rational and living in a specifically complex social structure that justifies us in sending humans, but not dogs or even monkeys to college. Self-consciousness gives higher animals more consideration than merely sentient ones. The Principle of Equality is merely the rule of impartiality: Apply your principles in a disinterested manner, according to the relevant criteria, not according to irrelevant ones. In the words of Aristotle, "Treat equals equally, and unequals unequally." It is purely a formal principle without any substantive force, one that could be used (as it was by Aristotle) to justify slavery and to justify the secret killing of innocents. It is compatible with Nietzsche's Superman, with his magnificent will (read "preference") for power.

Let's sum up the discussion of Singer's utilitarianism version of animal liberation. He has made a good case for rejecting speciesism and for regarding animals as morally considerable. Probably some higher animals are persons with strong claims to better treatment than we are affording them. What isn't clear is that his or any brand of utilitarianism, which compares hedonic states of humans and animals, is a plausible moral theory. Most of us will find it counterintuitive to prefer dogs and mice to our friends and relatives or to any normal human at all. Whether we are just speciesists is a question we must investigate further. We turn next to a theory that tries to deal with this issue within the framework of broad anthropocentrism.

5. THE SPLIT LEVEL THEORY

The Split Level theory is the name of a position, first set forth by Martin Benjamin, that aims at correcting the four positions above.[25] The Cartesian No Status view and the Indirect Obligation view contain the insight that rational self-consciousness endows human beings with special worth, but they err on two counts: (1) in holding that animals don't have this quality at all (we know now that some do to some extent), and (2) in holding that only rational self-consciousness gives one any rights, or makes one morally considerable. At the other extreme, the Equal Status view and the Equal Consideration view recognize the importance of sentience and the ability to suffer as morally considerable, but these views tend to underemphasize the aspect of rational self-consciousness as setting the majority of humans apart from the majority of animals.

The Split Level view combines the insights of both types of theories. It is nonspeciest in that it recognizes that some animals, like chimpanzees and dolphins, may have an element of rational self-consciousness and some humans may lack it (for example, fetuses and severely retarded people). The Split Level view recognizes that both sentience and rational self-consciousness are important in working out a global interspecies morality. This view rejects Regan's Sanctity of Life egalitarianism, but it also rejects Singer's equal consideration of interests principle. Rational self-consciousness does make a difference. A higher sort of being does emerge with humanity (and perhaps some higher primates and dolphins), so we ought to treat humans with special respect.

This theory distinguishes between *trivial needs* and *important needs*. It says that with regard to important needs, human needs override those of animals, but important animal needs override trivial human needs. For example, the need for sustenance and the need not to be harmed are important needs, whereas the need for having our tastes satisfied is a trivial need. So although humans have the right to kill animals if animals are necessary for health or life, we do not have the right to kill higher animals simply to satisfy our tastes. If there are equally good ways of finding nourishment, then humans have an obligation to seek those ways and permit animals to live unmolested.

This applies to higher animals who have a developed nervous system, enabling them to suffer and develop a sense of consciousness. Since no evidence shows that termites or mosquitoes have a sense of self, it is permissible to exterminate the termites and kill the mosquitoes when they threaten our interests. Of course, if we someday discover that termites and mosquitos are highly self-conscious, we will be obliged to act differently, but until we have evidence to that effect, we may continue our present practices.

The Split Level theory has been criticized as being unabashedly anthropocentric. Why should human criteria, such as rationality and self-consciousness, be the litmus tests for moral consideration? The response is that the capacity for moral agency sets rational agents such as humans apart, giving them inherent worth. Humans have special rights, but also special responsibilities to care for nature.

Which of these five theories is correct? The No Status theory and the Indirect Obligation theory seem to underrate the worth of animals, but the Equal Status theories seem to overrate it, leaving some form of the Split Level theory a victor by default. One would like to have a stronger argument, and I can appreciate that other thoughtful people have intuitions different from my own.

Vegetarianism

In the beginning of this chapter we noted some facts regarding animal mistreatment. Free-range grazing and farming have been largely replaced by the complicated technology of agribusiness, which promotes an impersonal process that tortures chicken, turkeys, cows, calves, pigs, and other animals. Since we have a moral obligation to eliminate gratuitous suffering whenever possible, we should cease to participate in the factory farming food production of our society. Rather, we should oppose it. Since more than 95 percent of the (nonfish) meat that reaches the market is factory bred, we have a strong duty to refrain from eating most of the meat that is available today. There is good reason to refrain from eating all meat. Why kill any animal when it's not necessary to do so? With very little effort, we can have a healthy diet consisting of vegetables, fruits, grains, and nuts. If our health depended on meat, as is the case in arctic climates and some less developed cultures, the injunction against causing unnecessary pain and suffering could be overridden. But this is not our culture. In fact, we can live healthier lives without meat. Given the hormones and antibiotics routinely added to cattle and poultry feed, and chemicals that may be added later, as the meat is processed and readied for sale, meat is becoming a health hazard. Since most dairy product production also involves cruel treatment of animals in factory farms, we should try to use only milk products produced from free-range farm animals.

Why do otherwise good people eat meat? When I ask my friends and students why they eat meat, they say they've just never thought about it—so deeply is it ingrained in our culture. Yet they would not think of eating dogs, who are typically not as intelligent as the pigs they eat. Or they say that they have a passion for steak or veal. Or it is a strong habit of meat eating. But habit and taste preference are not good moral reasons. Habit is simply a culturally derived practice, and taste is an aesthetic consideration. Morality trumps both cultural practices and aesthetics. What would you think if I said I love the look of red blood that bursts out of the veins of my victims as I cut their arteries? You'd rightly think that I was either crazy or morally depraved. But with the backing of culture and in the name of big business (which the meat industry is), we kill helpless animals for aesthetic reasons. Looked at objectively, from the point of view of a common Core Morality that requires us to avoid causing unnecessary pain and suffering and to do good whenever we can do so with minimal effort, meat eating is a vicious practice. Reflective moral people in a society like ours, where other kinds of food are readily available, become vegetarians.

Vegetarianism makes good sense from an energy-conservation point of view. We would save 90 percent of nutritional energy if we ate the grain and beans now fed to factory animals instead of the animals themselves. The argument, called the Trophic Levels argument, goes like this:

No transfer of energy from one trophic level to another is 100 percent. In fact, only about 10 percent of the chemical energy available at one trophic level is transferred and stored in usable form in the bodies of the organisms at the next trophic level. In other words, about 90 percent of the chemical energy is degraded and lost as heat to the environment. This is sometimes called the *ten percent law.* The percentage transfer of useful energy between trophic levels is called *ecological efficiency,* or food chain efficiency. For example, suppose a man eats some grain or rice containing 10,000 units of energy (calories). Ninety percent of the energy is lost in the transfer, so only 1,000 units reach him. Now suppose that a steer eats that same grain, containing 10,000 energy units, and the steer is slaughtered and eventually fed to the man. The steer got the 1,000 units, of which the man only gets 100 units, 90 percent of the energy being lost (as heat energy) in the transference process. Figure 13–1 illustrates this pyramid of energy transfer in aquatic grazing systems. Original producers of food are the phytoplankton, which are eaten by zooplankton, which in turn are eaten by fish, which in turn are eaten by humans. There is a 90 percent usable energy loss (which is turned into heat) at each trophic level. In this case the fishermen get only about 10 units of energy for every 10,000 original units. It would be 1,000 times more energy efficient if we could acquire a taste for phytoplankton salad!

Decreased efficiency occurs as we increase the distance between the primary producers of food and the ultimate consumers. We would get a lot more food value if we ate the beans and grains that are fed to animals, rather than the animals themselves. More than 80 or 90 percent of food energy could be saved in the process,

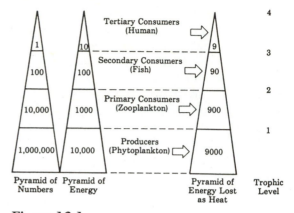

Figure 13.1

and thus more food could be made available to feed the global population.

So vegetarianism is both rational and moral. There are no compelling reasons for prohibiting the eating of dead farm animals, of course, but I doubt that this will hold much interest for meat lovers. Land presently used to graze animals can often be better used to grow food crops. Mary Ann Warren has pointed out that there may be environmental reasons for refraining from grazing free-range animals, for they greatly damage the ecology of fragile arid lands. She writes, "It might be better to do less grazing of domestic animals on marginal land, and go on feeding some animals with grain."[26] A compromise could be made, letting animals graze on free range, but feeding them mostly cultivated crops; those animals could provide our eggs and dairy products.

Some philosophers argue that if we didn't eat large quantities of meat, many domestic animals, such as cows and pigs would never live, since they are raised for food. Given that some life is better than none, we are justified in killing them for food. But this is a bad argument. We wouldn't breed extra people simply because "more life is better than none." It would be better that we didn't bring domestic animals into the world than to do so and kill them for food.

There are exceptions to strict vegetarianism. Sometimes animal populations need to be culled.

For example, many of our forests have too many deer, so hunting deer for food is sometimes ecologically warranted. I suppose eating insects, phytoplankton, and small sea creatures who lack a developed nervous system that produces a minimal sense of self-consciousness is permissible. Anyone care for termites for lunch?

Animal Experiments

We noted that millions of animals die in laboratory experiments each year. Richard Ryder puts the figure between 100 and 300 million worldwide.[27] Many of these experiments have been shown to be unnecessary and unjustified. More needs to be done to avoid unnecessary duplication and to enforce the laws requiring the use of anesthetics. Andrew Rowan and others have argued that alternative, nonanimal testing procedures, such as CAT and PET scans, in vitro cell and tissue cultures, and autopsy studies, can replace animal experiments in many instances. For example, CAT and PET scans have been valuable in the study of Parkinson's disease, visual physiology, and musculoskeletal tumors.[28]

Nevertheless, Regan's principle of rejecting all animal experimentation is to be rejected. Most proponents of alternative nonanimal testing procedures concede that the cessation of animal experimentation at the present time or in the foreseeable future would have serious adverse consequences for humans. If we accept the Split Level theory discussed above, then experimentation, with safeguards, should continue.

It is vitally important that we eliminate or control serious disease (cancer, heart disease, and infectious diseases such as malaria and AIDS), and to do this animal experiments are often necessary. Medical research on animals has helped bring about the treatment of diabetes, cancer, stroke, and heart ailments. "Dogs were used in the discovery of insulin and monkeys were used in the development of a polio vaccine."[29] We have no reason to believe that we can discover new treatments for diseases without experimenting on animals. We should

then use every safeguard in preventing abuse as we carry out our experiments. Most, if not all, university research centers now have institutional animal care and use committees to review and approve experimental protocols. But we can eliminate animal experiments in testing cosmetics, football helmets, and other items not vital to human flourishing. We should either do without these luxuries (cosmetics and football helmets—we might have to resort to "touch football") or find other ways of testing the products.

Singer, more moderate than Regan, would accept that some experimentation is justified. "Experiments serving no direct and urgent purpose should stop immediately, and in the remaining areas of research, methods involving animals should be replaced as soon as possible by alternative methods not involving animals."[30] However, this may be too restrictive. Henry Sackin has pointed out:

> Very often we simply do not know whether a path of scientific inquiry will ultimately lead to something important or useful. The discovery of the structure of DNA in 1953 would have been regarded by animal advocates as inappropriate and irrelevant. Yet it forms the basis of molecular biology that now makes it possible to genetically engineer pest resistant crops and provide adequate and inexpensive insulin for diabetics. Only those of us who possess divine omniscience can argue that certain animal experiments are less important than others. We simply do not know what is or is not important until after we understand the implications of that knowledge. This may explain why Nobel Prizes are often awarded years after the original discoveries were actually made.[31]

Hunting for Sport, Furs, and Zoos

Unless we subscribe to an egalitarian theory of animal rights, hunting for food seems morally permissible, and in some cases hunting may be warranted in keeping the animal population down. But hunting primarily for sport, trophies, or the fun of killing are activities much harder to justify from a moral perspective.[32] Perhaps they are impossible to justify. Here is a hunter's description of his killing of an elephant:

> The elephant stood broadside to me, at upwards of one hundred yards, and his attention at the moment was occupied with the dogs. I fired at his shoulder, and secured him with a single shot. The ball caught him high on the shoulder-blade, rendering him instantly lame; and before the echo on the bullet could reach my ear, I plainly saw the elephant was mine. I resolved to devote a short time to the contemplation of this noble elephant before laying him low; . . . I quickly kindled a fire and put on the kettle, and in a few minutes my coffee was prepared. There I sat in my forest home, coolly sipping my coffee, with one of the finest elephants in Africa awaiting my pleasure beside a neighboring tree . . .
>
> Having admired the elephant for a considerable time, I resolved to make experiments for vulnerable points. [The hunter misses the vulnerable points, further wounding the elephant, but finally succeeds in delivering a fatal shot.] Large tears now trickled from [the elephant's] eyes, which he slowly shut and opened, his colossal frame quivered convulsively, and falling on his side, he expired.[33]

Reflecting on this passage should be sufficient reason to condemn hunting for trophies.

If furs are necessary for people to keep warm, we may legitimately kill animals for their furs, but if less violent ways of producing clothes are available, we should take them. I confess that, as a hiker, my feet prefer leather shoes, but we probably can produce suitable nonleather alternatives. Of course, we could use the carcasses of dead animals for our leather. Aside from that, if we can produce good synthetic shoes, we should begin to do so. Leather sofas and coats probably are not morally acceptable since we can produce good-quality sofas and coats in other ways.

Zoos present a special problem. On the one hand, they provide a splendid source of amusement and education, and sometimes even opportunities for scientific research. On the other hand, keeping wild animals in captivity involves considerable suffering. Animals must be captured, removed from their native habitats, transported in confining vehicles, and maintained in an artificial environment. Do the benefits of zoos outweigh the suffering caused in removing animals from the wild and maintaining them in alien environments? Dale Jamieson has argued that they do not, concluding that zoos are not morally justified.[34] He argues that our amusement is not a good reason to perpetrate suffering, that we might be better educated about animals by viewing films and listening to lectures, and that very little research really goes on in most zoos. Moreover, zoos encourage dangerous speciesism:

> [Zoos] teach us a false sense of our place in the natural order. The means of confinement mark a difference between humans and animals. They are there at our pleasure, to be used for our purposes. Morality and perhaps our very survival require that we learn to live as one species among many rather than as one species over many. To do this, we must forget what we learn at zoos. Because what zoos teach us is false and dangerous, both humans and animals will be better off when they are abolished.[35]

Is Jamieson correct in advocating the abolition of zoos? Although his considerations have merit, the counterarguments need to be heard. Granted, the amusement factor is not itself a good reason for causing suffering; nonetheless, zoos can be made enjoyable habits for at least some animals. Forest-like habitats for chimpanzees and monkeys, large prairie areas for lions and tigers, and so forth, can approximate the wild, providing spacious prairies in which to roam, while at the same time protecting them from predators of the wild. Granted, they may become partially domesticated in zoos. Why is that wrong? There may be a presumption against taking an animal out of its native habitat, but surely this can be overridden if it will benefit the animal itself. Animals' life expectancy is typically greater in the zoo than in the wild. They are assured food and shelter, and they may very well flourish. At least we must do all we can to assure that they do. I grant that there's a deep issue here about what is "natural" and how we are to understand "benefitting animals." Perhaps it will turn out that some species of animals benefit and some do not. A lot more research on animal psychology needs to be done, but I confess I see no argument enjoining an absolute prohibition on domesticating wild animals.

Furthermore, Jamieson may underestimate the educational value of zoos. Here I have no statistics but can only attest to the joy and wonder I felt as a child—and still feel—when I visited the Brookfield Zoo in Illinois. Watching monkeys at play, noting the resemblance between chimpanzees and humans, hearing the lion roar, gazing at the long neck of the giraffe, studying sharks and dolphins, and learning to identify snakes constituted one of the most profound learning experiences of my childhood, and I imagine that others can testify to the same experience.

Animals in zoos should be treated kindly, and conditions must be such that they benefit from these conditions. If we can do this, then zoos can probably be justified. Perhaps safari parks should replace zoos for larger animals.

Conclusion

All conscious beings are morally considerable, since they can suffer and be aided in flourishing; but unless we want to stop killing harmful (to us) bacteria, we can agree that some animals are more valuable than others. Those that have a sense of personal identity, are rationally self-conscious, and have plans and projects, deserve special consideration. So the Split Level view seems, on balance, to be the correct position. Regarding important needs, human needs in general override the needs of lower animals, but regarding trivial needs, the important needs of animals override the nonvital needs of humans. Speciesism is a vice, like racism, if it gives an irrational sense of privilege to humans simply because they are human, but because humanity as a species is superior to other species, no evil is involved in developing general policies that reflect that fact.

The basic principle that should be at work in our relations with animals is the Principle of Nonmaleficence. We ought not to cause unnecessary harm or suffering. Is there a better way to live and eat? If so, we should take it. Do we need to do all of the research and animal experimentation in which we are presently engaged? If not, we should cut out the unnecessary experimentation. Are hunting and trapping necessary for human flourishing? If not, we should work toward the elimination of these activities. For the rest, we should be kind to all creatures of the earth, trying to make this cruel jungle into a closer approximation of the Garden of Eden.

Look again at Regan's three goals: (1) The total abolition of the use of animals in science; (2) the total dissolution of commercial animal agriculture; and (3) the total elimination of commercial and sport hunting and trapping. If the Split Level analysis is correct, all of these goals may be rejected as absolutist, but each has a point. Except in situations of special need, we should cease eating meat, but free-range produced dairy products are permissible. Abuses must be eliminated in research, and animal factories must be abolished. Hunting and trapping for sport should, in general, be prohibited, but exceptions might be permitted—for example, when a deer population is reaching a dangerous surplus and a die-back is likely. Animals might be trapped as humanely as possible for fur where severe climates exist.

Schematically put, here are the results of our analysis:

JUSTIFIED ACTIVITIES

1. Using milk products from free-range animals, especially if they are necessary for a community's well-being or survival. Note that since cows and goats eat grasses that are not digestible by humans, no energy loss occurs when these cows and goats are eaten.

2. Important biomedical experiments to increase scientific knowledge and find cures for diseases. However, safeguards must be built into these experiments, minimizing the harm done to the animals. Unnecessary duplication should be prevented.

3. Zoos enable city dwellers to learn about animals. They must meet minimum standards of decency for animals, including spacious areas so that cats such as lions and tigers can roam.

4. Hunting for food or when an animal population is out of control, but not for sport.

5. Trapping for fur where severe climatic conditions exist and perhaps where this is the traditional clothing of indigenous people.

ACTIVITIES NOT JUSTIFIED

1. Animal factories, where the suffering of animals is terrible and unnecessary.

2. Eating meat that involves killing animals, except when hunting to keep a population under control.

3. Nonvital experimentation, such as for cosmetics or football helmets.

4. Other luxury activities for which animals are unnecessarily exploited: hunting for sport, trapping for fashion fur, bullfights.

At the end of *Animal Liberation,* Singer issues a challenge for us all.

> Human beings have the power to continue to oppress other species forever, or until we make this planet unsuitable for living beings. Will our tyranny continue, proving that we really are the selfish tyrants that the most cynical of the poets and philosophers have always said we are? Or will we rise to the challenge and prove our capacity for genuine altruism by ending our ruthless exploitation of the species in our power, not because we are forced to do so by rebels or terrorists, but because we recognize that our position is morally indefensible?[36]

While we have warrant for using some animals for human good, we ought to modify many of our practices, realizing that animals have interests and are morally significant.[37]

Study Questions

1. Discuss the two quotations at the beginning of this chapter. Is either of them true or close to the truth? Explain.
2. What are the implications of the moral principle "Do no unnecessary harm"? Would it lead us to abolish factory farming? eating meat? some animal experimentation? all animal experimentation? hunting? Explain your position.
3. Do animals have rights? Are they morally considerable? Discuss the five theories on the moral status of animals outlined in this chapter. Which position seems the best to you? Would that position call for changes in your actions?
4. Is it morally permissible to eat meat? Under what circumstances would it be moral or immoral to do so?
5. Discuss the trophic pyramid. What are the implications for our diets?
6. Is hunting for sport morally permissible? Consider the description of a hunter's killing an elephant in the section on hunting in this chapter.
7. Robert White and Henry Sackin, among others, have argued that without experimentation on animals the cures for many diseases would not have been discovered. Does this justify experimentation on animals? Explain your answer.

Endnotes

1. The Office of Technology Assessment (OTA) put the number of animals produced for laboratory experiments each year at 35 to 50 million. Andrew Rowan, who has made one of the most thorough studies of the matter, told me that he had downscaled his estimate from between 60 and 70 million animals to a figure close to that of the OTA. For helpful discussions of the scientific literature on the ethics of animal research, see M. T. Phillips and J. A. Sechzer, *Animal Research and Ethical Conflict* (New York: Springer-Verlag, 1989) and Andrew Rowan, *Of Mice, Models and Men: A Critical Evaluation of Animal Research* (Albany, NY: State University of New York Press, 1984).

2. The material in this section on animal experimentation is taken from Richard Ryder's *Victims of Science: The Use of Animals in Research* (London: National Anti-Vivisection Society, 1983); Andrew Rowan, op. cit.; Peter Singer, *Animal Liberation*, (2d ed. New York: New York Review of Books, 1990); Muriel the Lady Dowding, "Furs and Cosmetics: Too High a Price?" in *Animals, Men and Morals* ed. Stanley and Rosline Godlovitch and John Harris (New York: Taplinger Publishing Co, 1972), and Phillip Zwerling, "Animal Rights, Human Wrongs," *Animal Agenda* (December 1985).

3. Singer, op. cit., 29f. Other reports tell of dogs that are driven insane with electric shocks so that scientists can study the effects of insanity. Cats are deprived of sleep until they die. Primates have been restrained for months in steel chairs allowing no movement, and elephants have been given LSD to study aggression. Legs have been cut off mice to study how they walk on the stumps, and polar bears have been drowned in vats of crude oil to study the effect of oil spills in polar regions.

4. Singer, op. cit., 80.

5. The material in this paragraph is based on John Robbins' *Diet for a New America* (Walpole, NH: Stillpoint Publishing, 1987).

6. James Rachels, "Vegetarianism," in *World Hunger and Moral Obligation,* William Aiken and Hugh LaFollette (Englewood Cliffs, NJ: Prentice Hall, 1977), 180–93.

7. René Descartes, *Discourse on Method,* in *The Philosophical Works of Descartes,* ed. Haldane and Ross, (Cambridge: Cambridge University Press, 1911) vol. I.

8. From Nicholas Fontaine, *Memoirs,* quoted in Peter Singer, *Animal Liberation* (New York: Avon, 1976), 220. Nineteenth-century British philosopher P. Austin modifies this Cartesian view (named after Descartes) by stating that while we have no positive duties to animals, we ought not to be cruel to them. "Animals should be treated with personal indifference; they should not be petted, they should not be ill-treated. It should always be remembered that they are *our slaves,* not our equals and for this reason it is well to keep up such practices as hunting and fishing, driving and riding, merely to demonstrate in a practical way man's dominion."

9. William Whewell, *Lectures,* cited in *Animal Rights and Human Obligations,* ed. Peter Singer and Tom Regan (Englewood Cliffs, NJ: Prentice Hall, 1976), 131.

10. Cited in M. T. Phillips and J. A. Sechzer, op. cit., 75.

11. Some Christian vegetarians point to this passage, which instructs humans to eat only plants, as a justification for vegetarianism. Meat eating was permitted only after the flood in Genesis 9.

12. Thomas Aquinas, *Contra Gentiles* (London: Benziger Brothers, 1928) Book III, Part II, ch. 112.

13. Immanuel Kant, *Lectures on Ethics,* trans. Louis Infield (New York: Harper & Row, 1963), 239.

14. K. McCabe, "Who Will Live, Who Will Die." *The Washingtonian* (August 1986).

15. Tom Regan, "The Case for Animal Rights" in *In Defense of Animals,* ed. Peter Singer (Oxford: Blackwell, 1985), 13–26.

16. Ibid, 13.

17. For a fuller discussion of this point, see my article "On Equal Human Worth: A Critique of Contemporary Egalitarianism" in *Equality,* ed. L. Pojman and R. Westmoreland (Oxford: Oxford University Press, 1997).

18. There are exceptions to this point. We do establish social contracts with our pets. If I give my dog or cat reasonable expectations and he or she does the same for me, so that we rely on one another, this may well constitute a moral contract.

19. Tom Regan, *The Case for Animal Rights* (Berkeley, CA: University of California Press, 1983), 284f.

20. Jeremy Bentham, *The Principles of Morals and Legislation* (1789), ch. 17, section 1. The main weakness of Bentham's account is that it equates humans and animals, so if a chicken and a child are suffering equal pain and we have only one pain reliever, we have a genuine moral dilemma on our hands. We might consider giving it to the chicken.

21. Peter Singer, *Animal Liberation,* op. cit., 5.

22. Peter Singer, "Animals and the Value of Life," in *Matters of Life and Death,* ed. Tom Regan (New York: Random House, 1980), 236.

23. Peter Singer, *Animal Liberation,* op. cit., p. 22.

24. Peter Singer, *Animal Rights and Human Obligation* (Englewood Cliffs, NJ: Prentice Hall, 1976).

25. Martin Benjamin, "Ethics and Animal Consciousness," *Social Ethics,* ed. Thomas Mappes and Jane Zembaty (Englewood Cliffs, NJ: Prentice-Hall, 1982); Mary Anne Warren, reprinted from *The Monist,* vol. 57, no. 1 (January 1973); Donald Van De-Veer, "Interspecific Justice" in *People, Penguins, and Plastic Trees,* ed. Donald Van DeVeer and Christine Pierce, (Belmont, CA: Wadsworth Publishing Co, 1986); Louis Lombardi, "Inherent Worth, Respect, and Rights," *Environmental Ethics* 5 (fall 1983). See also James Sterba, "Environmental Justice: Reconciling Anthropocentric and Nonanthropocentric Ethics" in *Environmental Ethics,* ed. Pojman (Belmont, CA: Wadsworth Publishing Co, 1998). Warren's position is that all sentient animals, capable of having experiences, have moral rights, but they are not of equal strength as those of persons.

26. Mary Anne Warren in correspondence, 25 January 1991.

27. Ryder, op. cit.

28. Rowan, op. cit.

29. Henry Sackin, "An Ethical Basis for Animal Experimentation" (unpublished paper).

30. Peter Singer, *Animal Liberation,* op. cit., 32.

31. Sackin, op. cit.

32. Robert Loftin, "The Morality of Hunting," *Environmental Ethics* 6 (fall 1984).

33. Quoted in Richard Carrington, *Elephants* (New York: Chatto and Windus, 1958) 158.

34. Dale Jamieson, "Against Zoos" in *Reflecting on Nature,* ed. Lori Gruen and Dale Jamieson (New York: Oxford University Press, 1994), 291–298.

35. Op. cit., 298.

36. Peter Singer, op. cit., 258.

37. John Kleinig, Michael Levin, Trudy Pojman, and Sterling Harwood made helpful criticisms on a previous draft of this chapter, for which I am grateful.

Chapter 14

World Hunger and Population

[Everyone has] the right to a standard of living adequate for the health and well being of himself and his family, including food.

UNITED NATIONS DECLARATION ON HUMAN RIGHTS, 1948

Feeding the hungry in some countries only keeps them alive longer to produce more hungry bellies and disease and death.

JOSEPH FLETCHER, "Give If It Helps But Not If It Hurts"

More than one third of the world goes to bed hungry each night.[1] Ten thousand people starve to death each day. Nearly a quarter of the human race lives in absolute poverty, with incomes less than one dollar a day. Eight hundred forty-one million people are chronically undernourished, and the United Nations Food and Agriculture Organization (FAO) estimates that almost half of these are children. In Africa the *number* of hungry people has more than doubled, and the *proportion* of the population that is hungry has increased 13 percent in the past twenty-five years. The FAO predicts that if current trends continue, 265 million Africans (the size of the present population of the United States) will suffer hunger in 2010, an increase from 148 million in 1981 and 215 million in 1992. While famines have ravaged parts of Africa and Asia, another third of the world, the industrialized West, lives in relative affluence, wasting food or overeating. The rich get richer and the poor get poorer.

World hunger is one of the most intractable problems facing humankind today. It is an environmental issue because it is tied to population growth, deforestation, soil erosion, and the just distribution of resources. Poor farmers in the rainforest cannot afford to worry about saving endangered species or the rainforest itself, because they are compelled to work to feed their families, even at the expense of the environment. World hunger is a global environmental issue. What can be done about it? What obligations, if any, do we in the affluent West have to distant, needy people, those who are hungry or starving? To what extent should population policies be tied to hunger relief? These are the questions discussed in this chapter.

I will discuss three responses to these questions: (1) the neo-Malthusian response set forth by Garret Hardin; (2) the conservative (or libertarian) response represented by Thomas Hobbes, Robert Nozick, and others; and (3) the liberal response, exemplified by Peter Singer and Richard Watson. After this I will suggest alternative positions, taking into consideration the valid insights of each of these other positions.

Four Ethical Responses to World Hunger

The contrast between neo-Malthusians and liberals can hardly be greater. Liberals assert that we have a duty to feed the hungry in famine-ridden areas either because the hungry have a right to it or because of utilitarian reasons maximizing welfare or happiness. Neo-Malthusians deny such a right and assert that we have an opposite utilitarian duty to refrain from feeding the hungry in famine-ridden areas. Conservatives take the middle road in this debate, asserting that although we do not have a duty to feed the hungry, it is permissible and praiseworthy to do so. It is an act of supererogation, an act going beyond the call of duty. We begin with the neo-Malthusians.

NEO-MALTHUSIANISM

The Reverend Thomas Malthus (1766–1834) held that population size tends to outrun food production, leading to misery, until war, disease, famine and other disasters restore a natural balance. Partly due to modern agricultural technology and the spread of birth control devices, Malthus's predictions haven't been universally fulfilled. In the United States and Canada, for example, food production has been substantially above what is needed for their populations. Neo-Malthusians are ecologists who accept Malthus's basic thesis but modify it in the light of technological innovation. A nation that is not maintaining the proper food-to-population ratio should not be helped from the outside by increments of food. To feed such sick societies is, to quote Alan Gregg, former vice president of the Rockefeller Foundation, like feeding a cancer. "Cancerous growths demand food; but, as far as I know, they have never been cured by getting it."[2]

The most prominent neo-Malthusian today is Garrett Hardin, Emeritus Professor of Human Biology at the University of California at Santa Barbara, who in a series of articles set forth the idea of Lifeboat Ethics.[3] Hardin's position can be succinctly stated through three metaphors that he has made famous: "lifeboat," "tragedy of the commons," and "the ratchet." Let us examine his use of each of these.

1. Lifeboat The world is compared to a sea in which a few lifeboats (the affluent nations) are surrounded by hordes of drowning people (the populations of the poor nations). Each lifeboat has a limited carrying capacity, which is such that it cannot possibly take on more than a tiny fraction of the drowning without jeopardizing the lives of its passengers. Besides, the need for a safety factor always dictates that we ought to leave a healthy margin between the actual number on board and the possible number. The optimum population is somewhat below the maximum population. According to Hardin, the affluent nations currently are right around that optimum figure, probably beyond it, so it is self-destructive to rescue the world's poor. Not only must we adhere to a population policy of zero-growth, but we must have stringent immigration policies that prevent immigrants from swamping our boat.

2. Tragedy of the Commons Imagine a public field (a "commons") where shepherds have been grazing their sheep for centuries. Because of the richness of the field and the poverty of the shepherds, the field is never overgrazed. Now there comes a time when the carrying capacity of the field is reaching its limit. At this point it is in the short-term rational self-interest of each farmer to add one more sheep to the commons in spite of its limitations. The farmer reasons that by grazing yet one more sheep, he will be reaping a positive factor of 1 (the value brought on by the extra sheep) and losing only a fraction of the negative unit 1, the loss of the field's resources, since all of the herdsmen share that equally whether they participate in overgrazing or not. So it is in each shepherd's interest to overgraze, but if too many shepherds act in their short-term self-interest in this way it soon will be against their interest, for the pasture will be ruined. Hence the tragedy of the commons! A similar tragedy is occurring in our use of natural resources. We are in danger of depleting the world's resources through wanton overuse. To prevent such a tragedy, we must have mutually agreed upon, mutually coercive laws that govern population increase, overgrazing, overfishing, deforestation, pollution, and the like. Each nation must manage its own commons, and if one fails to do so, it must be left to its own misery. Benevolent intervention on the part of misguided do-gooders is likely only to increase the overall misery. This leads to the next metaphor.

3. The Ratchet Hardin argues that there is a natural relationship in ecosystems such that once a species has overshot the environment's carrying capacity, nature takes care of the situation by causing a die-back on the population of the species and eventually restores a balance (Fig. 14–1). For example, when there is a serious decline in the natural predators of deer in an area, the deer population tends to increase exponentially until it overshoots the carrying capacity of the land for deer. The land cannot provide for this increase, so the deer begin to starve, causing a die-back in their population, until conditions are such that they can again increase at a normal pace. The same relationship applies to human population systems. Once people in a given area have exceeded the carrying capacity of the environment, there will come a period of scarcity, resulting, à la Malthus, in famine, disease, and war over scarce resources, which results in a die-back or lowering of the population below the level of the carrying capacity. Nature will take care of

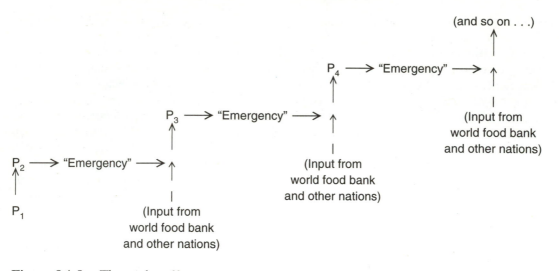

Figure 14-1   *The ratchet effect*

the tragedy of the commons. When people refuse to constrain their procreative instincts, nature intervenes and does it for them.

Now let some well-meaning altruists intervene to thwart nature's iron law. The altruists send food to the starving, fending off the effects of famine for a time. But what happens? The people procreate and the population increases even further beyond the carrying capacity of the land. Soon there are even more people starving, so another even greater altruistic effort is needed to stave off the worsening situation. A herculean effort is accomplished, and the population is saved once again. But where does this process lead? Only to an eventual disaster. The ratchet effect keeps raising the level of the population without coming to terms with the natural relationship of the population to its environment, and that is where Malthus's law is valid (Fig. 14–2). Sending food to those who are not taking voluntary steps to curb their population size is like feeding a cancer.

For Hardin, it is wrong to give aid to those who are starving in overpopulated countries because of the ratchet effect. It only causes more misery in the long run. "How can we help a for-

eign country to escape overpopulation? Clearly the worst thing we can do is send food. . . . Atomic bombs would be kinder. For a few moments the misery would be acute, but it would soon come to an end for most of the people, leaving a very few survivors to suffer thereafter."[4]

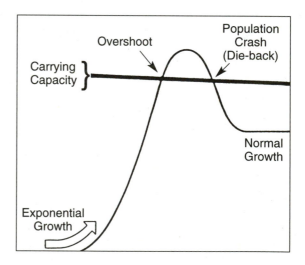

Figure 14-2   *The relation of the carrying capacity of an environment to exponential population growth*

Furthermore, we have a natural duty to our children and to posterity to maintain the health of the planet as a whole. By using resources now for this short-term fix, we rob our children and future generations of their rightful inheritance. The claims of future people in this case override those of distant people.

In summary, Hardin has three arguments against giving aid to the poor in distant lands: (1) It will threaten our lifeboat by affecting the safety factor and causing our carrying capacity to become strained; (2) It will only increase the misery due to the ratchet effect; and (3) It will threaten the welfare of our descendants to whom we have prior obligations. For all of these reasons we are morally required not to give aid to the hungry.

What can be said about this kind of reasoning? Is Hardin right about the world's situation? Let us examine the arguments more closely. Consider (1), the lifeboat argument. Is the metaphor itself appropriate? Are we really so nicely separate from the poor of the world? Or are we vitally interdependent, profiting from the same conditions that contribute to the misery of the underdeveloped nations? Haven't colonialization and commercial arrangements worked to increase the disparity between the rich and the poor nations of the earth? We extract cheap raw materials from poor nations and sell those nations expensive manufactured goods (for example, radios, cars, computers, and weapons) instead of appropriate agricultural goods and training. The structure of tariffs and internal subsidies discriminates selectively against underdeveloped nations. Multinational corporations place strong inducements on poor countries to produce cash crops such as coffee and cocoa instead of food crops needed to feed their own people. Besides this, the United States and other Western nations have often used foreign aid to bolster dictatorships such as the Somoza regime in Nicaragua and the military juntas in Chile and El Salvador, which have resisted social change that would have redistributed wealth more equi-

tably. For example, in 1973 when President Allende of Chile requested aid from the United States, not only was he turned down, but our government also aided in bringing his reformist government to ruin. When the military junta that replaced Allende took power and promised to maintain American business interests, eight times the amount of aid Allende had asked for was given to that government.

Hardin's lifeboat metaphor grimly obscures the fact that we have profited and are profiting from the economic conditions in the third world. Perhaps a more apt metaphor that "lifeboat" might be "octopus"—a powerful multinational corporation octopus with tentacles clutching weapons and reaching out into diverse regions of the globe. Our nation protects, encourages, and even intervenes in the affairs of other nations on the basis of its relations to these corporations. But if that is the case, how can we dissociate ourselves from the plight of people in these countries? Keeping the poor out of our lifeboats might be permissible if we hadn't built the boats out of rubber taken from them in the first place. The fact is, even if you can justify the commercial dealings we have with the rest of the world, we are already involved with the hungry of the world in a way that the lifeboat metaphor belies.

The question of distributive justice haunts Hardins argument. He admits that ofttimes survival policies are unjust, but he argues as a utilitarian that survival overrides justice, that it is better for some to survive unjustly than to be just and let everyone perish. "Complete injustice, complete catastrophe." But this fails to consider a whole middle range of possibilities where justice could be at least a contributing factor to a solution that would take the need for one's own survival into consideration. Justice would demand that some attention be given to redistributing the world's wealth. At present the United States, with less than 4.5 percent of the world's population, consumes some 35 percent of its food (much of it thrown into garbage cans or rotting in storage silos) and 38 percent of its energy and is responsible for creating 33 percent of the world's pollution. If Hardin is so concerned about preserving the world's purity and resources for posterity, justice would require that we sacrifice the overfed, overweight, overnourished, overconsuming, overpolluting, greedy Americans who throw into garbage cans more food than some nations eat.

Regarding the carrying capacity and ratchet effect considerations, several objections are in order. First of all, how does Hardin know which nations have exceeded their carrying capacity? The very notion of the carrying capacity, given our technological ability to produce new varieties of food, is a flexible one. Perhaps experts can identify some regions of the earth (for example, deserts) where the land can sustain only a few people, but one ought to be cautious in pronouncing that Bangladesh or India or some region of the Sahal in Africa are in that condition. Too many variables abound. New agricultural or fishing methods or cultural practices may offset the validity of technical assessments.

Second, Hardin is too dogmatic in proclaiming the lawlike dictum that to aid the poor is to cause the escalation of misery. Granted, we can make things worse by merely giving food handouts, and a population policy is needed to prevent the ratchet effect against which Hardin rightly warns. However, intelligent ways exist to aid, such as providing agricultural instruction and technological know-how to nations committed to responsible population policies, promoting mutually beneficial international trade agreements, and seeking ways to eradicate conditions that cause famine and malnutrition. We should also set a good example of what a just, disciplined, frugal society should be. But to dismiss these options out of hand and simply advocate pushing people off our lifeboat is as oversimplistic as it is cruel.

Finally, Hardin's food-population theory ignores the evidence that, contrary to ratchet projections, population growth is affected by many complex conditions besides food. Specifically, a number of socioeconomic conditions can be identified that cause parents to have fewer offspring. Birth rates can fall quite rapidly, sometimes before modern birth control devices are available. These conditions include parental security and faith in the future, the improved status of women in society, literacy, and lower infant mortality. Procuring these conditions requires agricultural reform, some redistribution of wealth, increased income and employment opportunities, better health services, and fresh expenditures on education. Evidence suggests that people who perceive the benefits of a smaller family will act prudently. The theory that favorable socioeconomic conditions cause a natural decrease in birth rates is called "The Benign Demographic Transition theory" (BDT). Although it is controversial, it may give us some reason to hope that population growth will level off. How much hope? That issue is discussed below in more detail. We now turn to the second philosophical theory on world hunger, liberalism.

LIBERALISM

The liberal position on world hunger is that we have a duty to help the poor in distant lands. There is something inherently evil about affluent people's failing to come to the aid of the poor when they could do so without great sacrifice. Liberal theorists on this issue come in several varieties. Some are utilitarians who argue that sharing our abundance and feeding the poor very likely maximizes utility or happiness. Some are deontologists who argue that we have a fundamental duty to use our surplus to aid those less well-off. Some deontologists simply find it self-evident that the needy have a right to our resources. Witness the report of the Presidential Commission on World Hunger: "Whether one speaks of human rights or basic human needs, the right to food is the most basic of all. . . . The correct moral and ethical position on hunger is beyond debate."[5] Others appeal to the principle of justice, arguing that the notion of fairness requires that we aid the least well-off in the world. Still others are radical egalitarians—perhaps the label "liberal" doesn't strictly apply to them— who argue that the principle of equality overrides even the need for survival, so we should redistribute our resources equitably even if it means that all of us will be malnourished and risk perishing. I think that we can capture most of what is vital to the liberal program if we examine Peter Singer's theory, which covers the first two types of liberalism, and Richard Watson's theory, which is a version of radical egalitarianism.

Peter Singer's article "Famine, Affluence, and Morality,"[6] written on the eve of the 1971 famine in Bangladesh, sets forth two principles, either of which would drastically alter our lifestyles and require that we provide substantial assistance to distant, poor and hungry people. The *Strong principle* states that "if it is in our power to prevent something bad from happening without thereby sacrificing anything of *comparable* importance, we ought morally to do it." Although this has similarities to utilitarian principles, it differs from them in that it does not require the maximizing of happiness, simply the amelioration of suffering through sacrifice of our goods to the point that we are at almost the same place as the sufferer. The idea behind this principle is utilitarian: diminishing marginal utility, which states that transferring goods from those with surplus to those with needs generally increases total utility. For example, if you have $100 for your daily food allowance and I have no allowance at all, your giving me some of your money will actually increase the good that the money accomplishes, for my gain of, say, $10 will enable me to survive, thus outweighing the loss you suffer. But there will come a point where giving me that extra dollar will not make a difference to the total good. At that point you should stop giving. If we were to follow Singer's strong principle, we would probably be giving a vast proportion of our GNP (gross national product) to nonmilitary foreign aid in-

stead of the present 0.21 percent or the 0.7 percent advocated by the United Nations as a fair share for rich countries.

Singer's *Weak principle* states that we ought to act to prevent bad things from happening if doing so will not result in our sacrificing anything *morally significant.* He asks you to suppose that you are walking past a shallow pond and see a child drowning. You can save the child with no greater inconvenience than wading into the water and muddying your suit or dress. Should you not jump into the pond and rescue the child? Singer thinks it is self-evident that nothing morally significant is at stake in the sacrifice.

Although Singer prefers the Strong principle, he argues that the Weak principle is sufficient to ground our duty to aid needy, distant people, for what difference does it make whether the drowning child is in your home town or in Africa or Asia? "It makes no moral difference whether the person I can help is a neighbor's child 10 yards away or a Bengali whose name I shall never know, 10,000 miles away." He or she is still a human being, and the same minimal sacrifice is required. Furthermore, the principle makes no distinction between cases in which I am the only person who can do anything and cases in which I am just one among many who can help. I have a duty in either case to see that what is needed is accomplished. Call this the "No-Exception proviso."

Singer's two principles have generated considerable debate, and many ethicists have accepted one or both of them, but there are problems with each. John Arthur has noted in his critique of Singer that the Strong principle is too strong and the Weak principle is too weak.[7] With the Strong principle, our rights to our property and lifestyles are too easily overridden by the needs of others. For example, if I meet a stranger who is going blind and I could prevent her becoming completely blind by giving her one of my eyes, I should take steps to have my eye removed— even, according to the No-Exception proviso, if there are others on whom she has a greater claim to some assistance than she has on me. Likewise, if I meet a man about to lose his kidneys or lung functions, I have a *prima facie* duty to give him one of my kidneys or lungs, a duty that can be overridden only by finding someone on whom he has a stronger claim, who will donate his or her organ. Woe the person who meets someone in need of all three of these organs—an eye, a lung, and a kidney! If no one else is doing his or her duty, you are left with the responsibility of yielding your organs, even if this results, as it surely will, in a severe change in your lifestyle. So long as you have not reduced your lot to the level of the other person's, you must go on sacrificing, even for strangers.

Richard Watson's position is more severe that Singer's.[8] From a deontological perspective, he argues that the principle of equal worth of individuals calls for the equal distribution of the world's food. "All human beings are moral equals with equal rights to the necessities of life. Differential treatment of human beings thus should be based only on their freely chosen actions and not on accidents of their birth and environment." It is our sacred duty to share scarce resources with every needy person, even if this means that we all will be malnourished, even if no one will get sufficient food, and everyone perishes. Equality trumps survival, even the survival of the human race.

Watson's Equality-Absolute has problems. The equal absolute right of each person to life's necessities needs a defense, which Watson fails to afford. I don't see why I am obligated to sacrifice the lives of my children and myself simply because there is not enough food to feed all of us. Suppose you and your family and friends (50 people in all) work hard and grow enough food to feed 100 people for the next six months. If you feed only your 50 people, you will have enough food for a year, after which a new crop can be harvested. But there are 200 people who need food. If you share your food with all 200,

you will all die. If you share it with 50 others besides your family (100 in all), you all can survive for the next six months but must hope for outside aid after that. What is the morally correct thing to do? (1) Feed only our community (50 people who did the work)? (2) Feed these 50 and another 50 outsiders? (3) Feed all 200 and perish together? (4) Draw lots to determine who should get the food and live? I think we are morally permitted to opt for (1), because we have a right to try to survive and flourish so long as we are not unjustly harming others. As we argued in the early chapters of this book, we have a *prima facie* right to the fruits of our labor, so we need not divest ourselves of life's necessities to help others.

An adequate moral theory must make room for self-regarding reasons. I am required to make *reasonable* sacrifices for others, but not at the cost of what would severely detract from the quality of my own life. Watson explicitly rejects the notion of reasonableness in morality. Morality is often unreasonable, according to him, but I see no reason to accept that verdict. If morality were truly unreasonable, rational people would be advised to opt out of it and choose a more rational Quasi-Morality in its place. My thesis throughout this book is that moral principles are reasonable requirements. In general they are in our long-term interest.

Of course, you are free to go beyond the call of duty and donate your organs to strangers. It is certainly noble of you to volunteer to do so. But such supererogatory acts are not duties of as such. Extreme utilitarians and absolutist egalitarians confuse morality with extreme altruism or saintliness.

We turn now to Singer's Weaker principle: If we can prevent an evil by sacrificing something not morally significant, we should do so. This seems closer to the truth, but John Arthur has argued that it is too weak, for what is morally significant varies from person to person. For example, my record collection or collection of rare pieces of art might be a significant part of what makes life worth living for me, so to sacrifice them for the poor would be of moral significance. Is owning a television set or possessing a nice car or having a nice wardrobe morally significant? For many people they are. Nevertheless, there are occasions when sacrificing these things for the poor or needy might be morally required. Even when a child is drowning in a pond, you could refuse to jump into the water to save the child, using Singer's Weak principle, for you could argue that having clean, unspoiled clothes is morally significant for you. Of course, it would really have to be the case that they are morally significant, but for some people they are.

Singer could respond that Arthur's objection fails because he is overly relativizing morally significance to the individual. There is an objective truth to the matter of whether something really is morally significant. Singer would have to qualify his principle of what is morally significant by relational terms: In situation S, object O is morally significant to person P (whether he or she realizes it or not). Compared to saving someone's life, wearing clean, unspoiled clothes is not morally significant, whatever the misguided dandy might think to the contrary. Not every supposed morally significant trait is really so. If I believe that burning witches is the way to save our nation from the devil and I go around burning those who fit my description, I am simply misguided. Likewise, if I think that my baseball card collection is more important than saving my best friend's life, I have a bad set of priorities—friends really are more valuable than baseball cards. If I fail to realize this, I am missing a deep moral truth.

Singer's Weak principle, suitably qualified, can survive the kind of attack that philosophers like Arthur hurl at it, but it may not be good enough to get him the hunger relief that he advocates. Other factors have to be addressed. For example, do needy strangers have rightful claims on my assets even though I have done nothing to cause their sorry state? Do the starving have rights to my property? We turn now to the conservative position.

CONSERVATIVISM

Conservatives on world hunger argue that we have no duty at all to give aid to distant needy people. Representatives of the view in question are such libertarians as John Hospers, Robert Nozick, and Ayn Rand, and contractualists such as Thomas Hobbes and, more recently, Gilbert Harman, Howard Kahane and William Nelson.[9] Typically, conservatives, in the minimalist sense I am using the term, reject the notion that we have positive rights that entail duties on the part of others to come to our aid or promote our good unless there is a contractual agreement between us. The one right we have is that of freedom: the right not to be interfered with, the right to possess our property in peace. So long as I have a legitimate claim on my property (that is, I have not acquired it through fraud or coercion) no one may take it from me, and I may refuse to share it regardless of how needy others are.

We may not positively harm others, but we need not help them either. No moral duty obligates you to dirty your clothes by trying to save the child drowning in the muddy pond. Of course, it shows bad character not to save the child, and we should endeavor to be charitable with our surplus and support good causes, but these are not strictly moral duties. They are optional ideals. It follows that if hungry Esau is prompted to sell his birthright to that feisty chef, Jacob, so much the worse for Esau; and if a poor African country decides to contract with a Western corporation to shift from growing a high protein crop to a cash crop such as coffee, so long as no external force was used in the agreement, the contract is entirely just. The corporation need feel no guilt when the poor nation undergoes a famine and finds itself unable to supply its people with adequate protein. No rights have been violated. The country simply made a foolish choice.

If you believe that the contractual approach to ethics, examined in an earlier chapter, is the correct approach, the conservative position will appeal to you. It may have considerable merit, but it also has certain weaknesses. Contractualism, unless it is supplemented with a theory of natural duties, limits moral obligations to agreements made. But, as I suggested in Chapter 2, morality, in large part, has to do with the promotion of human flourishing and ameliorating suffering, so we have some duties to help others, even when we have not contracted ahead of time to do so. If a poor country agrees to accept hazardous waste from a rich country, morality has nothing more to say about the matter. Following the contractualist model, the thirty-eight people who for thirty-five minutes watched Kitty Genovese being beaten to death, who did not lift a finger to call the police or lift their windows to shout at the assailant, did nothing wrong. However, if we have a duty to promote human flourishing and ameliorate suffering, these onlookers did have a duty to do something on Ms. Genovese's behalf, and they are to be faulted for not coming to her aid.

It would seem, then, that there are positive duties as well as negative ones. Both utilitarian and deontological theories are better than contractual theories at recognizing positive duties to help others and promote human flourishing, even when no contract is in force.

A MODERATE ALTERNATIVE

There is a moderate position between the liberal and the conservative that accepts part of each position but rejects other parts. It goes as follows: morality originates in group living, tribes. People discover that certain rules are necessary for survival and happiness, such as rules against killing each other, promise breaking, violating property rights, lying, and cheating, and rules promoting justice, cooperation,

respect for others, and beneficence. Members of a society implicitly agree to live by this Core Morality. They resolve their conflicts of interest through compromise or impartial third bodies—the primitive origins of law. But they notice that some other groups do not respect their lives or property and that there is no way to resolve differences through impartial review. The Other is the enemy to whom the rules do not apply. Indeed, it is only by not respecting the enemy's life and property that one can survive and flourish.

Eventually, the two groups learn to accept an intertribal Core Morality. They begin with a mutual nonaggression pact, respect each other as equals, cooperate instead of fight with each other, and subject their differences to an impartial review. Nevertheless, in many situations, members of a tribe feel a greater responsibility to aid members of their own family and tribe rather than members of a neighboring one. If my child, a neighboring child, and a child of another tribe all need a pair of shoes, and I have only enough resources to procure one pair, I will feel a duty to give them to my child. If I can procure two pairs easily, I will give the first pair to my child but sell the second pair at a low price to my neighbor. If I go into the shoemaking business, I will still be likely to give favored treatment to my neighbor over the person from the neighboring tribe. Greater opportunity for reciprocity arises with my neighbor than with the family of the neighboring tribe, so it makes sense to treat that family as special.

Moderate moral theory recognizes special responsibilities to family, friends, and neighbors. This is the reason Singer's drowning child example is misleading. I can do only so much good. I can save only so many drowning children. I may have a duty to give of my surplus to help save drowning children in a distant land, but I have a stronger duty to help those with whom I have intimate or contractual ties.

This said, the other side of the coin must be turned over and the liberal program acknowledged, for another aspect of morality is the enlargement of the circle of benevolence and flourishing, the utilitarian aspect of maximizing good. We need to expand the small circle of moral consideration and commitment from family, community, and country to include the whole world. We need to do this for two reasons. First, it is simply good to do so. Helping as many people (and animals) as possible without harming yourself is part of the meaning of promoting the flourishing of sentient beings. Second, it is in our self-interest to do so. Unless we learn to live together on this small planet, we may all perish. Humanity is no longer innocent. Technology, through its inventions of atomic weapons, biological weapons, poisonous chemicals, and so forth, is available to destroy all sentient life. One nation's adverse environmental impact can affect the rest of the world. If one nation pollutes the air through spreading sulphur dioxide or carbon dioxide, the rest of the world suffers the effects. If the Brazilian or Peruvian farmers cut down large segments of the Amazon Rain Forest, we all lose oxygen and ecological diversity. We are all in each other's debt. If we don't hang together, we *hang* alone.

So the same considerations that led to mutual cooperation between the original tribes must inform our global policies. A rational Core Morality must reign internationally. Although we will still have priority commitments to family and friends, we cannot allow selfishness to hinder generous dealings with the rest of the world. Hardin's metaphor of nations as lifeboats has only limited applicability. It may justify careful immigration policies that prevent overcrowding, but it should not prevent assistance to other nations that may be helped and that someday may be able to help us. In a sense the whole earth is one great lifeboat in which we'll sink or float together.

However, something must be said in Hardin's behalf. He points to a crucial problem that deserves our concentrated attention: population policy. Even if we finally opt for the Benign Demographic Transition theory, many situations

may not wait for that policy to take effect. The population of the world is multiplying at an exponential rate. Since 1930 the earth's population has increased from 2 billion to 6 billion by 1999. In 1968 Paul and Anne Ehrlich wrote *Population Bomb,* warning that the population of the world (then 3.5 billion) was growing exponentially at a rate of 70 million per year and that if strong measures were not taken, we would likely have Malthusian problems of famine and disease. Critics pejoratively labeled such cautioners "doomsdayers," but they have been proved correct.

Crowded conditions prevail in many parts of the world. Famines have become worse in areas of Africa and Bangladesh. Today the global population is growing not by 70 million per year, but by 90 million. The growth rate is 1.7 percent, which means that the earth's population is likely to double in 41 years. It is projected to rise to about 11.2 billion by 2050 unless significant population control policies are implemented. A slight increase in the growth rate would result in a world population density like that of present-day New York City by the year 2300. Add to this the following: The innovative technological development of food has leveled off, top soil is being depleted, pesticide-resistant strains of pest destroyers are appearing throughout the earth's agricultural areas, and there is evidence of changing weather patterns, probably brought on by the greenhouse effect, causing diminished farm production.[10] And, as though this were not serious enough, the ocean fish harvests are declining.

I noted in the critique of Hardin that the Benign Demographic Transition theory (BDT) holds that we should concentrate on the root causes of population growth and let the process solve this problem. How does this theory work? It idealizes population changes in four stages. In stage 1, the *preindustrial stage,* the severe living conditions give rise to a high average birthrate and a high average deathrate, resulting in very little, if any, population increase. In stage 2, the *mortality transition stage,* the deathrate falls while the birthrate remains high, so the population increases. In stage 3, the *fertility transition* (or *industrial stage*), the average birthrate decreases due to availability of birth control, the improved status of women, lower infant mortality, general education, and the rising cost of raising children. In stage 4, the *postindustrial stage,* the average rates for both birth and death are low, tending toward zero growth. The population has leveled out but is much larger than it was at stage 1. There is some evidence that validates the BDT. Separate studies by Revelle, Brown, Eberstadt, and Rich have shown that several countries that have progressed in these areas have cut their birthrates dramatically.[11] Some demographers point to the fact that in the 1970s, China has brought its birthrate down from 40 per 1,000 people to 30 in about five years and Cuba has brought its birthrate down to 27 per 1,000. The conclusion is that we should go to the causes of overpopulation (the activities mentioned in stage 3) and not punish countries for their "overpopulation."

Others have argued that the Benign Demographic Transition theory has severe problems. Demographer Joel Cohen points out that some countries decreased their birthrates before industrialization or educational development. In other cases, improved public health measures caused an enormous rise in higher life expectancy in developing countries without significantly reducing the birthrate.[12] Furthermore, after China and India made significant progress toward cutting their fertility rates in the 1970s in spite of the growing benefits of industrialization, their fertility rates increased in the 1980s. Referring to the 1980s and 1990s, Cohen notes that population growth rates are rising. Seventy-eight million people live in countries with a total fertility rate above seven children per woman, and 708 million live in countries with six or more children per woman. Why did the trend reverse? For several reasons, one being China's softening of its austere one-child policy and another India's relaxation of its family planning policy.[13] The point is that the BDT is too

idealized a model. It may indicate a tendency in industrialization to lead to population stabilization, but there is no lawlike necessity about it. People must understand that it is to their advantage to have fewer children, and effective techniques of fertility reduction must be available.[14] Even with the benefits of industrialization and the availability of birth control, a high average birthrate may continue for a long time, increasing the population at a very high rate, putting a stress on the ecosystem, and exceeding the carrying capacity of the land. Famines in the coming years could have devastating effects.

We have cause for alarm, and if the shouts of neo-Malthusians such as Hardin and Ehrlich are needed to wake us up, let us thank them for waking us up—even as we work for kinder, more just solutions to the problem. The point is that hard choices must be made, and food aid should be tied to responsible population control for the survival and well-being of humanity.

A proposal that improves on Hardin's Lifeboat Ethics is the triage approach first set forth by Paul and William Paddock in *Famine—1975* and advocated by Joseph Fletcher.[15] The term *triage* (French for "sorting") comes from wartime medical policies. With a scarcity of physicians and resources to cope with casualties of battle, the wounded were divided into three groups: those who would probably survive without medical treatment, those who would not survive even with treatment, and those for whom treatment would make the decisive difference. Only this last group would receive medical aid. The Paddocks and Fletcher urge us to apply the same policy to world hunger. Given limited ability and scarce resources to help, we should not aid nations that will survive without our aid or those who will not be able to sustain themselves even with our help. We should direct all of our attention to nations for which our input could make a decisive difference. The aim should be to enable these people to become self-sufficient, responsive to the carrying capacity of their environment. As a Chinese proverb says, "Give a man a fish today and he will eat for a day. Teach him how to fish, and he will eat for the rest of his days."

As repulsive as the triage strategy may seem, it should not be dismissed out of hand. Perhaps at present no nation is hopeless and we still have time to forestall the nefarious effects of overpopulation. We should give the Benign Demographic Transition theory a chance to work, supporting social reform at home and abroad with our actions and our pocketbooks, but if we cannot effect global changes, the time for triage may soon be upon us. The doomsdayers are to be taken seriously. They may not be correct, but their warnings should be heeded.

Meanwhile, the broad-based Core Morality, outlined in the first chapters of this book, seems to require that we personally contribute to hunger relief organizations and urge that national policy provide appropriate agricultural know-how and technological assistance to nations in dire need. At the same time, we should support family planning programs both here and abroad, aiming to provide everyone with as high a quality of life as is possible. The option is not food *or* population control, but food *and* population control. The world must see these as two sides of the same coin, a coin that is the entrance fee to a better future for all people.

If the preceding discussion is correct, we do have a duty to give aid to the needy, both in our own country and in other lands. It is a duty to exercise benevolence to ameliorate suffering and promote human flourishing. We do not have a duty to reduce our lot to an equal poverty as Watson and Singer's Strong principle advocates, but we should be giving more than most of us are. No one can tell another person just how much he or she should be donating, but each of us must consult his or her conscience. We should be living as personal examples of ecological responsibility, as good stewards of the earth's resources, and we should call upon our leaders to increase nonmilitary aid to underdeveloped countries where the need is greatest.

Study Questions

1. Discuss the neo-Malthusian views, especially those of Garrett Hardin, on the relationship between population and food production. Evaluate his three arguments against giving aid to starving people in distant places.
2. What is the "Benign Demographic Transition Theory"? How strong is it, and what might be said against its use in policy development?
3. Examine Peter Singer's argument in favor of helping famine victims. Evaluate his principle "If it is in our power to prevent something bad from happening, without sacrificing anything else of comparable moral importance, we ought morally to do it." If we followed this principle, what would be the likely results? What moral considerations would outweigh our obligation to give aid to famine victims or to anyone else in need?
4. How would a contractualist deal with the problem of aiding famine victims? Evaluate this position.
5. A reviewer suggests this problem: Suppose a farmer in the rainforest says, "My principle duty is to feed my children, not to worry about the global effects of cutting down rainforests. You Americans are happy to ignore such special relations when you say that *I* should worry about the rainforest because it is a treasure to the world. Yet you rely on special relations when you think my country ought to worry about feeding its poor, and your country ought to worry about feeding your poor." How would you respond to this farmer? What is the link between hunger and environmental degradation?

6. Discuss the notion of triage. How does it apply to the problem of world hunger?

7. Sometimes we treat hunger as an abstract idea, forgetting just how terrible it is. I suggest reading a report or essay on the subject. You might want to read Knut Hamsun's *Hunger,* one of the most poignant portrayals of the personal, psychological agony of starvation.

Endnotes

1. Hunger is a condition in which people do not get enough food to provide nutrients they need for fully productive, active, and healthy lives. Malnutrition, which impairs both physical and mental health, results from undernutrition, which is the inadequate consumption of one or more nutrients.

2. Alan Gregg, "A Medical Aspect of the Population Problem," *Science* 121 (1955).

3. Garrett Hardin, "Lifeboat Ethics: The Case Against Helping the Poor," *Psychology Today* (1974); "Living on a Lifeboat," *BioScience* (1974); *The Limits of Altruism* (Bloomington, IN: Indiana University Press, 1977).

4. Garett Hardin, "The Immorality of Being Softhearted," *Stanford Alumni Almanac,* (January 1969).

5. Presidential Commission on World Hunger, *Overcoming World Hunger: The Challenge Ahead* (Washington D.C.: Government Printing Office, 1980).

6. Peter Singer, "Famine, Affluence and Morality," *Philosophy and Public Affairs* (1972).

7. John Arthur, "Rights and Duty to Bring Aid" in *World Hunger and Moral Responsibility,* ed. William Aiken and Hugh LaFollette (Englewood Cliffs, NJ: Prentice-Hall, 1977).

8. Richard Watson, "Reason and Morality in a World of Limited Food" in Aiken and LaFollette, op. cit.

9. John Hospers, *Libertarianism* (Los Angeles: Nash, 1971); Robert Nozick, *Anarchy, State and Utopia* (New York: Basic Books, 1974); Thomas Hobbes, *Leviathan* (1651); Gilbert Harman, "Moral Relativism Defended," *Philosophical Review* (1975); Howard Kahane, "Making the World Safe for Reciprocity" in *Reason and Responsibility,* ed. Joel Feinberg (Belmont, CA: Wadsworth, 1989), and William Nelson, *What's in it for Me?* (Oxford: Westview Press, 1991). Ayn Rand, *The Virtues of Selfishness* (New York: New American Library, 1964) also holds this position from an explicitly egoistic perspective.

10. Statistics are based on *Population and Vital Statistics Report of the United Nations Statistical Office* and *UN Demographic Yearbook* (1990). Information is available through the Population Reference Bureau, 777 14th St, N.W., Suite 800, Washington, DC 20005. See also the journal *Population and Environment,* especially vol. 12, 3 (spring 1991).

11. See Robert Revelle, "The Ghost at the Feast," *Science* 186 (1974); W. Rich, "Smaller Families through Social and Economic Progress," *Overseas Development Council Monograph* #7, Washington DC, 1973. Nick Eberstadt, "Myths of the Food Crisis" *New York Review of Books,* 19 Feb., 1976; Lester Brown, *In the Human Interest* (New York: Norton, 1974), 119; *World Without Borders* (New York: Praeger, 1974), 140f; and M. S. Teitelbaum, "Relevance of Demographic Transition Theory in Developing Countries," *Science* 188 (1975).

12. Joel Cohen, *How Many People Can the Earth Support?* (New York: Norton, 1995), ch. 4.

13. Cohen, op. cit., 64–65.

14. Ashley Coale lists three general prerequisites for declining fertility: (1) Fertility must be within the calculus of conscious choice. Potential parents must consider it an acceptable mode of thought and form of behavior to balance the advantages and disadvantages before deciding to have another child. (2) Reduced fertility must be advantageous. Perceived social and economic circumstances must make reduced fertility seem an advantage. (3) Effective techniques of fertility reduction must be available. Procedures that will in fact prevent births must be known, and there must be sufficient communication between spouses and sufficient sustained will, in both, to employ them successfully.

One of Coale's students summed up this position by saying "potential parents must be ready, willing and able to control their fertility." Quoted in Cohen, op. cit., 62. Cohen says that the most significant factor in reducing the birth rate is the availability of birth control.

15. Paul and William Paddoch, *Famine—1975* (Boston: Little Brown, 1968) and Joseph Fletcher, "Give if It Helps, Not if It Hurts" in Aiken and LaFollette, op. cit.

For Further Reading

Aiken, William and Hugh LaFollette, eds., *World Hunger and Moral Responsibility* (Englewood Cliffs, NJ: Prentice-Hall, 1977).

Arthur, John "Rights and Duty to Bring Aid" in Aiken and LaFollette, op. cit.

Brown, Lester, *Tough Choices: Facing the Challenge of Food Scarcity* (New York: Norton, 1996).

Cohen, Joel E. *How Many People Can the Earth Support?* (New York: Norton, 1995).

Fletcher, Joseph, "Give if It Helps, Not if It Hurts" in Aiken and LaFollette, op. cit.

Hamsun, Knut. *Hunger,* trans. Robert Bly (New York: Bard Books, 1967).

Hardin, Garrett, "Lifeboat Ethics: The Case Against Helping the Poor," *Psychology Today* (1974).

Hardin, Garrett, "Living on a Lifeboat," *BioScience* (1974).

Hardin, Garrett; *The Limits of Altruism* (Bloomington, IN: Indiana University Press, 1977).

Lappe, Francis and Joseph Collins, *World Hunger: Twelve Myths* (New York: Grove, 1986).

O'Neill, Onora, *The Faces of Hunger* (London: Allen & Unwin, 1986).

Paddock, Paul and William, *Famine—1975* (Boston: Little Brown, 1968).

Singer, Peter, "Famine, Affluence and Morality," *Philosophy and Public Affairs* (1972).

Chapter 15

War

Nothing is worth dying for.

PLACARD AT AN AMERICAN ANTIWAR RALLY

Strive against (jihad) the infidels and the hypocrites! Be harsh with them. Their ultimate destiny is hell.

THE KORAN 9:73

War is a means of resolving conflicts of interest by other than rational persuasion. In war, two or more groups resort to violence to settle differences. War is bloody, destructive, vile, and irrational, but it has been humanity's most startling way of asserting power and struggling to survive. I remember meeting a devout Catholic woman on board the Norwegian Liner *Bergenfjord,* in 1971 as I sailed back from Denmark to the United States. She was expressing outage at the decadence and secularity of our time and criticized Planned Parenthood and our whole contraceptive culture as *"man's* faithless means to prevent overpopulation." "We have no faith in God," she said regarding this aspect of social policy. "Why, God has always had His methods of population control." I asked what they were. "War, famine, and disease," she exclaimed, wondering how I could be so stupid as to have to ask. "Maybe 'man's faithless means' are better," I meekly offered.

Famine and disease, whether we want to blame God for them or not, have been scourges on humanity, but the means of destruction for which we may take peculiar credit is war. We seem mysteriously, almost religiously, addicted to this sadomasochistic enterprise. Why is this so? Why do we love the blood-dipped sword?

War in Western History: From Moses to the Present

The history of humanity is the story of violence, bloodshed, pillage, massacre, and plunder. What is more, it is the story of the *glorification* of violence, bloodshed, pillage, massacre, and plunder. Witness the military symbols in national anthems, the marches and parades in honor of past wars (for example, Veteran's Day marches and the parades honoring soldiers from the recent war with Iraq), the sense of pride in victory, the making of military heroes, and the dehumanizing of enemies. All this is part of the litany of lust for carnage and conquest that has haunted our history. The slain victims on our side are seen not as the cannon fodder of megalomaniacs

and incompetents but as heroes wreathed in immortality. Marble monuments in a thousand marketplaces mark their memory. The war tax is usually the highest item in a nation's budget and frequently the only tax people do not hesitate to pay—witness the sudden influx of money to the government of Argentina (a land where collecting taxes is well-nigh impossible) during the Falkland Islands War, while Argentina was supposed to be on the edge of bankruptcy. While the United States lacks funds to improve its inner cities and lift millions out of poverty, it finds the needed resources to fight a war a long way from its shores.

Only recently, our hearts were riveted by the spectacle of courage and genius in the service of death and destruction against the Iraquis in Kuwait. The answer to the question of why war is so attractive is that it brings all human talents and energies to their highest tension and sets a crown of immortality on those who courageously risk their lives and conquer. The very danger and horror of the moment is its thrill.

Homo sapiens is one of the few species that systematically kills members of its own species. Because of this and because of the threat of attack by rivals, societies deem defense systems necessary for their survival Note that over 90 percent of all nations that have ever existed have been destroyed, often because they have not been militarily strong enough to defend themselves. From Shalmaneser III of Assyria to President Yeltsin and President Clinton, the need for a strong defense has been duly recognized. The problem is that the "defensive" army all too frequently becomes offensive.

Some 93 major wars occurred in the 150 years between 1816 and 1965 (about seven per decade), and 75 wars (not all major) have taken place in the past 40 years. About 40,000 people are killed every month in a war. In the American Civil War more than 600,000 Americans lost their lives. In World War II between 40 million and 50 million people were killed. In the Viet Nam War a million Vietnamese and

57,000 Americans died. Death and destruction have been the hallmarks of human history. From the very onset of our culture this was so.

In the Old Testament, Israel, with Yahweh's approval, pursues genocidal war. The foundations of Israel were laid in the destruction of Pharaoh's army and the Egyptian first-born. God hardened Pharaoh's heart so that He could destroy him, and when the Israelites pledged themselves to Yahweh as His chosen people, the covenant to which they dedicated themselves included a prohibition against murder and a prescription in favor of annihilating their neighbors. "When my angel goes before you and brings you in to the Amorites, and the Hittites, and the Perizzites, and the Canaanites, the Hivites, and the Jebusites, and I blot them out, you shall not bow down to their gods, nor serve them. . . . I will send my terror before you, and will throw into confusion all the people against whom you come, and I will make all your enemies turn their backs to you. . . . You shall make no covenant with them or with their gods" (Ex. 23:23–32). The Psalmist, who can sing Zion's songs of praise to God with one breath, can sing the doom of revenge in the next: "O daughter of Babylon, you devastator! Happy shall he be who requites you with what you have done to us! Happy shall he be who takes your little ones and dashes them against the rocks" (Ps. 137:8, 9). Jehovah is a god of blood and thunder, His people the people of the sword. The *jihad* doesn't begin with Islam but is already found in the Hebrew Bible with ancient Israel.

The Greeks are no better. The *Iliad* is one long recital of how Diomedes, Ajax, Sarpedon, Achilles, and Hector killed. Greek history, as William James rightly tells us, is a "panorama of jingoism and imperialism—war for war's sake, all the citizens being warriors. . . . Their wars were purely piratical. Pride, gold, women, slaves, excitement, were their only motives."[1] The Spartans, led by one of the greatest military geniuses of all time, Lycurgus, were the paradigm of a military state, in which everyone, male and female, learned to kill from childhood. So keen on war did they become that peace posed a threat to their social cohesion.

During the Peloponnesian war in the fifth century B.C.E., the Athenians asked the inhabitants of Melos, hitherto neutral, to acknowledge their lordship. The envoys met and held a debate, which Thucydides gave in full, and which for sweet reasonableness of form stood out in candor and eloquence. The Melians demurred and said that they refused to be slaves. They appealed to the gods for help.

The Athenian general replied: "The powerful exact what they can and the weak grant what they must. Of the gods we believe and of men we know that by a law of nature, wherever they can rule, they will. This law was not made by us, and we know that you and all mankind, if you were as strong as we are, would do as we do. So much for the gods; we have told you why we expect to stand as high in their good opinions as you."[2]

Thereupon the Athenians put to death all who were of military age and made slaves of the women and children. They then colonized the island, sending thither 500 Athenian settlers.

The Greeks gave us the notion of *Realpolitik*— kill or be killed; conquer or die. War no longer is seen as divinely inspired but as a mechanism for survival and power in which the Brazen Rule predates the Golden Rule—"Do it to others before they get a chance to do it to you."

In the New Testament Jesus advocates pacifism in the Sermon on the Mount. "Love your enemies. Do not resist evil. If someone strikes you on the right cheek, turn to him the other also." The early Christians were pacifists and generally refused to serve in the Roman army. In the second century, Tertullian summed up the Christian position on military service. "There is no agreement between the divine and human sacrament, the standard of Christ and the standard of the devil, the camp of light and the camp of darkness. One soul cannot belong to two lords—God and Caesar." Regarding

Peter's use of the sword on the night of Judas's betrayal of Jesus, Tertullian writes, "The Lord in disarming Peter, unbelted every soldier."[3]

However, once the Church came to power, it changed its mind and reinterpreted the message of Christ to apply to saints. The beatitudes and Sermon on the Mount consisted in "Councils of Perfection," not strict duties. Augustine (354–430) developed the idea of a just war. The Crusades were launched against Islam, Catholic and Protestant have killed each other in the name of God, and a presumption of God's approval has accompanied warriors against those of other creeds. Christian civilization has wielded the sword as readily and deftly as others.

Three Attitudes Toward War

Historically, Western culture has had three major philosophical attitudes toward war: romanticism, abolitionism, and realism. The *War-Romantics* believed that war is good for humanity in that it purges the dross of society, so that only the fit survive, and it brings out the best in humanity: courage, perseverance, knife-edge concentration, endurance, resilience, heroism, and intelligence. Hegel believed that war cleanses the nation and that humanity must accept war or stagnate. Napoleon spoke of war as glorious. Nietzsche said, "a good war hallows every cause." War is a natural activity that opposes Christianity with its slave morality, "accentuating humility, submissiveness and turning of the cheek." Helmut von Moltke put it this way:[4]

> Perpetual Peace is a dream—and not even a beautiful dream—War is an integral part of God's ordering of the Universe. In War man's noblest virtues come into play: courage and renunciation, fidelity to duty and a readiness for sacrifice that does not stop short of offering up Life itself. Without War the world would become swamped in materialism.

Similarly, Von Treitschke wrote, "The state's first duty is to maintain its power in relation to

other states—war is the one remedy for an ailing nation."[5] War is the process by which the truly civilized nations express their strength and vitality; life is an unending struggle for survival, war is an instrument in biologic evolution, killing off the less fit. Von Treitschke, with his racist tones, is the philosopher who inspired the Italian Fascists and German Nazis.

War is manly, strong, and brave; peace is feminine, weak, and defeatist. The *jihad* will bring immortal glory. Look at the quotations at the beginning of this chapter and contrast the protestor's pusillanimous placard with the misguided message of determined courage conveyed by the Koran. The first signifies the triumph of banality, the leveling of values, for if *nothing* is worth dying for, can anything be worth living for? While the passage from the Koran seems to enjoin fanaticism, at least it signifies a commitment to the good and true. That is the one truth in the romantic's message: life is serious and our deepest values are worth preserving even to death.

We turn to the *Abolitionists* with the question Is war inevitable or can we replace it with a lasting peace? Abolitionists argue that the abolition of war is possible and that we should assume the attitude of peace and nonviolence now. As noted earlier, the early Christians were persecuted pacifists. But after Emperor Constantine saw the vision of the cross at the battle of the Milvian Bridge and made Christianity the official religion of the Roman Empire (313 A.C.), Christians promptly embarked on a policy of persecuting heretics and battling infidels. Under Augustine pacifism gave way to the concept of the just war, which we will examine shortly. Nevertheless, the Abolitionist tradition perdured as a minority voice in the choir of theology from Erasmus (1467–1536) to George Fox (1624–91) and the Quakers to the Roman Catholic Bishop of Atlanta. Erasmus condemned the use of war as a great evil that opposes everything that humans have been created for. Men and women are born not for destruction, but for love, friendship, and service to fellow humans. Kant wrote a guide to the commencement of perpetual peace. Bertrand Russell conceded that, if it came to that, we are better red than dead. Tolstoy, Gandhi, and Martin Luther King Jr. practiced nonviolent resistance in the name of pacifism, proving that it could achieve more than some might have expected. Pacifism is reemerging in our country as a serious option. The Roman Catholic Bishop of Atlanta has said that in a nuclear age there is no such thing as a just war. In a recent, well-acclaimed study, *On War and Morality* (1989), philosopher Robert Holmes argues that because innocents are killed in war, the whole enterprise of war is immoral and cannot be justified.

While these sentiments are praiseworthy, there are serious problems both with pacifism itself and with the argument from innocence in particular.

Pacifism holds that it is immoral to engage in war even to defend yourself from attack. The problem with this is that on one hand, pacifism tells us not to kill others because they have a right to life, while on the other hand it tells us that we may not defend our right to life even against evil attacks! This is a strange kind of *right* that cannot be defended.

We may put the argument this way:

1. All humans (qua innocent) have the right not to be treated violently.

2. If we have any rights at all, we have the right to use force to prevent the deprivation of the thing to which we have a right.

3. Pacifism says both that we have some rights and that we may not use force to protect them.

But what is a *right* if we do not have the *right* to protect it? The very notion of a right entails an accompanying liberty to defend it for oneself and for others. The pacifist's logic is confused, its doctrine incoherent.[6]

Of course, having a right to defend our right to life doesn't require us to defend it. You can sacrifice your own right to life or right to protect your life, but what you cannot do is require others to sacrifice their right to prevent the unauthorized abrogation of their right to life. Further, you may have a duty to defend other people's right to life by preventive measures.

To what lengths may we go to defend our right to life? Here the notion of *proportionality* comes in. We may use just enough force to get the job done. But if the only way to defend a right to life against an aggressor is to kill the aggressor, that act is morally justified.

Applying this to war: if it's moral to defend your family, friends, or innocent people from an assailant by killing the assailant, then it's moral to defend your country or another friendly country from being taken over by an aggressor by attacking that aggressor.

If we have to kill some shields (innocent people or hostages placed in front of the aggressors) to save our family, then we may justifiably kill innocent people in the enemy country, if that is the only way to get to the aggressor.

Remember, the pacifist's claim is not that we *may* give up our right to self-defense, but that we morally *must* give it up. It is immoral to kill the aggressor who is torturing our children or about to blow up a bus with innocent civilians on it, even if killing him or her is the only way to save these innocent people.

Of course, Jesus and the early Christians held to pacifism with a difference. They held that this life was not worth defending because it was only the gateway to a better life, and the sooner we get there the better. By this logic the murderer does his victim a favor, so there is no reason to resist violence. If people believe this, pacifism may make sense, but given that most of us have doubts about immortality and would like to make this world as just as possible, pacifism does not have a lot to recommend it.

The pacifist argues that his or her position has the advantage that if it were universalized, there would be no war. This is shortsighted. We could also universalize the thesis "Never go to war unless another nation is seriously threatening to attack you" and still obtain the same results: a principle that, if universally followed, would prohibit war.

A weaker version of pacifism argues that while we may defend ourselves and others against direct personal violence, war is never morally justified because it involves the killing of innocent people. Richard Wasserstrom states the argument this way:

> Even in war innocent persons have a right to life and limb that should be respected. It is no less wrong and no more justifiable to kill innocent persons in war than at any other time. Therefore, if innocent persons are killed in a war, that war is to be condemned. The argument can quite readily be converted into an attack upon all modern war. Imagine a thoroughly unprovoked attack upon another country—an attack committed, moreover, from the worst of motives and for the most despicable of ends. Assume too, for the moment, that under such circumstances there is nothing immoral about fighting back and even killing those who are attacking. Nonetheless, if in fighting back innocent persons will be killed, the defenders will be acting immorally. However, given any war fought today, innocent persons will inevitably be killed. Therefore, any war fought today will be immoral.[7]

The argument may be analyzed in this form.

1. Killing innocents is immoral.
2. In war innocents are killed.
3. Therefore, war is immoral.

The argument is fallacious, committing the fallacy of composition: faulty reasoning from the part to the whole. For example: "Every atom in the Empire State Building is so small as to be invisible to the naked eye. Since the Empire State Building is composed entirely of atoms, it must be so small as to be invisible to the naked eye." Or "Every person in America has a mother. Therefore, America has a mother." Just because

parts of war are immoral doesn't mean that the whole is immoral. There are abuses in business, sports, education, families, and government, but that doesn't mean that on the whole business, sports, education, families, and government are evil. They may be moral without being morally perfect.

There is no absolute purity in this life, no absolute good in human activity, and to make that a precondition for any activity is to condemn oneself to inaction.

We need to appreciate the principle of the *Lesser Evil*. Tragic situations occur in which no purely good solution is available. Recall the trolley car example from Chapter 8. Noticing that the brakes of the trolley car have failed, you, the driver, have the choice between doing nothing and allowing five workmen to die and turning the trolley off onto a spur where you will kill one person. Either way, someone will die. Not to choose is still to choose. It is to choose to allow the greater evil to take place for which you are responsible. Likewise, recall Sophie's tragic choice in William Styron's *Sophie's Choice*. The young inmate of the Nazi concentration camp must choose whether to sacrifice her son or her daughter. Otherwise, the Nazis will execute both children. Moral choice sometimes means doing evil, when it is the lesser of evils in a situation in which all options result in some evil.

If Romanticism and Abolitionism are invalid positions, *Realism* will seem attractive. Some realists have cynically opted for a theory of total war with no holds barred ("All's fair in love and war"), but most realists, believing that human sinfulness made war inevitable, advocate mitigating constraints, aiming to limit the damage. Realists are to be distinguished from the War-Romantics, for they do not like war but see it as a necessary evil. Machiavelli (1469–1527) thought that war was inevitable, not because humans were evil (he thought humanity was weak and stupid, not evil) but because of the activity of malign fate, which is always forcing humans to arm themselves against adversity. Machiavelli held out no hope that war raised humanity to a higher plane; the prince is condemned to seek victory in war merely to survive in a hostile world. In times of peace a ruler should not sit with hands folded but should always be improving his state's military power against the day of adversity.

Thomas Hobbes (1588–1679) thought that war is not the act of fighting but the disposition to fight that exists in situations in which no common superior ensures that violence shall not be permitted. Only through the establishment of a commonwealth (that is, a superior law-enforcing agency, the *Leviathan,* to which all people are subject) can war be avoided and peace and civilization ensured.

Morality and the Just War

Given the broadly realist conception of war, it remains to examine ways of mitigating its violence through moral constraints. Three classic theories of morality—Utilitarianism, Contractualism, and Deontologism—prescribe three different strategies. Utilitarian theories, which seek to maximize goodness ("The greatest good for the greatest number"), enjoin a cost-benefit analysis to determine the likely outcomes of diverse strategies. When nations are in conflict, war becomes one option that may be considered as a means of conflict resolution. The only question to be asked is "How likely is it that war will bring about a better total outcome than any alternative policy?" If after careful analysis war is judged likely to bring about the greatest total benefit, war is justified.

A *Realpolitik,* prevails. No civilian-combatant distinction exists. If you can accomplish more by killing civilians, you are justified in so doing, although this may set a bad precedent—so be careful! The decision to drop the atom bomb on Hiroshima was justified from a utilitarian perspective. Reflect upon the words of President Truman:

Having found the bomb, we have to use it. We have used it against those who attacked us without warning at Pearl Harbor, against those who have starved and beaten and executed American prisoners of war, against those who have abandoned all pretense of obeying international laws of warfare. We have used it in order to shorten the agony of war, in order to save the lives of thousands and thousands of young Americans.[8]

Assuming that more good will be done by sacrificing the enemy lives to American lives, the argument has utilitarian traits. Save some lives by killing others.

Of course, Truman's reasoning could also be construed as simply enlightened self-interest, a view held by contractualist types of ethics. According to the contractualist, war is justified for a country whenever it is in that country's self-interest to go to war. Egoist-enlightened self-interest is the leitmotif of contractualism, which leads nations to sign treaties. Once bound to treaties, nations may support one another in battle. When no contract exists, no moral obligation exists, and when a contract exists the obligation must be surrounded with sanctions. Otherwise, the treaty is void, for, as Hobbes noted, "covenants without the sword are but words, and of no strength to secure man at all." Generally, if it is in a country's self-interest to make a treaty that includes the promise to defend another country, that treaty should be adhered to, for you will probably need that country's aid in the future, and backing out of a treaty is a poor advertisement to others. So if our government has a treaty with Saudi Arabia, Kuwait, or Israel, we should honor it and defend these countries when they are attacked or threatened. Interestingly enough, the United States had no treaty with Kuwait when it went to that country's aid.

As was the case with utilitarian theory, contractual theory recognizes no special rule distinguishing civilians from combatants. All are fair game.

We turn to Deontologic Ethics and the famous Just War theory. Augustine (354–430), Thomas Aquinas (1225–1274), and Francisco Suarez (1548–1617), a Roman Catholic Jesuit in the Middle Ages, believed that war, although an evil, could be justified if certain conditions were met. As deontologists, they reject simple cost-benefit calculations and the whole notion of total war—that all is fair in love and war. They distinguished between moral grounds for going into war (*jus ad bellum*) and right conduct while engaged in war (*jus in bello*). *Jus ad bellum*, the right to go to war, could be justified by the following circumstances. The war must be:

1. Declared by a legitimate authority. This would rule out revolutionary wars and rebel uprisings.

2. Declared for a just cause. The Allies' World War II declaration of war on the Japanese and Germans, who were seen as bent on destroying Western democracy, is often cited as the paradigm case of such a just declaration of war. The Gulf war against Iraq was allegedly about the integrity of Kuwait as well as the perceived danger to Saudi Arabia, Syria, and, especially, Israel. It was also about the control of oil in the Middle East.

3. Declared as a last resort. Belligerence may commence only after a reasonable determination has been made that war is the only way to accomplish good ends. In the Gulf war against Iraq, some argue that serious efforts at negotiation had failed and sanctions were not working, so war was the only alternative.

4. Declared with the intention of bringing peace and holding respect (and even love) for the enemy. The opposition must be respected as human beings even as we attack them.

Regarding carrying on the war (*jus in bello*) two further conditions are given:

5. Proportionality. The war must be carried out in moderation, exacting no more casualties than necessary for accomplishing the good end. No more force than necessary to achieve the just goal may be exercised. Pillage, rape, and torture are forbidden. There is no justification for cruel treatment of innocents, prisoners, and the wounded. Nuclear war seems to violate the principle of proportionality.

6. Discrimination. Contrary to utilitarian and contractualist theories, the Just War theory makes a distinction between combatants and noncombatants—those deemed innocent in the fray. It is impermissible to attack nonmilitary targets and noncombatants. Civilian bombing is outlawed by international law. The massacre of civilians at My Lai is viewed as the nadir of despicable behavior by American forces in the Viet Nam War.

Criticism of Just War theory centers on its idealized constraints. Critics contend that it is a holdover from the confined Medieval battlefield, with knights on horses voluntarily engaging the enemy in the name of the king, with spectators looking on from the safety of a promontory. It has little to do with the modern world, where political legitimacy is often open to question, where conscription may force young men and women to do a dictator's bidding, where the whole infrastructure of a nation may be relevant to the outcome, and where the enemy does not abide by the rules of proportionality and discrimination.

The first condition seems dubious. What is a legitimate authority? One set up by a democratic election? One widely recognized by its subjects? If so, all revolutions, including the American Revolution, are immoral. This seems counterintuitive. The notion of political legitimacy is a deep and difficult issue about which we can disagree. In the United States, only Congress has the authority to declare war, yet in the last fifty years the United States has been involved in full-scale wars in Korea, Vietnam, and the Middle East, not to mention military actions in Grenada, Lebanon, Libya, and Panama, without a declaration of war by Congress.

Few would question conditions 2, 3, and 4, since they seem self-evidently necessary to doing any lesser evil, but utilitarians would urge us to reject the sixth condition, discrimination. If by bombing a city in which 10,000 civilian lives were lost we could save 15,000 soldiers, we should bomb the city, maximizing utility. Whatever does the least total evil (or promotes the greater good) ought to be done, regardless of the status of the victims, be they civilians or combatants.

Where utilitarians waver is when practices such as torture are considered. If we could save ten of our soldiers by torturing one enemy soldier, should we do it? Is torture one of those unspeakable evils that should transcend (or nearly transcend) the utilitarian calculus? Perhaps utilitarianism is plausible when comparing lives but not when heinous acts such as torture are involved. But then is torture really any worse than mass killing, leaving children orphans, or using nuclear weapons to accomplish purposes of state? Note that it has recently been revealed that Israel tortured Arab prisoners to gain vital information. Suppose a terrorist has planted a bomb to go off in two hours. If we think that his wife knows where the bomb is, are we justified in torturing her to ascertain the location of the bomb? Deontologists would hesitate to justify this kind of treatment, but utilitarians would likely urge us on.

The moral distinction between innocents (more correctly *noncombatants*) and combatants is especially problematic. Sometimes civilians are wholehearted supporters of a war effort and soldiers are poor youths who have been conscripted against their desire. Soldiers, by the very nature of their profession, take on special risks of life and limb. A soldier is fair game for enemy fire—until he surrenders or is put out of action through being wounded.

Some Just War theorists, such as Paul Christopher, hold that soldiers have an exceedingly strong duty not to jeopardize civilians, even at the cost of putting their own lives in danger. For example, during the Korean War, North Korean units put civilian hostages in front of them as they attacked U.S. forces. The U.S. forces had the option of retreating, thus losing vital ground, or killing civilians. What should they have done? Christopher, in accord with his interpretation of Just War theory, says that the U.S. soldiers should have attacked the Koreans with bayonets to discriminate between civilians and soldiers. "Once we accept that it is part of the ethos of the soldier to behave courageously and to protect innocents, even at the risk of one's own life, then it becomes clear that it is the civilians' lives that must be safeguarded, not the lives of the soldiers. In this case, for example, the men could assault the enemy/civilian formation and use bayonets to engage the combatants."[9]

This seems extreme. Surely soldiers had a right to defend themselves against the North Koreans and advance their position. The Koreans, not the Americans, risked the lives of the hostages. Utilitarians and Contractualists have no difficulty justifying shooting at the soldiers, even though they foresee that some civilians will die. What does Just War theory say?

An analogy may be helpful. If a murderer who is using a hostage as a shield is about to kill you and your family, and you may save your family, as well as your own life, only by shooting through the hostage to the murderer, is it morally permissible to shoot the hostage? Although many Just War theorists, such as Thomas Nagel and Christopher, contend that it is impermissible to kill the hostage, I think a broad interpretation of the theory would permit it. The same is true for killing civilian shields in the war effort.

Just War theory is typically taken to prohibit preemptive strikes. We may attack only in defense, which supposes that the enemy is already at our door. Given modern weaponry, that may be too late to do any good. The Six Day War began on June 5, 1967, with Israel launching a first strike against Egypt. Israeli intelligence had ambiguous reports of an imminent Arab attack, and the Egyptian government had put its troops on "maximum alert," but the evidence was still unclear. Yet Israel felt that its survival as a nation was in jeopardy. Michael Walzer, a supporter of Just War theory and of Israel, argues that "Aggression can be made out not only in the absence of a military attack or invasion but in the (probable) absence of any immediate intention to launch such an attack or invasion. The general formula must go something like this: states may use military force in the face of threats of war, whenever the failure to do so would seriously risk their territorial or political independence."[10]

This practice of preemptive strikes changes the game. Now it is a matter of figuring out who is plotting against you and hitting first.

Just War theory doubtlessly has value in setting forth rules of engagement that limit the destruction of war to minimal evil. Even a utilitarian may accept the stipulations as rules of thumb to be overridden only in emergency—which comes up all too often in war. Whether these rules have validity apart from an effective world government to enforce them is a difficult question.

Nuclear War

Whatever your conclusion on which moral theory deals best with war, the threat of nuclear war puts the very concept of a Just War in serious doubt. Consider the facts. The atomic bomb that fell on Hiroshima on August 6, 1945, killing 60,000 people, had an explosive force of 12,000 tons of TNT. The nuclear warhead on an American Minuteman missile has an explosive force of 1.2 million tons of TNT, 100 times the force of the bomb that fell on Hiroshima. A larger 10-megaton hydrogen bomb has an explosive force 800 times that of the Hiroshima

bomb. The United States and the former Soviet Union together have about 50,000 nuclear warheads. France, Great Britain, China, India, and Israel all have nuclear weapons, for a total of more than 60,000 nuclear warheads.[11]

Here is what would happen if a 1-megaton bomb exploded in a populated area of the United States. While conventional bombs produce only one destructive effect—the shock wave—nuclear weapons produce many destructive effects. At the moment of explosion, when the temperature of the gasified weapon material reaches stellar levels, the pressure is millions of times the normal atmospheric pressure. At the same time, radiation (gamma rays, a high-energy form of electromagnetic radiation) flows into the environment, destroying whatever is in its path, killing all humans within a 6-mile radius (destroying or polluting most vegetation and animal life as well), so that the survivors could not eat anything in the area.

Simultaneously, an electromagnetic pulse is generated by the intense gamma ray radiation. At a high altitude this can produce such a surge of voltage that it would cripple communications throughout the United States. If a bomb exploded in the stratosphere over the center of the country, it could generate an electromagnetic pulse strong enough to cripple the nation's electrical circuits and bring its economy to a screeching halt.

When the fusion and fission reactions of the bomb have taken place, a giant fireball takes shape. It expands, radiating harmful X-rays into the air in the form of a thermal pulse, a wave of blinding light and intense heat that can cause second-degree burns in exposed humans in an area of 280 square miles (a 20-megaton bomb would do this over a 2,460-square-mile area). The fires from the thermal blast will cause raging fires, which will destroy everything for miles around.

At the same time, the total reaction of the explosion causes an enormous blast wave to be sent out in all directions. The blast wave of an air-burst 1-megaton bomb can flatten all but the strongest buildings within a radius of 4½ miles (a 20-megaton bomb can destroy everything within a 12-mile radius).

As the fire ball burns, it rises, condensing water from the surrounding atmosphere to form the characteristic mushroom cloud. This mixture will return to earth as radioactive fallout, most of it in the form of fine ash. This fallout will be carried downwind for thousands of miles, exposing human beings to radiation disease, an illness that is fatal if intense enough.

One of the global effects of the detonation would be the partial destruction of the ozone layer in the stratosphere. The nitrogen oxides from the explosion would flow upward and cause chemical reactions that would result in the depletion of the ozone layer, which filters the sun's harmful ultraviolet rays. As much as 70 percent of the ozone layer could be destroyed, resulting in an epidemic of cancer.

Another effect would be the nuclear winter. The ashes and soot cast up from the explosions would cloud, thereby blocking, the sun's heat from the earth, causing a new Ice Age to ensue and killing most human life.

The effect of 300 1-megaton bombs on the United States would be the destruction of more than 140 million people in a few days. Since 60 percent of the population lives in an area of 18,000 square miles, they could be annihilated with fewer than 300 bombs in a short time. Jack Geiger wrote:

The landscape would be strewn with millions of corpses of human beings and animals. This alone is a situation without precedent in history. There would be an immense source of pollution of water and food. If you read the literature concerning natural disasters such as floods and typhoons, you find that there is always an associate danger of cholera or typhoid. The corpses would also feed a fast-growing population of insects. . . . Naturally, medical measures to fight disease would not be taken, since the blast would have destroyed virtually all medical facilities."[12]

The living might well envy the dead, for their lives would have little to look forward to. Strontium-90 (which resembles calcium in its chemical composition and so gets into milk products and then into humans through the milk) eventually causes bone cancer. Most animals, especially large ones such as cattle, and most trees would die; lakes and rivers would be poisoned by radiation; and the affected soil would lose its nutrients and, consequently, its ability to produce food. "In sum, a full-scale nuclear attack on the United States would devastate the natural environment on a scale unknown since early geologic times, when, in response to natural catastrophes . . . sudden mass extinctions of species and whole ecosystems occurred all over the earth."[13] What would survive? Mainly grass and small insects. The United States would become a republic of insects and grass.

A nuclear war violates the principles of a Just War. It violates principles 4 (aiming at bringing about peace in which the enemy is respected), 5 (proportionality), and 6 (discrimination between combatants and noncombatants). This is why the Roman Catholic Bishops have declared that using nuclear weapons is inherently immoral.

Utilitarians and contractualists also generally condemn nuclear war. The short-term and long-term destruction of such a war would be so terrible that it defies the power of words to describe. However, these theories might justify the selective use of nuclear weapons, as theorists from both of these camps justify the use of the atomic bomb on Hiroshima and Nagasaki to bring Japan to surrender and thus save hundreds of thousands of lives. For utilitarians the principle of the Lesser Evil applied. Do whatever will minimize evil! For contractualists the bombing was an instrument of enlightened self-interest.

Both utilitarians and contractualists agree that we must prevent a nuclear war. In the shadow of a nuclear holocaust, the deontologicst, utilitarian, and contractualist tend to converge, as do abolitionist and realist positions. Such an act of madness violates Just War principles, it violates the principle of utility, and it is not in anyone's interest. The threat of nuclear war provides a powerful incentive for all people throughout the earth to learn to live together in peace.

Conclusion

War has typically been a sacrament of state, a holy rite of passage for young males, bringing out the virtues of courage, discipline, devotion, decisiveness, and endurance, as well as engendering the thrill of strenuous competition as does no other activity on the face of the earth. The horror is the thrill. Now, however, given the threat of a nuclear holocaust, we can no longer afford to play that game, except arguably where nuclear weapons are excluded, although even here the sport becomes increasingly futile. As the globe shrinks and the powers of destruction grow, we need to use more rational means for the resolution of conflicts of interest.

Nevertheless, the high virtues and heightened tension of mortal powers recognized in war deserve recognition and an outlet. Other institutions must substitute for war, giving pride of place to valor, devotion, creative intelligence, endurance, and the thrill of difficult accomplishment. This is my reason for tolerating sports such as football and hockey, which are otherwise crude and dangerous. They may be, in the words of William James, the "moral equivalent of war." Humans beings, at least at this stage of evolution, need the challenge of great heights, of physical endurance, of great causes to which to devote themselves. On to Mt. Everest, the football field, the Peace Corps, the Environmental Protection Program, the Space Program, sacrificial service in the poorest, most dangerous quarters of the globe, but away from war! A Peace Army into which every young person would be conscripted for two years to serve human need instead of human destruction should eventually replace present practices of war armies.

The horrors of My Lai, Bosnia, Kosovo, and Rwanda urge us, in the name of humanity and all that is rational, to find peaceful ways to solve our disputes. Economic boycotts and international censure must replace armed conflict, and arms sales to belligerent nations must be curtailed. Eventually, nation states will have to relinquish some sovereignty to a global peacekeeping institution such as the United Nations, which at present is the only agency able to adjudicate international conflicts of interests. Ensuring its impartiality and moral integrity and increasing its power to act against aggression without itself being despotic are two of the colossal challenges of the twenty-first century. International law based on an objective morality, such as was outlined in Chapter 3, with a fair and effective judicial body will be necessary if we are to live together in peace and justice.

Meanwhile, nations like our own must wield power adroitly and responsibly. As guerrilla warfare and terrorism increase, new fine-tuned forms of defense will become necessary. The grim irony of technophobic, convicted Unabomber Ted Kazynzsky's use of sophisticated technological know-how to kill people whom he saw as perpetrators of technological dominance over the human spirit should not be lost on us. The wise use of technology, technology as a deferential servant to moral ends, to preserve peace and allow the human spirit to thrive and flourish, is an imperative par excellence. But as malice rachets up its technological prowess, so must virtue. For the foreseeable future a strong national military will be necessary, but it must be more flexible, innovative, intelligent, inventive, and moral than all previous armies. International peacekeeping missions, such as those operating in Bosnia and that might have helped in Rwanda, will become more common. It may even be necessary to use military might to guard our global resources, such as the rain forests.

Although human nature, containing both good and evil and generating conflicts of interests that ignite to violence, causes us to arm ourselves in the name of goodness, still we must live in hope for a better world. Our vision should be for the peaceable kingdom in which:

The wolf shall dwell with the lamb
and the leopard shall lie down with the kid,
 and the calf
and the lion, and the fatling together
The cow and the bear shall feed;
Their young shall lie down together;
And the lion shall eat straw like the ox,

They shall not hurt or destroy in all my holy
 mountain.
[A righteous judge] shall judge between the
 nations.
And shall decide for many peoples;
and they shall beat their swords into plow-
 shares,
And their spears into pruning hooks;
Nations shall not lift up sword against nation,
Neither shall they learn war any more.

(*Isaiah* 11:6–8; 2:4)

Study Questions

1. Discuss the three major philosophies of war. What are the strengths and weaknesses of each?
2. Discuss pacifism. Is it a deeply moral position or, as Jan Narveson argues, a fundamentally incoherent position?
3. What is the Just War theory? What are its principles? Distinguish between *jus ad bellum* and *jus in bello*. Do these principles apply to modern warfare? Would adhering to these principles handicap one side against a ruthless enemy who stopped at nothing to prevail?
4. Is there a clear distinction between combatants and noncombatants as posited by Just War theory? Or are all who contribute to the enemy's effort in any way to be viewed as legitimate targets of aggression?
5. What should be our policy toward nuclear weapons? Should we work for universal nuclear disarmament or maintain nuclear weapons as a credible deterrent?

Endnotes

1. William James, "The Moral Equivalent of War," *The Writings of William James*, John J. McDermott, ed. (New York: Random House, 1967), p. 661.

2. Dionysius of Halicarnassus, *On Thucydides*, trans. W. Kendrick Pritchell, quoted in Michael Walzer, *Just and Unjust Wars* (New York: Harper & Row, 1977), 6.

3. Tertullian, quoted in *History of Christian Ethics* George Forell (Philadelphia: Fortress Press, 1972), 123.

4. Helmut von Moltke, quoted in *War and Civilization*, Arnold Toynbee (Oxford: Oxford University Press, 1950), 16.

5. Quoted in Toynbee, *ibid*, p. 16.

6. I am indebted for this argument to Jan Narveson's article "Pacifism: A Philosophical Analysis," in *War and Morality*, Richard Wasserstrom (Belmont: Wadsworth, 1970).

7. Richard Wasserstrom, "On the Morality of War: A Preliminary Inquiry," in *War and Morality*, ed. Richard Wasserstrom (Belmont, Calif.: Wadsworth, 1970).

8. Address to the Nation by President Harry S. Truman, 9 August 1945, quoted in *The Just War*, Robert Tucker, (1960), 21f.

9. Paul Christopher, *The Ethics of War and Peace* (Englewood Cliffs, NJ: Prentice-Hall, 1994), 174–75.

10. Michael Walzer, *Just and Unjust Wars* (New York: Basic Books, 1977), 85.

11. I am indebted to the account given by Jonathan Schell in his brilliant work, *The Fate of the Earth* (New York: Alfred Knopf, 1982), ch. I, for my account of the destructiveness of nuclear weapons

12. Ibid, p. 68.

13. Ibid, p. 64.

Selected Bibliography

Code: D = Deontological; U = Utilitarian; C = Contractualist or Egoist; O = Objectivist; R = Relativist.

I. Ethical Theory

Baier, Kurt. *The Moral Point of View.* Ithaca, NY: Cornell University Press, 1958. This influential work sees morality primarily in terms of social control. (C) (O)

Dawkins, Richard. *The Selfish Gene,* 2d ed. Oxford: Oxford University Press, 1989. One of the most fascinating studies on the subject, defending limited altruism from the perspective of self-interest. (a type of C)

Frankena, William K. *Ethics,* 2d ed. Englewood Cliffs, NJ: Prentice-Hall, 1973. A succinct, reliable guide. (D) (O—Intuitionism)

Gert, Bernard. *Morality: A New Justification of the Moral Rules,* 2d ed. Oxford: Oxford University Press, 1988. A clear and comprehensive discussion of the nature of morality. (C)

Hobbes, Thomas. *Leviathan* (1651). Indianapolis: Bobbs Merrill, 1958, Parts I and II. Classic work in contractarian ethics.

Kant, Immanuel. *Foundations of the Metaphysics of Morals.* Trans. Lewis White Beck. Indianapolis: Bobbs-Merrill, 1959. A classic work in D.

MacIntyre, Alasdair. *A Short History of Ethics.* London: Macmillan, 1966. A lucid, if uneven, survey of the history of Western ethics.

Mackie, J. L. *Ethics: Inventing Right and Wrong.* London: Penguin, 1976. A modern classic defense of relativism. (R)

Mill, John Stuart. *Utilitarianism.* Indianapolis: Bobbs-Merrill, 1957. A classic work in U.

Nielsen, Kai. *Ethics without God.* Buffalo: Prometheus, 1973. A very accessible defense of secular morality. (U)

Pojman, Louis. *Ethical Theory: Classical and Contemporary Readings,* 3d ed. Belmont, CA: Wadsworth, 1999. An anthology containing readings on all the major positions.

———. *Ethics: Discovering Right and Wrong.* Belmont, CA: Wadsworth, 1989. An objectivist perspective. (O)

Quinton, Anthony. *Utilitarian Ethics.* London: Macmillan, 1973. A clear exposition of classic utilitarianism.

Rachels, James. *The Elements of Moral Philosophy.* New York: Random House, 1986. One of the clearest introductions to moral philosophy.

Singer, Peter. *The Expanding Circle: Ethics and Sociobiology.* Oxford: Oxford University Press, 1983. A fascinating attempt to relate ethics to sociobiology. (U)

Taylor, Richard. *Good and Evil.* Buffalo: Prometheus, 1970. A lively, easy-to-read work that sees the main role of morality to be the resolution of conflicts of interest. (C) (R)

Van Wyk, Robert. *Introduction to Ethics.* New York: St. Martin's Press, 1990. A clearly written recent introduction to the subject. (O) (attacks versions of C—minimal morality)

II. Applied Ethics

Aiken, William and Hugh LaFollette. *World Hunger and Moral Responsibility.* Englewood Cliffs, NJ: Prentice-Hall, 1977. The best collection of essays on the philosophical implications of world hunger.

Arthur, John. "Rights and Duty to Bring Aid" in William Aiken and Hugh LaFollette, op. cit.

Battin, Margaret Pabst and David Mayo, eds. *Suicide: The Philosophical Issues.* New York: St. Martin's Press, 1980. A set of contemporary essays, especially those by Brandt, Mayo, Martin, and Battin.

Beauchamp, Tom L. and James F. Childress. *Principles of Biomedical Ethics,* 2d ed. Oxford: Oxford University Press, 1983. An accessible work showing how ethical theory applies to issues in medical ethics.

Beauchamp, Tom L. and Seymour Perlin, eds. *Ethical Issues in Death and Dying*. Englewood Cliffs, NJ: Prentice-Hall, 1978. The best collection of essays on the subject.

Bedau, Hugo Adam, ed. *The Death Penalty in America*, 3d ed. New York: Oxford University Press, 1982. A helpful set of readings, reflecting all aspects of the contemporary debate.

Bernat, James, "A Defense of the Whole-Brain Concept of Death" *Hastings Center Report* vol. 28:2 (1998). A defense of whole-brain death as the most coherent standard for determining death.

Berns, Walter. *For Capital Punishment: The Inevitability of Caprice and Mistake*. New York: Norton, 1974. A retributivist defense of capital punishment.

Capron, Alexander, "Death and the Law" *Hastings Center Report* vol. 27:5 (1997). A good overview.

Cohen, Joel E. *How Many Peple Can the Earth Support?* New York: Norton, 1995.

Coope, Christoper Miles, "Death with Dignity," *Hastings Center Report* vol. 24:5 (1997). A useful discussion.

Cowart, Dax and Robert Burt, "Confronting Death: Who Chooses, Who Controls?" *Hastings Center Report* vol. 28:1 (1998). A dialogue on patient autonomy.

DeSpelder, LynneAnne and Albert Lee Strickland. *The Last Dance: Encountering Death and Dying*. 4th ed. Mountain View, CA: Mayfield Publishing Co., 1996. A comprehensive examination of issues in death and dying.

DesJardins, Joseph, *Environmental Ethics*. Belmont, CA: Wadsworth Publishing Co., 1997. A fine overview of the subject.

Devall, Bill and George Sessions, eds. *Deep Ecology: Living as if Nature Mattered*. Salt Lake City: Peregrine Smith, 1985. A good anthology of readings on deep ecology.

Devine, Philip E. *The Ethics of Homicide*. Ithaca, NY: Cornell University Press, 1978. The best treatment from a conservative perspective of the issues discussed in this book.

Ehrlich, Paul, Anne H. Ehrlich, and Gretchen Daily, *The Stork and the Plow*. New York: Grosset/Putnam, 1995. A plea of population stabilization.

Feinberg, Joel, ed. *The Problem of Abortion*. Belmont, CA: Wadsworth, 1973. A valuable anthology containing classic articles.

Frey, R.G. *Rights, Killing and Suffering*. Oxford: Basil Blackwell, 1983. The best work opposing animal rights.

Gerber, Rudolph and Patrick McAnany, eds. *Contemporary Punishment*. Notre Dame: University of Notre Dame Press. A helpful anthology with important articles by Hart, Wasserstrom, Flew, Mabbott, Packer, Menninger, Lewis, and others.

Glover, Jonathan. *Causing Death and Saving Lives*. London: Penguin, 1977. A U examination of several moral problems.

Hamsun, Knut. *Hunger*. Trans. Robert Bly. New York: Bard Books, 1967.

Hardin, Garrett. "Lifeboat Ethics: The Case Against Helping the Poor." *Psychology Today* (1974), reprinted in Aiken and LaFollette, op. cit. A modern classic of the neo-Malthusian perspective.

Hardin, Garrett. *The Limits of Altruism*. Bloomington, IN: Indiana University Press, 1977.

Harris, John. *The Value of Life*. London: Routledge & Kegan Paul, 1985. A succinct but penetrating work in medical ethics, covering many of the topics discussed in this book.

Hopkins, Patrick, "Bad Copies," *Hastings Center Report* vol. 28:2 (1998). A revealing essay on how the media influences public opinion on ethical issues and specifically human cloning.

Kass, Leon, "The Wisdom of Repugnance" *New Republic* (June 2, 1997). A blistering attack on the idea of human cloning.

Kleinig, John. *Valuing Life*. Princeton: Princeton University Press, 1991. The most thorough study of the value of life.

Kohl, Marvin, ed. *Beneficent Euthanasia*. Buffalo: Prometheus, 1975. An excellent collection of articles.

Lackey, Douglas. *The Ethics of War and Peace*. Englewood Cliffs, NJ: Prentice-Hall, 1989. A clearheaded discussion of pacifism and the Just War theory.

———. *Moral Principles and Nuclear Weapons*. Totowa, NJ: Rowman and Allenheld, 1984. A comprehensive study of the moral aspects of nuclear arms policy.

Ladd, John, ed. *Ethical Issues Relating to Life and Death*. Oxford: Oxford University Press, 1979. Contains nine important articles.

————, eds. *Biomedical Ethics,* 2d ed. New York: McGraw-Hill, 1986. An excellent set of readings on abortion, euthanasia, and the concept of death.

Leopold, Aldo, *Sand County Almanac*. New York: Oxford University Press, 1949. A Classic in Environmental Ethics.

Mappes, Thomas and Jane Zembaty, eds. *Social Ethics,* 3d ed. New York: McGraw-Hill, 1986. An excellent anthology with succinct selections on most of the issues discussed in this book.

————, eds. *Biomedical Ethics,* 2d ed. New York: McGraw-Hill, 1986. An excellent set of readings on abortion, euthanasia, and the concept of death.

Menninger, Karl. *The Crime of Punishment*. New York: Viking Press, 1968. A defense of rehabilitation as a way of dealing with criminals.

Munson, Ronald, ed. *Intervention and Reflection,* 5th ed. Belmont, CA: Wadsworth, 1996. One of the best anthologies in medical ethics, especially on abortion and euthanasia.

Murphy, Jeffrie, ed. *Punishment and Rehabilitation,* 2d ed. Belmont, CA: Wadsworth, 1985. An excellent collection of articles on the subject of punishment and its alternatives.

O'Neill, Onora. *Faces of Hunger*. Boston: G. Allen & Unwin, 1986. A careful Kantian discussion of the principles and problems surrounding world hunger.

Paddoch, Paul and William. *Famine—1975*. Boston: Little Brown, 1968.

Pence, Gregory E. *Classic Cases in Medical Ethics,* 3rd ed. N.Y.: McGraw-Hill, 1999. The best single-authored text on medical ethics.

Pence, Gregory, ed. *Flesh of my Flesh* Lanham, MD: Rowman & Littlefield, 1998. An anthology on human cloning, just published.

————. *Who's Afraid of Human Cloning?* Lanham, MD: Rowman & Littlefield, 1998. A timely, well-written work supporting human cloning.

Perlin, Seymour, ed. *A Handbook for the Study of Suicide*. Oxford: Oxford University Press, 1975. A helpful series of articles.

Pojman, Louis and Frank Beckwith, eds. *The Abortion Controversy*. 2d ed. Belmont, CA: Wadsworth Publishing Co., 1998. A comprehensive anthology on the 25th anniversary of Roe v. Wade.

Pojman, Louis, ed. *Life and Death: An Anthology*. Wadsworth Publishing Co., 1999. A companion to this book, containing readings on every topic discussed here.

Rachels, James. *Created From Animals: The Moral Implications of Darwinism*. Oxford: Oxford University Press, 1990. A provocative study with relevance to the issue of the sanctity of life and animal rights.

————. *The End of Life*. New York: Oxford University Press, 1986. A clear defense of voluntary active euthanasia.

Regan, Tom. *The Case for Animal Rights*. Berkeley: University of California, 1983. The most comprehensive philosophical treatise in favor of animal rights.

————, ed. *Matters of Life and Death,* 3d ed. New York: McGraw-Hill, 1993. An excellent set of essays on euthanasia, suicide, war, capital punishment, animal rights, and environmental ethics.

Regan, Tom and Peter Singer, eds. *Animal Rights and Human Obligations*. Englewood Cliffs, NJ: Prentice-Hall, 1976. The best anthology on animal rights.

Robbins, John. *Diet for a New America: How Your Food Choices Affect Your Health, Happiness, and the Future of Life on Earth*. Walpole, NH: Stillpoint, 1987. A strong case for vegetarianism.

Rohr, Janelle, ed. *Animal Rights: Opposing Viewpoints*. San Diego: Greenhaven Press, 1989. Elementary essays on the subject.

Schell, Jonathan. *Fate of the Earth*. New York: Knopf, 1982. An excellent book on the dangers of nuclear war.

Simon, Arthur. *Bread for the World*. Mahway, NJ: Paulist Press, 1975. A poignant discussion of the problems of world hunger and some thoughtful suggestions for improving the situation.

Singer, Peter. *Animal Liberation,* 2d ed. New York: New York Review of Books, 1990. The classic work on the subject. The second edition contains recent data on animal experimentation and factory farming.

———. "Famine, Affluence and Morality." *Philosophy and Public Affairs* (1972).

———. *Practical Ethics.* Cambridge: Cambridge University Press, 1979. A helpful U approach.

Singer, Peter and Deane Wells, *The Reproductive Revolution: New Ways of Making Babies.* New York: Oxford University Press, 1984. Still worth reading.

Sorell, Tom. *Moral Theory and Capital Punishment.* Oxford: Blackwell, 1987. A clearly written, thoughtful work for beginning students.

Steinbok, Bonnie, and Ron McClamrock, "When Is Birth Unfair to the Child?" *Hastings Center Report* vol. 24:6 (1994). A good discussion of the issue.

Sterba, James, ed. *The Ethics of War and Nuclear Deterrence.* Belmont, CA: Wadsworth, 1985. The best anthology on the subject.

Stoessinger, John G. *Why Nations Go to War,* 4th ed. New York: St. Martin's Press, 1985. A fascinating essay on the causes of war in the twentieth century.

Szumski, Bonnie, Lynn Hall, and Susan Bursell, eds. *The Death Penalty: Opposing Viewpoints.* St. Paul: Greenhaven Press, 1986. Contains short but important articles. Basic.

Tooley, Michael. *Abortion and Infanticide.* Oxford: Oxford University Press, 1983. A sustained case for a liberal position on abortion.

Truog, Robert D. "Is It Time to Abandon Brain Death?" *Hastings Center Report* vol. 27:1 (1997). He argues that the concept of brain death is incoherent and should be replaced.

Van de Veer, Donald and Christine Pierce, eds. *People, Penguins and Plastic Trees.* Belmont, CA: Wadsworth, 1990. A good set of readings on environmental issues, including animal rights.

Veatch, Robert M. *Death, Dying and the Biological Revolution.* New Haven: Yale University Press, 1976. A thoughtful discussion of issues relating to death and dying.

Walzer, Michael. *Just and Unjust Wars.* London: Penguin, 1977. A penetrating, and very readable study of morality and war.

Wasserstrom, Richard, ed. *War and Morality.* Belmont, CA: Wadsworth, 1970. Contains excellent articles.

Index